84
84
84
53
___
302

75.5

4) 302
28
___
22
20
___
20

18
16
___
24

89
90
81
84
___
344

86
4) 344
32
___
24

REACHING FOR THE STARS

REACHING FOR THE STARS

BY

Nora Waln

The fashions of this world are in continuous
change and I would concern myself with things
that are abiding.
— JOHANN WOLFGANG VON GOETHE

BOSTON
LITTLE, BROWN AND COMPANY
1939

For three gentle persons steadfast in a troubled generation: my mother-by-affection, *Shun-ko* of Hopei; my ideal Quaker, *Charles Francis Jenkins* of Pennsylvania; and my friend, *Ellery Sedgwick* of Boston

CONTENTS

REACHING FOR THE STARS

I

A DAY IN JUNE

IT was the last Saturday in June, 1934. A soft summer day, the sun's radiance tempered by a breeze.

Motoring leisurely across Belgium, my husband and I stopped in Spa at noon for lunch. We chose an open-fronted restaurant facing on the town square, shaded by awnings striped a cool green and white. My husband has the habit of resting after midday food. While waiting for our salad to be mixed he glanced about in a way which I recognized to be a search for a quiet corner; and I gave my attention to the possibility of having a look at Spa, preferably with a resident of the place.

Recently I had read *Ereignisse und Gestalten* by Kaiser Wilhelm II. Inheritor of the kingdom of Prussia with the emperorship of all Germany and German responsibilities beyond the seas, he abandoned his position, at the threat of German revolution, in a hasty flight from Spa, thus losing for his descendants the power which a notable line of ancestors had won, by military victories and political strategies, for the House of Hohenzollern. So Spa was of interest to me just then, not as a Belgian town but as related to him.

The restaurant proprietor kindly sent for his daughter, whom he introduced as an educated woman, a teacher before her marriage. She generously offered to escort me and we set forth.

Keeping to the paths of the wooded rise above the town square, she pointed out the direction from which the German army had come in the summer of 1914; the buildings they had used as staff headquarters; the château where their Kaiser had dwelt; the road down which he had fled to seek sanctuary in Holland in the autumn of 1918; and the way the evacuating troops had gone.

"I helped the officers billeted on us to pack," she said. "They were stunned by the necessity to go home before the war was won. The invaders went in an orderly manner. I was nine when the German army arrived. I was thirteen when I sat on yonder hill to watch them depart."

She flung her comely hands in a wide circle: "There is where the Germans were. They succeeded in seizing all our land except a tiny corner. German orators now moan over the radio about their bleeding frontiers — but who first tore at the frontiers? Do they forget that they snatched as much as they could from their neighbors and clung to it as long as they could hold? They groan to high heaven about the Ruhr and Rhine occupation, yet they made use of everything in each place they invaded as if it were their own. Quartered on other people's homes, they shouted, whipped, and shot if their commands were not obeyed. More than four years they sat on us. It took the allied help of half the world to move them out of Belgium and France. They would have been here still if America had not helped. You may feel that the Treaty of Versailles is bitter. So it is. The Nazis contend that Germany would have written a less vindictive settlement had she won the war. That should be so. It should be easier for conquering invaders to be magnanimous than for the nearly exhausted invaded and their allies."

She was trembling. We sat down on a rock. As quickly as she had lost control, she quieted herself and began to ask me questions about myself.

"Your husband is English, but you are not?"

"I am an American, a Pennsylvanian."

"Where did you marry?"

"In China."

"Are you on the continent only to enjoy yourselves?"

I explained. Music has always been my husband's avocation. It was given a secondary place in his education, and before he was of age he was started on a career in government service in China. His vacations he spent in study with private teachers and at the Royal College of Music in London. Now he had resigned. He had just completed eighteen months of music study in France and was going to Germany to study.

"Do you know the Germans?" she asked.

I told her that I had known many people of German descent in my native Pennsylvania; in China we had made a point of becoming acquainted with the German community in each post where we lived, entertaining them in our home and visiting in theirs; as successor to a French nurse we had had a German governess for our daughter, and at Tientsin had sent her to the German school.

"Did you send her to school when you lived in France?"

"Yes, to the French public school."

"And where is she now?"

"At a school in Switzerland."

"You aren't taking her with you into Germany?"

"We are not willing to send her to school there until we find out how the schools are under the Nazi government."

"What is your opinion about war?" she requested abruptly.

"It is uncivilized."

"I agree with you — but who is right and who is wrong when it does occur?"

"Nobody is right.   Everybody is wrong."

"That is loose thinking.   The invaders are wrong.   The German Kaiser sinned against civilization when he gave orders for his soldiers to march beyond his own frontiers, and every man who obeyed that command and set his foot on neighboring soil sinned against his fellow men."

"It would seem from the book he has written," I offered lamely, "that Kaiser Wilhelm II did not want war."

"Perhaps not," she conceded.   "I have read his book. I imagine he saw himself as the conductor of an orchestra of Siegfrieds.   He may have believed that he had but to send them forth in operatic step, blowing a heroic E flat on shining trumpets, and all Europe would awaken to join joyously in a Pan-Germanic chorus.   But they were equipped with bayonets, hand grenades, machine guns, bombs, poison gas, and submarines for an emergency." She shrugged her shoulders.   "Wilhelm II is an old man now.   He is no longer important, except as an example of the self-deceptions the emotional Germans permit themselves.   A young conductor has picked up the baton he dropped."

We were silent, each busy with her own thoughts — I

longing selfishly, as I have done so often since I came to live in Europe, to run far away from this war-scarred continent with its clatter of weapons now being collected for further fights.

"I have a boy of three," she began. "I would be content if I could be confident that he could have a life free from war. A few years ago here in Europe we founded a league of women pledged to bring our sons up never to kill each other. The German women were keen about the idea. We numbered many thousands. There was a member in Germany as companion to every member in Belgium and France. When the Nazi government came into power they outlawed our society. Pacifism is treason in Germany now."

"Do you think that a people so intelligent as the Germans will long endure such autocratic rule?"

"A dictator does not rise," she asserted, "unless his temperament, technique, and objective are in tune with the people from whom he emerges. Power and glory are certainly the aim of many Germans, otherwise they would not have been tempted to listen to Nazi theories, and in Belgium we hear that Monsieur Hitler is a master in the art of shaping the state to this end. The Germans desire to be hypnotized by their leaders so as to feel sure that what they want is unquestionably right. He seems to possess this ability. Under such circumstances they will surely bear all that he imposes upon them, not only willingly but with enthusiasm, just so long as he inflates German importance."

We walked on a little way and sat down again before she asked, "Have you read Monsieur Hitler's book?"

I replied that I had read the English edition.

"That tells you nothing," she declared impatiently. "The vital parts are left out. He has forbidden foreign circulation of the book in full. Get *Mein Kampf* as issued to Germans."

"How did you get it?" I queried.

"My mother's family are Flemings. I had the book from a cousin. The German invasion of Belgium is continued anew now. The arms are propaganda. The Nazis are calling to the Flemings of Belgium to join in a brotherhood of race. They would weaken our country by fomenting dissension among us."

She built a little structure of twigs and brushed it aside. "It isn't that Germans are intentionally wicked. It is that they befuddle themselves into faith that good can be achieved through evil. They have consciences that prick them and they quiet their troublesome doubts, not by self-correction, but by repeated self-assurance of the best intentions. Once a German is convinced that the Germans know how to order life for everyone's good, he is converted to Pan-Germanism. The means is but the way to that perfectly beautiful end."

No words for argument came to me. Therefore I was silent, and she continued: "After the Germans had settled down on us they were kind to children who obeyed them. In their leisure they whittled toys for us. They were homesick for their own children. They showed us pictures of their wives and little ones. As we learned to understand the language they told us anecdotes from their home lives. They wanted Belgian children kept clean. They took our schoolhouses as hospitals for their wounded, but they used their medicine for us when we were sick and even helped to nurse us. They always wanted the battles to cease for Christmas. Bringing evergreen into the house, they celebrated the festival as in their homeland. I was meek. I have flaxen hair. 'Princess Golden' the soldiers quartered in our house called me, and every year they trimmed a little fir tree. Also in the famine winters they shared their rations. Ashamed of my lack of patriotism, I grew fond of them. I really missed the eldest when he was gone from our house."

Her voice hardened: "But my childhood holds other memories. Hours of my mother's weeping. The fate of my brother. The sight of relatives and friends corralled and commandeered as they were bent to the will of the conquerors. Keys to cellars and storerooms had to be given up. Secrets disclosed. In the occupied areas the battles could be heard and we could get no news from outside. Even little children who slipped past the front to find their fathers were executed as spies if caught. Belgians young and old were detailed to till the fields and operate the mills for the benefit of the invaders. My brother was eleven when they came. He was a stout-hearted boy with more courage than I possessed. He refused to plant potatoes to feed men who had no right in Belgium. He was taken away. We never saw him again. His fate was that of all who disobeyed. It is the fate of all who refuse to do and think as they are told in Germany to-day."

My husband beckoned from below. We rose and moved toward the car which was to carry me into life in Germany.

"God be with you," she said in parting.

Soon we were off. Climbing through lovely country, we came to a glorious panoramic view. Then dipped to the frontier over a moor golden with early gorse.

A Belgian in uniform stopped us. He was a guard on duty. Here, on land that had been German before 1914 and used then for the peacetime manœuvres of Rhineland troops, a Belgian regiment was holding manœuvres. Shooting made the road dangerous. We could wait until five o'clock when the exercise would be over for the day, or go around. We chose to detour. The Belgian appeared bored with life, but brightened when my husband gave him a packet of cigarettes. He kindly stepped on our running board and came a distance with us to make certain that we understood the way.

His right sleeve hung empty. "Lost at Lantin," he said. "I was nineteen then." Gunfire to the east punctuated his weary voice. "We must practise to defend ourselves . . . every shot blows away money we need in Belgium . . . and wastes a man's time. . . . Germany, forbidden by the peace treaty to rearm, is arming . . . our scientists are no match for hers . . . tanks that travel sixty miles an hour . . . bullets that can cut steel . . . aeroplanes directed by electric waves . . . new poisonous gases . . . all these I hear Germany has. What use our practice?"

Suddenly his voice tightened. "Our governors said in the past: 'While God is in His heaven the Germans shall not pass over Belgium.' Fine words. Fine words. I for one am not going to do any more fighting."

He got down at the crossroads. Astonished, I stared after him as he made his way back to his post.

Further on, in an area of sparse hill farms, we were hailed
again. This time by a German. He had been running;
sweat marked a broad line along his suspenders; his words
were breathless. In his house his son's wife was danger-
ously ill — the child refused to be born — the doctor needed
things from the nearest pharmacy — he had been sent out
to flag a car to help.

Beaming his thanks, he got in.

A tall, lean mountaineer, his hands were calloused, his
face seamed. He spoke, with a simple pride, English
learned in a war prison camp. A man for work rather
than reading in those days, so he told us, he had missed
the news of the war until, looking up from a furrow, he
saw soldiers marching past his fields to defend the Fatherland. He did not wait for his conscription to join. Three
years he fought. Then he was taken prisoner by the
British.

He got home a year after the Armistice to find his native place, which had always been a part of the Fatherland,
held by the enemy.

"We were promised a vote. An unfair plebiscite in
1920 fastened Belgian rule on Eupen and Malmédy. We
Germans of Eupen-Malmédy wait to be reunited to the
Fatherland. The Saar first. Then our Leader will rescue
us. That is right. They have suffered most. It takes
long. It will come — but it takes long — and I am old."

When we left him at his house door he promised to let
us know about his daughter-in-law by postal card to Bonn.

Turning east into a wooded road, along which a lonely
tram track ran, we passed the Belgian Customs. Some

yards further on the way was barred by a slender pole swung as a gate between two posts and neatly painted red and white, the colors of love and innocence.

"Heil Hitler," exclaimed a young man in a uniform of green jacket, black trousers, and high black boots.

"Heil Hitler," we responded to the convention.

Beyond the barrier, atop a pole of stouter proportions than the one used to close the road, waved the Nazi flag — a scarlet flag with a circle in pure white bearing a hooked cross in black. It was a banner of no flimsy stuff, but an ensign cut from a notable weaving. The branches of trees had been trimmed to give it space.

Three frontier officers were in view. The one giving us his attention came to our car and bowed. He spoke politely, exchanging comment on the weather and inquiring my husband's reason for wishing to enter Germany. Then he escorted my husband and his credentials into a small roadside building. I waited.

Up the shady road out of Germany swung an open roadster, halting across the gate from me. The shiny car was a gray Mercedes-Benz, upholstered in bright blue leather and driven by a plump man, dressed to match in a gray suit and bright blue shirt. His round head was shaven as clean as his genial pink face. Beside him sat a slim girl with fair hair and big blue eyes; pretty in a sleeveless white sports frock and without a hat.

He wanted a ride through the Belgian mountains — an hour or so. He had passports and some money. He did not have a permit to take money out of Germany. Good-naturedly he handed his wallet over to the custody of the officer questioning him, and was allowed to take from it "pocket cash" — a few coins. Then pressure of the officer's foot on a lever lifted the red and white pole. Their right hands raised high in salute, the man and the girl cheered "Heil Hitler" as their car leaped forward and whizzed by.

Trams from Belgium and from Germany met at the frontier to exchange passengers. An officer in a green jacket stood at each end of the barrier. People entering walked round the right; those going out round the left. Every man, woman, and child had to show a card with a photograph on it, and respond to the "Heil Hitler" salute. A woman from the Belgian side who persisted in saying "*Grüss Gott*" instead could not pass. She went away in the tram in which she had arrived.

An officer came from the roadside office. He bowed to me and, opening the hood of our car, copied our engine number on his pad. He asked about our luggage. I gave him my keys. He undid one bag, glanced in, closed it carefully, returned the keys, bowed again, and went back into his office.

With blithe "Heil Hitler" three workmen bicycled round the barrier into Germany, tin dinner pails swinging on their handlebars. A boy of eight or nine would have bicycled out as casually, but he was stopped. "I'm on my way to my grandmother's and late," he protested. "You officers all know she lives just over there. Her house was in Germany before war shifted the boundary." He was turned home to get his pass card.

The day was lazy, but the German officials did not loiter or chat. Alike in a mannered courtesy, they performed their duties with dispatch. Even when idle they did not lounge.   They stood seriously, their shoulders straight and their heads high.   I was surprised by their youth.

Our car's international *carnet* signed, the Customs satisfied, and my husband's passport stamped, we were assured that all was in order for our entry.   I have a passport. An American passport.   My husband forgot to offer it and he was not asked for credentials for me.   Some months later, when we were settled in a house, the local police just put me on their registry as *Ehefrau* or housewife, a title of which I am proud and to which I have not the least objection.   There was considerable concern about my husband's desire to bring in and keep over an indefinite length of time a motorcar of English manufacture, but seemingly no concern about his bringing in a woman.

The barrier opened.   We entered the land which French friends had warned me is a land of *Die Herren der Schöpfung*, a civilization where man is the master of creation. I turned in my seat to watch the frontier close behind me.

Life in Germany had begun.

Within Germany the road we traveled was smoothly laid.   It widened down a charming hill, curved and bent over the valleyed Eifel, and followed the course of the water along the banks of the Ahr and the Rhine as we circled to Bonn.   Our way led through carefully kept forests clean of underbrush and gnarled trees, by tidy farmsteads, past terraced vineyards, and in and out of neat hamlets and towns each with its own tall church spire.

At places where the view was best good benches were set; and frequently a rest house at which to procure beer, milk, coffee, or wine.   We found the roadside, even in isolated places, cleared of useless growth. Eatable berries and pretty flowers were let grow. Poppies and cornflowers, buttercups and bouncing Bet, scattered their beauty lavishly; brown-eyed Susan, Queen Anne's lace, John-go-to-bed-at-noon, and the prim daisy were as much at home here as in the countryside of my childhood.

Half-timbered black and white houses, with a window box of petunias or bright geraniums blooming on every sill, had charm for us. We saw many geese, plump brown ducks, and on the pond in each town a pair of stately swans.

Children were numerous. Clean, winsome children who stared wide-eyed and called *"Ausländer"* at us, but were quick to answer smile with smile.

The highland soil was thin. The Rhineland valley a rich loam. Rich or thin, it was tilled as by those who know their craft. Tall rye swayed in the breeze. Oats were full-grained; winter wheat in fine head; the first clover crop stacked, the second deep enough to cover well the larks' nests. Much of the timothy was already out; in many fields men were pitching the hay into wagons where women arranged the fragrant load. Often a little boy or girl held the driving lines. In avenues approaching the villages and in orchards cherries were ripe, apples and pears coming on. Within garden fences a few very late strawberries gleamed sweetly in beds where the leaves were turning. Raspberries were in season, currants nearly ready, gooseberry bushes laden with fruit, and the vegetable gardens had all been nicely hoed. Clear of weed, asparagus was growing up in feathery plumes.

At frequent intervals we passed under white cloths let-

tered in black stretched across the road high above our
heads and read: "Thinkest thou, German man, and thou,
German woman, of the Saar?" — "My dear German folk,
forget not thy kin in the Saar" — "Germans! While you
enjoy life in the Fatherland, remember your brothers in the
Saar" — in German, of course.

Commercial advertisements were few. We spoke of
this at a place where we bought gasoline. We were told
that an order had been issued from Berlin for the removal
before 1936 of all those now defacing the landscape.

It was Saturday afternoon. In the towns people were
buying and selling in preparation for Sunday. In the
country they toiled late before a day of rest. Horses were
in use, but on the steeper hills the farmers plodded after
oxen, slow and patient in their movements as their beasts.
Many were harrowing their fields. Others ploughed stub-
ble under. Or were busy setting a root crop where hay
had been harvested.

We saw a little girl, whose flaxen plaits hung from beneath a blue-checked sunbonnet, slip under roadside bars
carrying a napkin-covered basket. "Papa! Papa!" she
called. The man at work in the field put down his scythe
to greet her, stooping to kiss her before he took the
basket.

Further on we passed a group of schoolboys hiking on
stilts, accompanied by a master also stilting. They had
flushed, happy faces and were making fast progress.

At the posthouse in Blankenheim we stopped for coffee.
With "My balcony is best in June," the inn host ushered
us through to a porch on the edge of a ravine. The
ravine's further side rose above us in steep cliffs; and on

the loftiest crag stood a stone castle, its massive outline dark against the pale sky. Unfurled from the highest turret floated the banner of the black cross. The time was after six and the slanting light of the sun had set panes of gold in the castle windows.

We were seated at a table by the rail. "The castle was the home of the Knights of Blankenheim until destroyed by henchmen of Louis XIV of France," our host told us as he spread the cloth. "Hitler Youth have rebuilt it with their own hands. It is in use as a hostel; just now a Labor Corps is there."

As he placed our cups he chatted on, and en route to his kitchen he took time to dial a radio bringing to us the "Unfinished Symphony" of Franz Schubert. The players were well begun, and to the sweet rise of the composition's theme we heard the nearer homely grind of a coffee mill, the flow of a tap, the rattle of an iron stove. Then the silence held only Schubert's music until, from somewhere hidden quite close, came the notes of a thrush. Evening shadows lengthened while we listened. The bird, gifted with but a narrow scale, sang clear and true, adding his voice with all a thrush's power to Schubert's message. As I listened, for no common-sense reason there swelled in my heart a renewed confidence in the affairs of the world.

Suddenly we lost the melody of thrush and Schubert in the boom of the "Horst Wessel" song; "*Die Fahnen hoch*" — the clang of castle gates and the tramp of booted feet; "*Die Reihen dicht geschlossen*" — down the cliff trail men climbed; "*S.A. marschiert mit ruhig festem Schritt.*" Like the crack of a whip their shouted words — "*Kam'raden, die*

Rotfront und Reaktion erschossen" — resounded across the ravine. In double file they passed down the village street. *"Es schaun aufs Hakenkreuz voll Hoffnung schon Millionen"* — each measure clipped, and a measure of heavy tread. *"Der Tag für Freiheit und für Brot bricht an"* (The day of freedom and of bread is dawning) — a chanted line and a voice pause for the march of feet to be heard. Timed as to the beat of a metronome.

Thirty-two young men, near six feet tall and handsomely built; stripped to the waist, their smooth skins reddened by sun and wind; trousered in gray-green cotton cloth freshly laundered; booted to the knees in stout leather — they strode along in the vigor of physical health and mental contentment, holding between them a rope. Thus the first German Labor Corps I saw went by, their eyes glancing neither to the right nor to the left.

"Heil! Heil!" cheered the villagers. "Heil! Heil! Heil! — Heil! —— Heil!"

"Fine strapping fellows," said our inn host as he brought a tray to our table. "They go down to the meadow in the evenings to exercise in a game of tug-of-war."

The coffee was good, the cream thick, and the innkeeper gave us cherry tarts newly baked. The reckoning was fifty cents. Before we rose to go the thrush sang again.

"Hitler — Arbeit und Brot" we read painted on an arch of a railway bridge spanning the river below Altenahr. "Hitler — Work and Bread" we read again on a white banner set in the vineyards of Walporzheim.

"Thank the Führer for 415,673 hours of work" we read where the road widened into a fine boulevard. The new cutting was not an ugly gash in the mountainside because the raw banks had been sodded as a lawn to the end of the completed work. It was Saturday afternoon. The road builders were away. They had left their machines protected by fitted waterproof covers and their hand tools, so we presumed, were locked up in the neat red shed on wheels.

"Heil Hitler!" called two boys standing in the middle of the road beyond Remagen to signal us. They asked our destination and a lift that far. "We are Hitler Youth," they told us.

Both wore rucksacks, and the elder had a guitar hung on a shoulder strap. Fair-haired, freckled, clear-eyed; square hands clean even to scrubbed nails; blue shirts elbow-sleeved and open-throated; black cotton shorts, laced boots, and thick socks. We gave them our back seat.

They quickly slipped off their packs, making themselves comfortable. Frankly glad of this opportunity to practise English learned at their school in Hamburg, they used it eagerly, their voices courteous. One was fifteen. The other twelve. They had recently been in the Black Forest and were now visiting the Rhine and its tributaries, spending the summer in learning to know their country.

At night they slept in Youth Hostels. They assured us there were plenty of these places all over Germany, each equipped with facilities for keeping one's self and clothes as a German should, as well as providing shelter and the comradeship of other Hitler Youth.

"We have serious conversations, evening campfires, and music," explained the elder.

"Rüdiger plays well," added the younger, touching the lute.

This was the smaller boy's first season of Youth Travel. The elder had him under his care. Rüdiger had been started in the same way three years ago by an experienced boy. He now knew Hannover, Thüringen, and Bayern — in fact, most of his Fatherland with the exception of East Prussia.

"East Prussia is the most important province to study, because it is into the East that our nation must expand," Rüdiger told us. "A journey there is difficult. The Polish Corridor separates that part of our nation from the Fatherland. I can't get across. The technicalities are too many. But next year I shall go by boat."

"I'll go by boat, too," put in the younger.

"Yes, you can come. We must all understand East Prussia."

We asked if they had traveled in any other countries but Germany.

"No, that we cannot do. It would be interesting, but our Leader forbids. He wants German youth to be German, not to pick up other ways: and we have plenty to see in our own beautiful Fatherland. Also, Germany is poor. We haven't money to spend outside."

"I'd like to see France," said the twelve-year-old. "My mother went to Biarritz with her parents when she was young."

"Flat-headed sheep is what the French call us Germans," the older boy told him. "They would take the Rhine away from us if they could."

"Would they?"

"Sure, they would — and they have mines laid all along the border. All they have to do is to press a button in

Strassburg to blow up our western frontier. That is what
the League of Nations has let them do."

"I would like to see France," the little one persisted.
"My mother liked Biarritz."

"We are a generation who cannot do things because we
like." The older boy spoke firmly. "We must live, not
for ourselves, but for Germany."

On entering Godesberg we found the streets garlanded
with swastikas. The boys were keen to know why. We
stopped to let them ask. The policeman consulted answered them politely. Adolf Hitler had come to the Hotel
Dreesen yesterday afternoon and the decorations had not
yet been taken down.

"The proprietor of the Hotel Dreesen is our Leader's
lifelong friend," Rüdiger informed us.

"If we had come yesterday we might have seen *den
Führer.*"

"Have you ever seen him?" I asked.

"Rüdi three times and I once."

"Our Leader is the best man in the world," exclaimed
Rüdiger, his eyes shining like stars.

From Godesberg on, the back seat was quiet. Once I
turned to look. Within the circle of the older boy's arm
the little one was asleep, his head cradled on the other's
shoulder. As we approached Bonn, Rüdiger whispered
directions. When we drove up before a Youth Hostel
he woke his companion gently.

"Thank you," "Good-bye," and "I hope we meet again,"
were their words as they shook hands with us.

"My name is Otto. You forgot to ask," remarked the
little one when he had hoisted up his pack.

"Why not exchange addresses and birthday dates?" exclaimed the elder, and we did.

"Heil Hitler!   Heil Hitler!   Heil Hitler!" we heard in a medley of cordial young voices as they were welcomed into their hostel.

We went on to a hotel.   The hotelkeeper came out to the curb, greeting us as if truly glad we had come.   He asked after the health of the little girls, our daughter and our niece, who had stopped here with my husband in the early spring.   His remembrance of them pleased me, making me feel that I had come to live among a warm-hearted people.

Then he said: "Bonn is full.   This is the best tourist season we have had in Germany for many years.   The privilege of registered marks combined with curiosity as to whether we Germans have cloven hoofs is bringing people into our country."

"You haven't rooms for us?"

He hastily assured us that he had received our letter and reserved a place.   The rooms were nice.   The charge, inclusive of meals, which were excellent, and the 10 per cent for service, was twenty marks a day, "as you are staying longer than a fortnight."

We dined in a small room where full-length portraits in color of Field Marshal von Hindenburg, wearing uniform, and Reichskanzler Adolf Hitler, in a trench coat, looked down on us.   I could see other portraits of these two leaders of the German people on the walls of a brilliantly lit café across the street.   This café was filled with singing people.   As we sat down they were chorusing in slow rhythm, starting low and rising high, a folk song which begins: *"Es liegt eine Krone im tiefen Rhein"* — and goes, in English translation: —

> There lies a crown in the depths of the Rhine,
> 'Twas conjured from jewels and gold so fine,
> Whoever retrieves it, receives with it power,
> He's crowned in Aachen the very same hour.

> From the Belt to the Danube his lands all combine
> To make him the Kaiser, the Prince of the Rhine.

> There lies a lyre in the depths of the Rhine,
> 'Twas fashioned of gold and of ivory fine.
> Whoever the lyre from the depths doth raise,
> From his lips pour forth enraptured lays.

Immediately this was finished a man rose up from a table by the open window and began to sing in solo: —

"Gold und Silber lieb ich sehr, kann's auch gut gebrauchen, Sei's des Mondes Silberschein, sei's das Gold der Sterne."

None of this crowd were young. All were well past middle age. The women wore their long hair in knots on the top of their heads and used side combs. Most of the men had the local summer haircut, a clean shave, leaving them bald and shiny pink. All were neatly dressed in good clean clothes. They were orderly people. Quiet except for their music. The waiter told us that the café was filled with rival singing clubs, come in from near-by villages to enjoy Saturday night in town.

They sang in emotional voices as people do who have pleasure in sentimental melody. At times a group would sing while all the others listened. Then the folk round another table would take a turn, sometimes repeating the last song, giving it a different interpretation. Several times quartettes came out on the pavement and, turning, sang through the open windows to their companions inside. Often there were solos.

Between songs waiters served these people with food and beer. The women buttered bread for their men and put on slices of meat or cheese. Hearty eating and drinking did not hamper the volume of their romantic songs, but a woman's hand sometimes covered a man's glass and she said: "Thou hast had enough."

"*Ach, Frauchen*," the man would exclaim, and perhaps his "little wife" would let him have another. But not always.

Their concert went on all the time we were eating dinner and long afterwards. My husband went out to visit a bachelor friend, named Hans Schmidt, and I listened on to the singing. Upstairs, I found a balcony to my room and sat there in a low chair. It was like a concert, but I enjoyed it more than any formal concert I have ever attended. Here in Bonn, the birthplace of Beethoven, on my first evening of residence in Germany I heard *Rhein-Lieder*, *Volkslieder*, and songs from Brahms, Schubert, Schumann, Löwe, Mendelssohn, Wolf, and others of the German constellation of composers. All sung as if folk songs.

As I prepared for bed a quartette of male voices were giving a song which they announced had been used by a city watchman of a bygone day. There was a verse for every hour of the night watch and a chorus repeated after every verse. This is what I heard: —

"Hark to what I say, good people,
The clock struck ten from our steeple,
Commandments ten God did decree,
To them let us all faithful be.

Chorus:

"Human guarding cannot aid us,
God must guard us, God who made us,
Lord, by thy grace and might,
Grant to us a peaceful night.

"Hark to what I say, good people,
Eleven has struck from our steeple,
Eleven disciples steadfast were,
Grant that we die not in despair."

Thus, in serene Christian faith, a German city watchman of a bygone day had marked the passage of time from curfew until dawn, and German people of the twentieth century still cherished his words. Here was a peace like that in the *Deutsch* communities of my own dear Pennsylvania. These people had the same substantial build and the same homely ways of their kinfolk far across the seas whom I knew so well in my early youth.

Memory told me these were people I could love and trust. Our Pennsylvania Germans do not sing in public cafés, but this scene below had a domesticity solid as in a home. Less homesick than at any time since I came to Europe, I listened. It seemed my bed could be in Lebanon County; it had the good comfort and linen smelling of fresh garden lavender.

On the wings of their song I drifted to sleep.

II

"DIE FLEDERMAUS"

I awoke to the ring of church bells. It seemed the natural sequel to the watchman's song. I felt rested and at peace. *"Die Welt steht auf dem Kopf,"* the maid who brought my morning coffee told me, and to this information that the world stands on its head I buttered my first German Sunday bread. She lingered, and realizing that perhaps the Rhinelander, like folk in China, enjoys a friendly chat and has time for it, I did not discourage her.

"We Germans have Adolf Hitler sent by God to help us. The poor people in other lands have nobody to help them," she declared in preface to a detailed and romantic account of his recent activities as given to her by a cousin, a waiter at the Hotel Dreesen near Godesberg. She and her cousin had spent yesterday afternoon, their free day, walking in the Königswald.

She told how the Führer had come to the Hotel Dreesen on Friday afternoon, looking tired and worn. The usual vegetarian meal had been carefully cooked for him, but he did not notice food and it was understood by all that he wrestled with some serious government problem. She said: "Ordinarily, it is his habit to thank those who serve him."

Dr. Joseph Goebbels, whom she called "Our Joe," Herr Viktor Lutze, and other aides had been there with the Führer. "Others give what advice and help they can, but the strain of every decision for our German good rests on our Hitler," she averred.

Dr. Goebbels and the Führer had left the party gathered round a table and walked on the Rhine terrace, Dr. Goebbels talking to Herr Hitler in a comforting voice. The context of his speech could not be heard, but Germany, Germany, Germany, throbbed through his words. Then the Führer walked alone, back and forth, back and forth, struggling toward decision. The hour advanced beyond midnight, a fog gathered over the Drachenfels. The orchestra, which had played all the evening, played on and on, giving such help as it could, choosing the Führer's known favorites from Wagner and the National Socialist hymns.

Back and forth, back and forth, he walked. Dispatches interrupted him and after each he stared long at the Rhine, running past in its solemn flow. Finally, there came a telephone call from Berlin. The Führer himself must be brought to the phone. He listened, but did not speak beyond an occasional monosyllable. When he had hung up, he walked alone again, paler now, his dark eyes sunken in sadness. Suddenly he turned and gave the command: "We go."

An order was put through to the Bonn aerodrome for a Junkers plane to be got ready. The Führer and his party left the hotel. "Since then our Hitler has striven for us, putting down a revolution before it started. He lives only for Germany. He is our father and our mother, keeping us safe from all harm," the maid stated as she took my tray.

Downstairs I asked the hotel manager about this revolution. "Yes," he acknowledged, "there is serious trouble in Munich and in Berlin, but our Leader has it competently in hand. Here in the Rhineland there is not the least disturbance. Come to the door and observe the tranquillity of Bonn."

I walked with him to the door and saw that a Sunday peace rested on the tree-shaded avenue. Elderly people strolled there, quietly and neatly dressed, many of them accompanied by small children, some turning into a near-by church; folk in ages between the elderly and the very young, athletic of figure, hurried by dressed for various sports.

I went down to the tree-protected promenade along the Rhine. In the coolness here equally peaceful people were enjoying a Sunday leisure, while in and on the water several swam and many had pleasure in boats. Tiny yachts sped by, their owners wearing natty seafaring rig. Some people brought folding canoes to the bank; quickly setting them up, they paddled off.

At fairly frequent intervals passenger vessels passed, churning a wide wake of foam. Their decks were filled with happy-looking throngs, many of them singing. All the boats were cleanly painted, usually white with a trim of blue, green, or red and aflutter with flags and gay banners. One had a lilac ribbon lettered in gold stretched from prow to stern proclaiming it an outing of a metaphysics association and giving the name of their town. The metaphysicians were chorusing in fine harmony with their orchestra of wood, wind, brass, and strings.

On the opposite bank from where I walked a populace less refined than the quiet people here made merry. There a calliope played amid the white tents of a circus. A merry-go-round and Ferris wheel revolved. Theirs was an exuberant pleasure, noisy with boisterous laughter.

A ship, with a notice inviting everyone to come on board and view a state exhibition of things made by German hands, stood docked below Bonn bridge. I was about to go up the gangplank when my husband and Hans Schmidt arrived. They came to announce their decision that after two days of motoring we needed a real walk. So we crossed by motorcar to the foothills of the Siebengebirge and parked in a *Platz*. A dirt road on which cars were forbidden led up from here.

Donkeys for hire, saddle horses, victorias, and a miniature railway train offered conveyance to those who wished to begin their pedestrianism after arrival at the wooded summit. We joined those walking up the long hot broadway. They were a friendly sort, joking about the toil of lifting one foot after the other, quoting proverbs on the merits of exercise, and exchanging fun with those so lazy as to ride. None appeared concerned with any revolution.

Donkey men were persuasive and parents lenient, so that many children climbed the hill on donkey back. The timid clung to an adult hand while in the saddle. The bold gave themselves airs, flapped the reins, and dug in their heels. The result of this was several times disastrous. More than one young rider came down and had to suffer the mockery of the crowd: "*Wer den Schaden hat, braucht für den Spott nicht zu sorgen.*" Thus is the loser laughed at in many lands.

Everybody took the hill at an easy pace excepting a

column of little girls dressed alike in black shoes, short blue skirts, white blouses, and brown jackets much too warm for the day. Their hair, drawn severely from centre partings into tight plaits, was damp above their brows. Sweat poured down their earnest faces. Some were of fine physique, others sadly marked by undernourishment. Sound limbs and ricket legs keeping the same forward step, they swept by singing with ardor as they marched. In face and figure they were children still — children whose honest faces were lit by a shining radiance, such as I once saw on the young converted at a Christian Revival Service in America.

"*Bund Deutscher Mädel*," commented Hans. "The Hitler Maids."

This is what I heard them sing: —

> "*Deutschland,*
> *Du wirst leuchtend stehn,*
> *Mögen wir auch untergehn.*
> *Vorwärts! Vorwärts! Schmettern die Heldenfanfaren.*
> *Vorwärts! Vorwärts! Jugend kennt keine Gefahren.*
> *Ist das Ziel auch noch so hoch,*
> *Jugend zwingt es doch.*

Kehrreim:

> "*Unsre Fahne flattert uns voran,*
> *In die Zukunft ziehn wir Mann für Mann.*
> *Wir marschieren für Hitler durch Nacht und durch Not,*
> *Mit der Fahne der Jugend für Freiheit und Brot.*
> *Unsre Fahne flattert uns voran.*
> *Unsre Fahne ist die neue Zeit,*
> *Und die Fahne führt uns in die Ewigkeit.*
> *Ja, die Fahne ist mehr als der Tod!*"

(Germany,
Thou wilt gleaming stand,
Even though we perish.
Forward! Forward! Resound the heroic fanfares.
Forward! Forward! Youth knows no hazards.
Be the goal ever so high,
Youth will yet achieve it.

Chorus:

Our flag flutters before us,
Into the future we move man for man.
We are marching for Hitler through night and
    through danger,
With the flag of youth for freedom and bread.
Our flag flutters before us.
Our flag is the new time,
And the flag leads us into eternity.
Yes, the flag is greater than death!)

Verse after verse of their hymn drifted to us when they had passed, their clear young voices penetrating the distance even when we had turned from the broadway into a narrow path leading to the quietness of the wood. It was pleasant here under the deep foliage of hardbeam and beech. Hans had a footpath map of this district and told me that one can buy such maps in any town in Germany. Paths have been laid out all over the country and are kept in repair for no other reason than to give refreshment to the minds of walkers. Our way was not crowded. Neither was it lonely. We met solitary walkers, occasional couples hand in hand, and many family groups, one in which two sturdy boys marched before their parents and a little girl was merry on her father's back.

In technicalities beyond my education, my companions talked of the composition of symphonies, dwelling on Beethoven's carefully weighed decisions and his intelligent courage, passing through consideration of his *rondo finale* to discussion of Brahms, and on to Schubert's C Major, which they called a "reckless, glorious steeplechase." We passed a class of school children out with their teacher identifying plants and trees. Beyond a rustic bridge we met two young girls wearing green tunics and barefoot sandals and a young man dressed in matching green shirt and shorts. They were playing guitars. Swinging along three abreast, they kept step to their music, singing as they walked: *"Wer recht in Freuden wandern will, der geb' der Sonn' entgegen —"* I liked the idea that those who would wander with joy must go toward the sun.

It was an idyllic day. A lovely sylvan day. Furred and feathered creatures were friendly along our paths as in a Buddhist land. Sweet-voiced songsters fluttered beside us, many very charmingly colored and of species I did not know. Robins chirped from branch to branch. Tits were really cheeky. Red squirrels wanted nuts. Most of the German folk had provisions for the inhabitants of the wood. There were several people who inspired such confidence that birds flew to their hands for tidbits. To my delight, when I tried they came to my hands, too.

We stopped for lunch at one wayside place and for coffee in another. In both I was surprised by the quality of the food. I had yet to learn the high standard in comfort and diet which the German counts a necessity.

People were friendly everywhere. At lunch, when I made some remark about life, a stranger leaned across from her table to tell me that in some thirty poems a German poet named Mörike has summed up all one needs to know. As proof she recited several beautiful verses which made me want to read his works.

Where we stopped for coffee we found a crowd gathered round a man with a long gray beard. He played a lute and gave a lead in singing whatever songs he was asked. Since leaving China I had not expected ever again to find a minstrel in a modern world, but here, they assured me, was one. A minstrel in a shabby brown velvet coat. It made me absurdly happy. The customers of the coffee inn applauded him with an enthusiasm that would have gratified a bard in any tea house.

Back at our hotel the man who came to take our dusty shoes asked if we had enjoyed our walk.

"I never miss mine," said he. "Thursday is my day off. My wife goes with me. We start from home at six in the morning so as to have a good long day. Eleven years we have been married. Rain or shine, except when she couldn't because of the baby, she has never missed coming along. He is a big boy now. Goes to school. He eats dinner at his grandmother's on Thursdays. Packs a tasty lunch for us, my wife does. Always a surprise in it for me. When we want a drink we stop in some place for a coffee, a beer, or maybe a nice glass of wine. We don't sit in long. It is out-of-doors we like. That is what I minded most during the war — no freedom to wander."

Before we crossed the frontier into Germany I had been apprehensive about living with the National Socialists. Not only did I know what I had heard in France and read in newspapers and magazines, but I had been in Heidelberg on a brief visit at the very time they came into power and I had been turned against them by what I saw there. My feeling had been so strong that I had refused even to come into Germany in April with my husband when he came to make arrangements for work he wished to do in German music. This although I knew that he had cherished a desire to study here through twenty-eight years in China.

Now, ashamed of my behavior in the spring, I set forth to find a furnished house in which to make a home during our sojourn. Child of a Pennsylvania Quaker and a Swedish mother, and wife to an Englishman whose favorite composers are German, I have always lived in homes with doors wide open for German visitors. During the Great War I was neutral, as were all my kin. Neither then nor since had it ever occurred to me that one group of the peoples involved was any more to blame for those four long years of reversion to barbarism than the other. I knew people who had been caught up in the tides of patriotism on both sides. I had mourned dead who fell facing each other's guns.

I had some German friends and many German acquaintances, but my knowledge of things German was exceedingly superficial. I knew well one German book, a drama, and I was not entirely ignorant of Germany's poetry; but I did not have the habit of reading her literature, nor had I given her philosophies more than a casual glance. From an early age my attention had centred on things of the Orient, but the influences round me had tended to my acceptance of the Germans as belonging to the coterie of the civilized. Also my heart was soft to them because they had been defeated. People invited to any house where I was hostess were not asked again if they were stiff to German guests met there.

On this Monday morning, July 2, 1934, I reasoned that the National Socialists of Germany are Germans, a people of violent temperament, but a moral people who, when they do wrong, soon long to make it right again. A hotel maid had gossiped of further revolution, but there could be nothing serious happening in a land where people were so serenely unconcerned in demeanor as here. I thought of the French Revolution and of the Russian Revolution, as I achieved a reasoned pardon for the violence attendant on the National Socialist assumption of control in Germany.

Since I must live in Europe, this country now suited me as well as any other. Moving from France had interrupted a book I was writing about Ch'in Shih Huang-ti, the builder of the Great Wall of China. As my publisher wanted the remaining chapters as promptly as possible, I had a concern to get my domestic affairs in order quickly that I might finish my book.

Monday and Tuesday, and until late afternoon on Wednesday, I searched with a quiet heart; then my complacency was shaken. The estate agent took me to Marienburg, an attractive suburb of Cologne. We stopped before a house which was occupied.

"This is the place you want," said he; "it has every requirement you have specified. I can only show you the location to-day, but by to-morrow morning I will have an order to view."

"Who lives in it?" I asked.

"A man named Abendroth."

"The musician?"

"Yes — "

"Why is he moving?"

"He has been dismissed from all his Cologne appointments."

"Abendroth dismissed! I thought he was one of the few important men in music left in Germany and Cologne's pride. Is he a Jew?"

"Pure Aryan," he answered.

"Who dismissed him?"

"The local government."

"Why?"

"It is not usual to question acts of government here. It borders on treason."

"Is Herr Abendroth banished from Germany?"

"No. As soon as the news spread that he had been dismissed from Cologne, the rival musical city of Leipzig invited him there."

"So Cologne loses him to Leipzig! Didn't any of the citizens of Cologne protest?"

"Foolishly, thirty-five did. I believe that they were elderly professors, probably most of them musicians. Two young officials in government uniform received the deputation. When the officials had explained to the petitioners the seriousness of the misdemeanor they were committing in presenting a petition against a government decision, thirty-three of them had the sense to slip away."

"And the other two?"

"They persisted in reading the petition and were beaten insensible. One was a fine organist at one of our biggest churches. I have heard that his hands are ruined." The estate agent coughed nervously. "You must not judge ours a bad government. We have got to be ruled hard until things are straight. Our country would have gone Communist if the Nazis had not saved us. Hitler's government is benevolent to all who willingly obey. Our Führer knows that we must be a people of one Will if we are to regain our place among the strong nations of the world."

He offered to show me other houses, but I felt that I needed to think before using any more of his time, and I went back to my hotel. What shocked me more than the violence of the young officials was that thirty-three elderly men had slipped away. If thirty-five men had prepared the petition, then thirty-five should have supported it. A country which bred old men weak in courage had not my respect.

Wanting to think things over quietly, I went to Bonn University campus next morning. I took the morning mail along to read, and en route I bought copies of the local papers. My husband had said that he intended staying here, so I was prepared to study them in my quest for a house.

We had a postcard of greeting and "again thanks" from Rüdiger and Otto, the Hitler Youths whom we had given a lift on Saturday. Also a letter from the German farmer met in Eupen-Malmédy. He had a fine grandson safely born. Mother and child were doing well. Would we be godparents? This request touched my heart. Next I read a letter from my brother in America, and one from friends in China.

Then I opened the German papers. They reported troubles in other parts of the world. Unrest in France, misery in Russia, a serious shipping strike in California, the

breaking up of the British Empire, and hopelessness in the
Danube countries.   Reading here, this seemed a sorry
planet; but in Germany at least there was peace.   There
had been an insurrection over the week-end within the
National Socialist Party, but the Führer and his aides had
soon brought this to order.

Twelve years in China detached me from newspaper
reading as a regular habit, but my husband has *The Times*
sent to him from London wherever he is, and several copies
had come together, catching up with our new address.   I
opened them leisurely, half my attention on a rusty-coated
blackbird in the tree above me who was singing notes as
liquid as if the month were May.   When I had them all
doubled back at the middle, where their principal news is
always hidden, I suddenly saw that Germany was in the
headlines: —

"Herr Hitler's Coup" — "A Midnight Descent on
Munich" — "Arrest and Execution of S.A.[1] Leaders" — "A
Party Purge" — "More Executions in Germany" — "The
'Clean-up' Complete" — "President's Thanks to Herr
Hitler" — "Ban on S.A. Uniforms" — "Attitude of Army"
— "Ex-Premier among Victims" — "Bodies Found on
Moors" — "Growing Death Roll in Munich."

Under these headings I read column after column of re-
strained English prose narrating the execution of an unknown number of Germans by their fellow Germans.
Then I read two editorials: "Purging a Party" and "Mediæval Methods."

The fair day darkened, time turned back, and memory
swung me across space. . . .

[1] *Sturm Abteilung,* the "brown-shirts," Hitler's political army.

It was a summer day in China and I had stepped out of a hotel at the Nankow pass under the shadow of the Great Wall. My chair bearers, who were to carry me on a visit to friends in the northeast, sat waiting. Before us on the plain, soldiers were drawn up in regimental formation. Discipline was in process among them. Every ninth man in every ninth row was being called out to kneel, bare his neck, and bow his head to the executioner's sword. Silently, they were meeting death.

Then, as now, the fair green earth had waved before me in sickening black. I heard the voice of my head chair-bearer speak: "Come, Tai-Tai, we wait"; and my sight had cleared that I might walk to my waiting chair. The bearers set off in their usual deliberate trot, helping me to quietness by their steadiness, hastening their pace only when they could put a hill between us and what was going on. Then without a command from me the old bearer stopped the chair and put it down. "You had better have a drink of tea," he said kindly.

I could not put the scene from my mind and must ask questions. The chief bearer explained to me that their commander was an austere man who gave to every soldier in his army a set of moral edicts: no one in his ranks could loot, rape, swear, smoke, drink, or be untidy. Slackness had come into this regiment, and its members were being taught to obey the will of their Lord by this method of striking terror into their midst. There had been no court of inquiry. Justice resided in their commander.

My memory was broken in upon by a German voice: "We are professors of the university. We noticed that you have copies of the London *Times* and would appreciate sharing them." Thus two men introduced themselves. I gave them the papers and they sat down, both reading from the same sheet. Their faces went white as they read, yet neither made any comment. When they had finished, the professors folded the papers neatly, returning them with thanks.

I went back to my hotel. On the faces of the people whom I passed I saw no troubled anxiety, no harassed, apprehensive, bewildered look. Men, women, and children all appeared concerned only with their own affairs. I crossed a market square where fruits and vegetables were offered for sale; here *Hausfrauen* were busy at their marketing, intent on their purchases. Beside one mother a little girl waited, gayly skipping.

I told my husband that I intended to leave, and learned again that he meant to stay. After sitting a while embroidering, I realized that he was right. Violence may occur in any land. I had never left China because it occurred. I could not now run away. Deep in my heart I knew that it is a woman's first job in life to make her husband as comfortable a home as she can — in the place where he wants to be, regardless of geography.

The forenoon of our second Sunday we went to a pageant given on Bonn campus by citizens of the town. I had supposed from reading the papers that the S.A. were all on vacation, but men in the brown uniform were roping off the central grass when we arrived. In company with other observers we strolled under the trees, noticing the charm of fair children, the kindliness in the wrinkled faces of the aged, the feminineness of the girls' dresses and the eager attention

which they gave to young men, many of whom were
sabre-gashed, some with a nasty black gumlike paste on
their fresh wounds. Elderly ladies carried candies in pretty
little china or cut-glass boxes which they took from hand-
bags and passed to their relatives and friends.

A goodly audience had gathered before the citizens taking
part in the pageant arrived on horseback and in open horse-
drawn carriages. The men were gay in satin breeches,
lace ruffles, silk stockings, and buckled shoes; the women
gowned in dainty flowered silks and muslins. All wore
powdered wigs. Children were replicas of their elders.
With bygone ceremony they descended from horse and
carriage, greeted each other, and came on to the green to
dance minuets.

Sweeping curtsy and stately bow distinguished the leisured performance of the opening number, danced to music composed by Jean Baptiste Lully for the court of
Louis XIV. Then came a minuet from Haydn, light-
hearted and cheerful. This was followed by a graceful
and tender melody arranged by Mozart. And, lastly, we
were given one from Bonn's own Beethoven of quicker
tempo and more varied rhythm than any of those before,
dignified, yet with a spirit of romping fun in it. "A minuet
truly Rhenish," a woman standing near explained to me.

Later in the day we went to a memorial service held in
a private house for Dr. Willi Schmid, a music critic who
had lost his life at Munich during the previous week-end.
An obituary notice was read from the *Münchener Neueste
Nachrichten*, and a statement was made that he had been in
no way involved in politics. His executioners had arrested
and shot him instead of the wanted man. It was a case of

mistaken identity. The government had expressed regrets. No blemish of even suspected treason was attached to his reputation.

There was no prayer, and no discussion. The service consisted of a programme of selections from Bach's *Matthäuspassion*. The infinite tenderness and sorrow of this music filled the room for more than an hour. Then the radio was turned on that we might listen to Herr Hess, deputy to Herr Hitler, speaking at a National Socialist Congress at Königsberg in East Prussia.

Herr Hess began in a husky voice, each slow phrase emotionally controlled. In this manner he spoke of Herr Hitler's courageous action in carrying out a grave decision with severity and energy a few days ago, thereby saving Germany and the National Socialist movement from mutineers. The death of these ringleaders had prevented a civil war. It was necessary to save the lives of thousands, if not of tens of thousands, of the best Germans, among them possibly women and children.

He thanked all the organizations of the Party for their loyalty; particularly the Hitler Youth, among whom every boy looked up to the Führer as his idol, because he had always acted, especially in these days just past, in the way of an ideal heroic figure. In a few hours he had freed the nation from the thrall of a few abnormal, perverse beings, and restored to womenfolk their faith in the purity of the ideals for which their men and their children lived and strove under his leadership.

He gave no details of what had happened and mentioned no names, but went on to appeal to his East Prussian hearers

— as representative of soldierly German manhood, men who could best understand the Führer. He asserted that when the fate of the nation is at stake the degree of the guilt of an individual cannot be given meticulous judgment. To my astonishment he remarked that, severe though it may be, there is a deep significance in the old German system of crushing mutinies by shooting every tenth soldier, without putting the smallest question concerning his guilt or innocence.

His delivery quickened as he entered on the major part of his address, which was a discourse on war and peace. He mentioned that within a few weeks would occur the twentieth anniversary of the day which saw the beginning of the German soldiers' great heroic struggle. He said Germany now had the good fortune to be governed predominantly by her front-line soldiers, who had grafted the virtues of the front on to state leadership.

He paid a glowing tribute to all men who had fought at the front, on the enemy as well as the German side. Then in graphic and lengthy detail he painted a dramatic picture of the splendors and the agonies of warfare, drawn from his personal experience, and called on soldiers everywhere to prevent their governments from bringing about a repetition of these horrors.

After some caustic remarks about the men who had betrayed Germany, betrayed the German soldier, he warned the world not to confuse the Germany of to-day, the Germany of peace, with the erstwhile Germany, the Germany of pacifism. "The way is not open for a stroll through our land," he proclaimed, rousing his audience in Königsberg to loud and lasting applause, which came clearly through the radio.

"Exactly as the French people contested each hand's breadth of ground with their utmost powers in the Great War, so would we Germans do the same. The French-line soldier well understands us when we declare to those who are still playing with the idea of a war which would call others to the front: 'Just you dare attack us! Just you dare to march into the new Germany!' Then the world will learn something about the spirit of the new Germany! It would fight for freedom as heroically as any people have ever fought! Old and young would dig themselves into the soil of the Homeland! They would defend themselves with unprecedented fanaticism!"

He closed with a conclusion, under ten minutes in duration, that peace was wanted in Europe and throughout the world, asked for an understanding with France reflecting the will to peace and the mutual respect of the soldiers on the two sides of the frontier, and reminded the world that Herr Hitler had repeatedly declared that Germany only desired equality of rights in all spheres, including that of armaments. After the attainment of such an understanding between Germany and her neighbors, Germany could more easily content herself with that minimum of armaments which was necessary to secure her safety and therefore peace. A virtually defenseless country was a danger to peace, a temptation to other countries to make war on her.

When the radio talk was over there was no comment in the room where we sat. Soon the sincere simplicity of the *Matthew Passion* continued. Listening, I realized as never before how infinitely tender music can be when composed by a mature intellect seeking to teach humanity that only through love and understanding of each other can mankind be civilized.

During the following week the greater part of my time continued to be occupied with the search for a house. Finally, since we must have a home when our daughter and niece arrived for the summer holidays, we took temporarily an apartment near the botanical gardens at Cologne. We went to tell of this arrangement to some people who had been energetic in assisting us, and stayed to afternoon coffee.

Here, we did hear comment on Herr Hess's address. Our host and hostess denounced it in no uncertain terms. "The German people have a right to an adequate explanation of 'bloody Saturday'" . . . "We Germans are one of the foremost peoples in the world in the adequacy of our laws and the efficiency of our Courts of Justice" . . . "No Chancellor has the right to turn back to mediæval practices" . . . "Herr Hess has criminally evaded the issue with an emotional smoke screen" . . . "We hope that Herr Hitler, a Chancellor constitutionally appointed, will be more adequate when he addresses the Reichstag, which has been summoned to the Kroll Opera House to hear him on Friday, July 13." Those were things they said.

At eight o'clock on Friday evening, July 13, we went to the Cologne High School of Music. We had been invited to attend their graduation exercises. But we discovered that the ceremonies would not take place until after the broadcast of Herr Hitler's speech, to which all Germans must listen. He spoke for an hour and a half with furious animation and skillful technique. I had read his book, *Mein Kampf*, wherein he has explained his theories on public speaking. He fulfilled them all. He told nothing more than he wished his people to know.

The most important part of his oration, so I thought, was: "I am ready before history to bear the responsibility for twenty-four hours of the bitterest decision of my life, during which Fate has taught me, in anxious worry, to cling with every thought of mine to the dearest thing we possess in this world: the German people and the German Reich." And: "In this hour I was responsible for the fate of the German nation. Therefore the Supreme Court of the German people was myself."

"Audacious poetry!" exclaimed the stranger on my left as this remark from his Chancellor came out of the radio.

When the speech was over the Cologne High School of Music ceremonies began. The programme was ambitious and disappointing. The performance was not even equal to that which I had heard the previous year at the Royal College of Music in London, and I had expected much more from scholars in a land so natively musical as this.

Afterwards, feeling that Germans have no end of vitality, I went along on an invitation to hear some real music. Arrived at a fine house, four of our number, one of them a Jew, took up their instruments. They were businessmen. They said they had met together to enjoy music without interruption every Tuesday since they were young men — except when interrupted by the war, in which all had fought. Our host's promise that we should hear real music was no idle boast. They played superbly Beethoven's "Quartette in E flat," Opus 127.

Our host had both beer and champagne on the ice, and sandwiches, ready for a party. As he filled glasses he sang from *Die Fledermaus*: "*Glücklich ist, wer vergisst, was nicht mehr zu ändern ist!*" (Happy is he who can forget what cannot be altered.)

III

TOWARD NOVEMBER

"Still, sprich durch die Blume," was the reply when I asked a simple question as we sat drinking coffee on a Rhineland terrace.

"Hush, speak through a flower!" It seemed a curious answer. Because I looked puzzled, it was amplified: *"Regierungsbeamte und Parteimitglieder darf man höchstens loben"* (Do not speak the names of government officials or Party members unless you praise them). I felt hurt, for I had meant no harm. I probed no further that day. Mine had been but an idle curiosity.

Never before had I been so close to the frequent passing of tragedy, nor among a people who accepted tragedy as did these. Every few days I encountered stories that appeared incredible in a land as outwardly serene and gay as this. For instance, I saw a woman go by, tall and fair, her beautiful face so marked by pain that I must ask about her.

I was hushed and not answered until we were in our host's house. Then, after the servant had left the room, pillows were put down along the crack of the door, a wad of plasticine stuck in the keyhole, and the telephone — which in Germany plugs into a wall socket — pulled from its connection "because the inventions for listening in on families are most easily applied to the telephone and some chance remark overheard might be judged treason."

These arrangements completed, I was cautiously told the following about the woman. Two unknown men wearing the brown uniform of the National Socialist Party had entered the house while husband and wife sat at dinner, and taken the husband away. Three months later four young men wearing black uniform with the "death's head cap" had brought back a coffin, and informed her that her husband had committed suicide. It was forbidden to open the sealed casket.

My narrators carefully explained that the husband was not a Jew, but an Aryan, as they call non-Jews here, a distinction in tragedy of which I did not see the point. The Party officials stayed until after the funeral. The widow was made to pay five thousand marks for "burial services."

From what I could learn her husband had been a respected member of the community. Neither the community nor her kin had made any united protest. In fact no protest of any kind had been made. And this was explained with the sentence: "It is not wise to interfere between individuals and the Party."

Around us, as the summer advanced, trellised roses bloomed to meet the purple clematis. Stately delphinium, snapdragon, hollyhock, and sweet pea beckoned to the budding aster, the dahlia, and the chrysanthemum. The Rhineland is rural even where urban, and every man here a landed proprietor, be his estate but a window box.

In the Rhine Valley I never saw a no man's land of old tin cans and rubbish. I never came upon an ugly back-yard corner. Everywhere were flowers in array, neat paths, and pretty lawns; in each garden there was an arbor or a tree with a cleanly table and chairs set beneath its shade. Nearly always there was water — a trickling stream, a lily pond, or a fountain, if the location gave no view of the river.

"For us, where there is something growing, there is always hope," I was told, and this was added: "If you will look you will find the seed of blossom in every German heart. No matter how sordid the round of his daily life, tucked under the crustiest exterior each German has a sentimental love of forget-me-nots and rustic waterfalls."

Although the Rhine is a busy commercial river, at few places along its banks are warehouses permitted to press down to the water's edge; long stretches of riverside are kept open, some laid out in parks, others left in wild and rugged beauty. At the close of the Great War, the peace dictated by the Allied victors leveled the fortressed walls of patrician Cologne; the havoc and mess round the proud city were soon cleared away and its double-towered cathedral now looks down on an encircling green belt planted with trees and shrubs, furnished with swimming pools and playing fields. In lovely Düsseldorf, flowering vines clamber up houses built flush on the street. It seemed they must spring from the pavement. I learned that their roots are nourished in well-tended beds in the cellars of the houses, the trunk stems carried through wall and sidewalk in encasing tubes.

Stiefmütterchen or "little stepmother"; *Himmelsschlüssel* or "key of heaven" — these are names given the pansy and the primrose. The ever-flowering begonia is called "industrious Elizabeth." Each blossom has its *Kosename* or love name.

Walls do not generally shut homes from view. In passing one may enjoy the flower gardens, and also glimpse the householder surrounded by his family at coffee, or perhaps find him busy at cultivation. Even on huge estates, where there are gardeners enough, owners wheel heavy barrows, spade, plant, weed, and water, spray and train, in serene business.

"Politics spoil the character," according to a German proverb, and I found few people concerned with their government, except those actively employed in it. The people I met preferred to be occupied with other things.

Daily I heard what in America is called classical music, and under the following explanation I was assured that there is nothing curious about this. Effective melodies are invariably borrowed folk tunes, and all the great German composers were folk musicians, kin to the highway minstrel and troubadour of an earlier day. German folk songs were transformed into hymns by Martin Luther, who put religious words to them; still later their melodies appear in the chorals of Bach. In Bonn, Beethoven's birthplace, one can hear to-day the rustic dance melodies, cuckoo calls, and final serenity which the master put into his Pastoral Symphony. Schubert, Schumann, Brahms, Wagner, and the other great men arranged and rewrote what was already commonplace, enriching it with their own genius. Even the tune of "*Deutschland über alles*," taken from Haydn, was got by him from a Croatian folk song.

There may have been places where the political events of this time beat in upon these people differently than I saw. As far as my observation went their concern with politics was to keep free of it. "We love the Fatherland deeply, truly, reverently, but we are not temperamentally suited to the management of affairs other than our own," I heard again and again, while broadcast on the air every day were strange statements made by members of the National Socialist Party who quite frequently gave their remarks support by quoting phrases torn from the text of Schiller, Lessing, Fichte, and even Goethe.

"These Rhinelanders have wine in their veins, not blood," a Berlin friend who was visiting us said of them. "They need a firm hand before they can be properly incorporated into the Third Reich. They care more about carnival than politics and have a half-serious, half-mocking affection for both England and France. Given moonlight on the Rhine, they have always been willing to let who will tend to politics.

"But a new time is born now, a serious time, and soon their life and vigor must be harnessed more practically to the service of the state. That cannot be done, of course, until we have reoccupied the Rhine — a right the Versailles Treaty forbids us. These folk compounded of gentleness and coarseness, nimble wits and catholic piety, careless gayety and business genius, are a splendid people. They must be made more closely one with the rest of the Fatherland. Of course, some of the great factory owners here have supplied Hitler with gold, helping to make his rise possible. They gambled on him as an 'unknown soldier' who might be right in his fanatical belief that he is selected by God to bring back German prosperity."

Despite the great joy they took in their domestic gardens, no one here seemed quite at home in town; all had a nostalgia for the wilder country. At every week-end they hurried away, the wealthy in motorcars or river yachts, the less rich in small cars and on motor bikes, the populace pouring out on push bicycles and on foot.

They went in family groups to wooded hill and river-side meadow, freshly and neatly clad. The poorest showed no rags. Every garment they wore was cleanly washed and nicely patched. Little folk rode in baskets fastened on the bicycles of their parents, or were carried pickaback. They took their books and games along and the mothers had hampers of provisions. Picnicking in beauty spots everywhere, they left not the least scrap of litter. I often wondered if this was due to their innate tidiness or to train-ing and the strictness of the law.

I found the heavy summer heat in this valley more trying than any heat I had ever known, but the people here were not wilted by it. They were seemingly impervious to its discomfort. Boisterous in their enjoyment, they danced in the open, sometimes with flowers in their hair, the blonde heads of the women shining in the sun. Young people strolling with arms round each other's waists stopped un-abashed for long kisses. Aged couples laughed at them and did likewise. It was usual to see people whose hands were callous with toil playing musical instruments. No gather-ing was without its song. They scattered music over their great river, over their wine-clad hills, and along their forest ways.

Peals of laughter punctuated the pleasures of the popu-lace. The German language seems a hard-wrought struggle with thought. It lacks the ease of English, and the crystal-line clearness of meaning to which I had become accus-tomed in China and in France. To me it is barbaric and rough, a language of doughty vigor, plastic and unformed; yet possessed of a richness more polished tongues have lost. When spoken, High German breaks upon my ears like the rumble of a wooden drum, the gutturals hard and brittle, closely overlaid by flute tones. But on the tongue of the Cologne populace language turns into a melodious dialect. They put a soft roll on the *r*'s and add a rich cadence to expression, jeweling their speech with vivid phrases often vulgar, nearly always funny.

Very shortly after arrival I learned that there was pressure to cultivate selfishness in regard to places of recreation. The National Socialists were urging the Rhinelanders to exclude Jews from use of the river and its meadows, from the forested hills, from the swimming pools and playing fields, and to keep them out of the opera houses, theatres, and concerts.

Marie and Brenda, my daughter and niece, soon discovered this. And one afternoon I came home to be told that they were giving tea to Manfred, the son of a German neighbor. High voices arrested my attention before I opened the door to the room where they sat.

"The Jewish problem must be settled. It is a serious world problem," I heard Manfred say.

"It is no problem at all," put in young Brenda quickly. "The world is God's and we must live in it together peacefully."

"German soil is German," he said firmly. "They have to get off German soil."

"The German Jews are German," Marie said. "They helped to make this nation, and in its good and its evils are a part of it. You cannot rise up and crush them, neither can you stamp out the pacifists, the Masons, all who believe in the League of Nations, and every other element that does not bend to this wicked creed. Don't you know your own Hans Sachs?"

"Children, children," I admonished, but I have never been able to stay Small Girl on any of her determined courses. Her voice, clear and firm, subdued mine, repeating words she had learned long ago in China from a German governess, an East Prussian: —

> *"Also, ir lieben söne mein,*
> *Weil ir in lieb bleibt zusammen gebunden,*
> *Einer des andern schutz wil sein,*
> *So bleibt ir reich und auch unüberwunden.*
> *Halt ir nicht ob einander Schutz*
> *Und sucht jeder sein eigen Nutz,*
> *So wert ir gen zu grund in kurzen Stunden."*

> (And so, dear sons of mine,
> while you stay bound in love to one another,
> each one willing to be the protector of the other,
> so long will you stay rich and unconquered, too.
> But if you are not concerned to cherish each other,
> and each seeks his own gain,
> then you will perish in a few short hours.)

The three had stony faces.

To my surprise Manfred's face softened first, and he said: "You foreigners cannot have any idea how beset with difficulties we young Germans are. We have to join the Hitler Youth. We have to accept as gospel every Nazi word. Otherwise we have no future. We are told quite plainly that no job and no profession will be open to us if we do not accept National Socialism. I want to be a doctor. I have always intended to be a doctor. I am ready to take my final high-school examination next term. I cannot study further without a certificate that I have passed it. And no one is allowed to take the examination who does not have a reputation as a believing Nazi."

"You poor thing," I heard from Brenda. "Do take another piece of the chocolate cake."

Marie was filling his teacup, putting in plenty of sugar, as I closed the door to go away.

The people here were not entirely occupied with their own personal celebrations. Masses of them took part in each national celebration, as requested from Berlin, celebrating events with a fervent pageantry which often made me feel that we were a part of a Wagnerian opera. Torchlight processions were usual. National anthems, as romantic as they are violent, as sentimental as they are martial, assailed my ears. Local songs, drums, and full orchestras were supplemented by radioed programmes in which noise more thrilling than the words filled the air.

Into the outward serenity of this summer came the radioed news of a National Socialist uprising in Austria, the failure of a group who had tried to bring about an *Anschluss* with Germany. Music and noise were suddenly stilled, this gay world abruptly quiet.

"The *Anschluss* is right, Austria should be joined to us. This clause must be torn from the wicked Versailles Treaty, but, alas, the Austrian is a fumbler. Somewhere his timing has gone wrong," one heard said. It was known that Dollfuss was dead and there was sadness that he had not been allowed a priest before his death. The Rhenish Catholic folk with whom I listened were much moved when a broadcasting voice announced that his last words had been, "May God forgive them."

The great anxiety was: "Has Austria again plunged us into war?" Men and women mentioned radio broadcasts which, they said, had been going out from Munich, given by an Austrian National Socialist living in exile there, broadcasts against Dollfuss and his government. They spoke of thousands of Austrian National Socialists finding sanctuary in Bavaria — armed men organized into legions, camped near the Austrian frontier; men in training these eighteen months past in readiness to rescue their country when the signal should be given.

Anxiety deepened as word came across the wires, picked up from France and England and Luxembourg and other stations, that Frau Dollfuss was with Mussolini, and Italian troops were massing on the Tyrolean border. It was remembered that the German Chancellor, Adolf Hitler, was not a birthright German but an Austrian. "We have been sacrificed to Austria," white-faced people said. "War has come upon us."

Then suddenly spirits rose as quickly as they had sunk. Around the radio where I listened, people began to say: "*Heil! Heil! Heil!* He has saved us!"

News had come across the wires that Adolf Hitler was in Bavaria turning back the Austrian legions. "All National Socialists have taken an oath to obey implicitly the Führer's will and so there can be no question among them of disobedience," ran the murmur around me.

"He is standing on the road turning them back." Only

then was it remembered that in his book, *Mein Kampf,* Herr Hitler has written praise of Mussolini and expressed the view that a bond of friendship must be made and kept with him.

When it was known that a telegram had gone to President Miklas in Austria expressing President von Hindenburg's condolences on the "abominable outrage" of which Dr. Dollfuss was the victim, there was general approval.

"Twice within a summer month this Führer has saved us from war — from inner revolution by his action at the end of June, and from world war now," was said in these days, and I saw that many of an intellectual class who had been indifferent to him were won to his support by his conduct at this time. Conversations in ensuing days confirmed this.

Full meed of praise one heard, yet never a thorough discussion of the tenets of government. Instead of this, *"Vorsicht, leise sprechen"* became a phrase very familiar to me. I have a lively curiosity and I had never lived with people like these before. "Careful, be quiet," had not been a habit of my life. I found it hard to acquire. Resolved not to question, I would find myself questioning. "I would not bother myself if I were you," I was told.

The amusement places were full. Old men had their own corners in coffeehouses, certain chairs sacred to them; here they met the same friends for the same games at the same regular times. Women too had their groups and their own sacred tables round which they had met on the same date for years; a circle of girls, often from the same school, stout matrons now who once a week went *kondi-*

tor'n. They brought their handwork to the coffeehouse. Quite at home in this public place, they ate heartily of *Torte, Apfelkuchen mit Schlagsahne, Pfirsich-Melba Eis,* helped down by generous cups of coffee topped with whipped cream. Then they embroidered their gayly colored *Kissen, Tischdecken, Läufer,* and other things that would make nice presents at Christmas, discussing as they worked everything except the forbidden.

In places where there was music, usually out of doors in this fine weather, the young folk danced on a part of the paved terrace reserved for dancing. They have the custom that a young man may go to any table and with no introduction bow and ask a girl to dance. Strangers, they dance, and when the music stops he brings her back to her table and leaves her. They have this social freedom and yet a simple question on anything related to their government brought either extravagant speech lauding National Socialism or such a reply as this, said behind a hand: *"Wir haben zwar die Polizei, aber damit nicht genug. Wir haben die Geheimpolizei und die noch geheimere Polizei. Wer das ist, weiss keiner. Ich könnte einer davon sein, oder meine Frau. Hermann, hier, traktiert uns mit Bier, und das Geld dazu erhält er vielleicht für Spitzeleien."* (We have the police, but that is not the end. We have the secret police and the more secret police. Who they are nobody knows. I may be one. My wife may be one. Hermann, here, may be treating us to beer with money he gets as a secret agent.)

Men are not afraid of outspokenness if they really care about a thing. Nor women either. Where there is ardor of soul against a condition, people defy danger, courting

martyrdom.   Death is an experience common to each of us.
Stirred to defense of a conviction, men and women gladly
give their lives.   They are not halted by threat of arrest
or torture where feeling is strong enough.   People the
world over suffer, even die, gladly for any cause they really
cherish.   The Germans are no cowardly exception different from the rest of mankind.   I had known too many
of them to conclude this.

I found their desertion of the cause of free speech dis-
concerting, and their failure to stand by kin and neighbors
astounding.   I felt the desire for the illumination which
could come only from the German people themselves; but
at this period of my experience Rüdiger and Otto were
the only persons who took the task of my enlightenment
seriously.   I pondered on the fact that their own Goethe,
after a long lifetime spent in active contemplation of the
German heart, died with a prayer for "more light" on his
lips; but I could not stop my search for a solution; it became my habit to write queries to the two boys.   They
answered with detailed care.   Beyond this I had to educate
myself by observation.

Crossing the Cathedral square in Cologne one day, I
heard an order broadcast to all Germany.   On August 2
every church bell in the land was to ring at noon, tolling
for fifteen minutes in commemoration of the twentieth anniversary of the day when the flower of German manhood
set forth to protect the Fatherland from a war forced upon
it.   Flags were to be flown on every home and shop in
honor of the sons of the homeland who had shown a readiness to sacrifice themselves for the just cause of Germany.

No turret, balcony, or roof was to be without its banner.

The colors of the old and of the new Reich were to float there side by side. "The reborn nation is commanded to think in silent reverence of the incomparable spirit which they displayed in the path of heroism. Silent prayers are to be followed by church services, parades, and ceremonies in every corner of the Reich; these are to be inspired by the thankful knowledge that God has raised us out of want and shame to National Socialism," said the fervent broadcasting voice.

I bought a copy of the *Deutsche Allgemeine Zeitung* and there read: —

In the days of the collapse in 1918 and of the Versailles dictate it seemed as if all our sacrifices had been in vain. To-day we may say that, historically considered, we did not lose the war of 1914–1918, for the plan to dismember the German Reich, to break up the creation of Bismarck, and to set us back where we were before 1870 did not succeed. It did not succeed in the war, or in the post-war period, in spite of all apprehension. Since National Socialism seized power, the national spirit of self-assertion has been so renewed that skillful political leadership will be able to avert every future danger.

On August 2 the banners of the old and the new Reich floated side by side on castle and cottage, small shop and great factory; but they were at half-mast, draped in black, and the church bells ordered to toll in honor of the soldiers of the German army left on the field of battle now tolled for them and for the leader of that army.

Twenty years ago to-day the German government had informed the Belgian government that it intended to occupy Belgian territory in order to forestall an enemy attack from that direction. A few weeks later General von Hindenburg, who had fought as a young lieutenant in the battle of Sedan, which gave the Germans victory over invaded France in 1870, had been summoned from retirement to repulse a Russian attack in the east, and at the age of sixty-seven won the battle of Tannenberg. From that date until this, with rare intervals, he had been the embodiment of German hope. In belief that red revolution, such as had occurred in Russia, was rising in the Fatherland he had advised his Kaiser to seek refuge in Holland. Leading home his defeated army, he had striven since then to establish order, and he had served republican Germany for several terms as President. Now, early this morning, Dr. Goebbels sadly broadcast to the nation the news of his death. Around us I heard the question: "What will happen? Who succeeds to the Presidency?"

There was radio silence for half an hour after announcement of the death. Then Dr. Goebbels spoke again announcing the unification of the Presidency and the Chancellorship in Herr Hitler's person: "The bill giving this joint office to Adolf Hitler is in two parts. Firstly, the office of the *Reichspräsident* is united with that of the *Reichskanzler*, and in consequence the former powers of the *Reichspräsident* pass to the Führer and *Reichskanzler*, Adolf Hitler. He nominates his deputy. Secondly, this bill enters into force from the moment of the death of the *Reichspräsident* von Hindenburg."

This automatically gave to Adolf Hitler General Field Marshal von Hindenburg's place in the German army. It was made known to the people that General von Blomberg had sent an order to the services which read: "The

Field Marshal's example of service to the Fatherland until his last breath will forever be a lesson to us to pledge our strength and our lives to the new Germany. The door of this new Germany was opened to us by Field Marshal von Hindenburg, who called Adolf Hitler to the Chancellorship, thus fulfilling the dream of centuries of German history. Inspired by the heroic figure of von Hindenburg, we tread the path to the future of Germany full of confidence in the leader of the Reich and the German people, Adolf Hitler."

Soon all Germany knew that, division by division, the soldiers and sailors were pledging their loyalty with an oath: "I swear by God this sacred oath that I will render unconditional obedience to the leader of the German Reich and the German people, Adolf Hitler, the commander in chief of the services, and I will at all times be ready to stake my life for this oath."

"The army," I heard, "is the only force capable of resisting National Socialism. This shows that it stands behind the new law and the new order."

By evening Adolf Hitler had designated that he wished to be known as Leader and Chancellor, and that he desired the bill appointing him to this joint office to be submitted to a national plebiscite on August 19.

"There is nothing left for us to decide," a woman explained to me; "our part is to thank the Leader for what he is willing to undertake for us."

In dramatic detail Field Marshal von Hindenburg's funeral was broadcast to the world. Every step of the black horses drawing the hearse, a gun carriage covered with a war flag, was reported on its long journey from his estate to Tannenberg, — the scene of the greatest victory of the war, — where he was buried.

At 11.30 on the day of the interment all Germany paused for a moment; heads were bared in the streets, arms outstretched in salute, and bells rang from the steeples. In the schools children listened and were dismissed for the day. In shops and factories workers gathered around a wireless for the ceremony, spending the whole morning listening.

Every employer of labor had by government order to install a wireless set ready for this broadcast, and have it there for future use, so that it would no longer be possible for a worker to give the excuse that he had not listened to a government broadcast because no facilities were provided.

From this day on there was the bustle and stir of preparation for August 19, the day chosen for the plebiscite, or "thank you."

In the midst of this the Baptist World Congress in session at Berlin passed two resolutions: "Firstly, this Congress deplores and condemns as a violation of the law of God all racial animosity and every form of apprehension or unfair discrimination towards Jews, colored peoples, or subject races, in any part of the world. Secondly, this Congress urges governments throughout the world to declare themselves ready to surrender whatever of their national sovereignty it may be necessary to surrender in order to establish an international authority for the maintenance of peace on a basis of equality and right in the world."

This seemed fine to me, but I did not hear that it stirred governments anywhere to action.

The plebiscite sanctioning Adolf Hitler's election as Leader and Chancellor happened around me. There were crowds of excited people, often cheering, and hundreds sang.

People everywhere talked of the election. A man in the streetcar said: "Kaiser Wilhelm II broke the ship of state which Bismarck built, and now we have a man who is certain that by gift of God he has the power not only to repair that ship but to steer it."

There was much color. Banners and flags waved on every home and shop and on public buildings. There was much singing and marching to flute and drum, and endless parades. Even a parade for work horses, in which each horse wore a bow of the National Socialist colors. The trees that shade the streets all had *Ja*, or yes, on their trunks.

The radio broadcasts were tireless and a loud-speaker covered "every inch of Germany," so a man in the street told me. Men from every walk of life addressed the nation and the world. There was a twenty-minute biography of the life of Herr Hitler every evening.

An elderly woman who shared a tramcar seat with me explained the need for this, my request for information arising from the fact that the tram halted at a square where the broadcast came from a loud-speaker. She said that since the Kaiser and the kings left their thrones there have been many political parties — twenty-eight and more in some elections each putting up a candidate. People had become bewildered and tired of it all. Few knew the names of the Chancellors that have held office. Despite familiarity with Herr Hitler's name because of the "Heil

Hitler" salute, it was very likely that numbers of folk knew nothing further about him.

She knew because her second son lived in Bavaria and had been a member of Herr Hitler's party for twelve years. He had told her that Herr Hitler was a modest man who shunned publicity at first. In fact, early in Nazi history the party had been called "Riders of the Night" by the romantic. Then as they grew stronger the Führer had begun to make use of propaganda, and he had as his Propaganda Minister a man who was cleverer at this than any other man in the world. "In this hour of victory when he stands high as the Leader of all Germans within and without the present Reich, every man, woman, and child must know him," she concluded.

The twenty-minute biography given each evening portrayed a moral man, virtuous and steadfast; pictured his birth in a humble home on the German-Austrian border, his straitened childhood and unhappy youth, the loss of his mother, days of poverty in Vienna, his war service, his suffering from gas, and how he lived only to right German wrongs. Dr. Goebbels assured listeners: "Herr Hitler does not surround himself with pomp and circumstance." Herr Frick, the Minister of the Interior, said: "It is the business neither of the State nor of the National Socialist Party to attack the Christian churches. The State and Party leave every man to find salvation in his own way. What they will control is political activity under cover of ecclesiastical endeavor."

The Foreign Minister, Baron von Neurath, said: "All the shame and all the evil we have suffered since Versailles had their origin in our humiliation and disarmament by the

Versailles dictate. We must all stand solidly behind Adolf Hitler and show the outer world that his will and his demands are identical with those of the whole German nation."

Secretary Hierl, the Reich Labor Leader, said: "Let us show foreign countries which are befogged by a lying international press that Adolf Hitler is no dictator oppressing the German people by force, but the true Leader of Germany, raised to his position by the confiding trust and devoted love of a whole nation."

Speaking from Hamburg on the eve of the plebiscite, Adolf Hitler repeated his philosophy of authoritative personal government as against party government because a state governed by conflicting parties is without resolution. "The world must now know two things," he said. "First, the German Reich will never surrender its honor and its equal rights. The German people, internal relations and economics in order, will defend the nation against all. Secondly, the German government, like the German people, is filled with the unconditional wish to make the greatest possible contribution to the preservation of world peace. The German army does not need to rehabilitate the fame of its arms. . . .

"The time of the German revolution is past," he continued. "The National Socialist ideal has conquered. Germany is ruled by this philosophy. But in taking over, a loyal alliance has been made with many who did not spring from the movement. In practice this has proved beneficial to the German people. Millions of Germans who have earlier stood aside or opposed have been reconciled to a régime which has no wish other than to put

Germany's best and most capable men in the posts of public life.

"The gradual evolution of the Reich in coming decades under National Socialist leadership of the German peoples' state demands discipline at home, complete order, undisturbed tranquillity. Therefore, it is my inflexible resolve personally to bring to account any who should venture to hinder or oppose this development. I will not have the ignorant, misled, insignificant persons shot. But I will in all cases crush to earth the really responsible.

"The National Socialist State pledges itself to positive Christianity. It is my sincere aim to safeguard the rights of the two great Christian confessions, to preserve their doctrines from attack, and to create harmony between their duties and the requirements of the present state.

"The economic tasks ahead are great. They demand decision and endurance. But the skill of the German inventor, the ability of German economic leaders, the diligence and superior ability of the German craftsman, the industry of the land tillers, the area of the foodstuffs, and the richness of the soil will supply our needs if we are courageous in our struggle.

"Do not count on any standing in the eyes of the outer world other than that of the strength your brotherly solidity gives the Reich. . . . Not for my sake but for that of the German people I have requested this referendum. I do not need a vote of confidence to strengthen or maintain the position I hold. But the German people need a Chancellor supported before the whole world.

"I do not argue with those to-day who think they can do better in this place than I can. They have all failed.

They must admit that on the whole my fifteen years of struggle for you has been successful. I have created a movement from nothing and given the German people a new and better situation at home and abroad. Ever since I have been in the struggle one thought only has ruled me – Germany."

Just before the voting a remark from Bismarck was broadcast to the nation: "We Germans, placed in the centre of Europe, must hold together more than other nations. We must be one if we do not wish to be lost. We have no natural safeguard and must stand back to back if all the sacrifices of the past are not to be lost to us."

The published result of the election was that out of a qualified electorate of 45,473,635 there were 43,529,710 who took advantage of their right to vote. Of these 38,362,760 voted "yes" to Hitler's appointment to the position of Leader and Chancellor combined, 4,294,654 voted "no," and 872,296 marked invalid ballots. By radio Herr Hitler immediately thanked the nation, and then General von Blomberg for the army's oath of loyalty. He promised to uphold the integrity of the service and to consolidate the army as the sole bearer of the nation's arms. He reminded them that Christ had had one traitor among the twelve who stood nearest to him.

National enthusiasm was not allowed to subside into quietness at the conclusion of this successful election. Rally after rally for one cause and another filled the days. Events in one corner of the Reich were broadcast to every other corner. Thus a unified enthusiasm was kept astir. Greatest among these were the Saar rally at Coblenz and the *Parteitag* at Nürnberg. The rally at Coblenz had as its theme encouragement to the Germans of the Saar, who would in the winter have the opportunity of voting as to whether they would rejoin the Fatherland or not.

At this time a young American girl, member of Kappa Kappa Gamma, the sorority to which I belong, telephoned me. She was traveling in Germany, and she had a note to me. She came to stay in our apartment for a few days. On her travels she had made a friend, a young S.A. After she was gone he continued to come to offer his services in any way that would be of aid to us, despite the fact that he was very busy on the Saar rally. We did not see him for several days, as he had gone to Coblenz. I knew he had a ticket for a seat well to the fore in the assembly at which Herr Hitler would speak, and that he was eager to sit near to his Führer.

"Well, how did you enjoy your Führer's speech?" I asked when he returned.

"I did not hear it," he said simply. "I forgot my credentials and was found too near the Führer for one who did not possess them. So I was taken into the cellar of the building and locked there until I had been identified."

I expressed sorrow, but I did not find him sad for himself.

"We young Germans must learn to be silent, not only when we are dealt with justly, but to endure injustice with silence," he told me. "And I was not treated unjustly; I should not have forgotten my credentials." When I showed my surprise he added: *"Wir sind zu blindem Gehorsam verpflichtet!"*

"We are pledged to blind obedience," I repeated after him.

"Yes," he assured me solemnly.

It was a lovely fall. The mountain ash was gay with bunches of scarlet berries. The chestnut wore leaves of gold. The girls went off to school in Switzerland.

Every day I drove my car out into the country. One afternoon I halted in a tree-shaded street. This street was full of little boys. While I waited for them to pass a man spoke to me.

He said: "I see you have a large car and you don't look busy. Would you lend yourself to our service?"

I asked him what he wanted. He explained that he was a schoolteacher and here were ten thousand little boys called in to Cologne to march past Herr Dr. Joseph Goebbels, the *Reichsminister*.

"This marching is not good for their hearts. Many of them have come a long way. They have had this day of parade and now they must get home again. I and other teachers have made ourselves a self-appointed committee to ask kindly-looking people with cars to give conveyance to the little ones."

I said that I would gladly do what he asked and he filled my car to overflowing. Directed by the children, I took them home. At the very end I had just one more to deliver. We were in a small village about four miles from Cologne.

"Our house is the first beyond the church," the child directed me, adding, "I am the pastor's son."

I took him there. Before he got out he thanked me for the ride, shaking hands with great politeness, as all the others had done, saying, "*Auf Wiedersehen!*" And then, like his companions, clicking his heels together and lifting his right hand, the palm spread, he exclaimed: "Heil Hitler!"

He seemed so very young. I waited to see him safely in. His bang of the garden gate brought a woman to the house door, a fair woman about my own age. She stooped for his kiss.

His arms tight around her neck, he told her in high excited treble: *"Mutti, ich habe den ganzen Weg Schritt gehalten. Mutti, nicht einmal bin ich aus der Reihe gekommen. Wir sind nach Musik marschiert. Ich immer in den Fusstapfen des Jungen vor mir. Den ganzen Weg bin ich so gegangen."*

(Mummy, I kept step all the way. Mummy, I never once lost step. We marched to music. I kept marching in the tracks of the boy before me. All the long way I did.)

IV

NEIGHBORS

RABBITS nibbling in a field of clover display no corporate concern when a weasel slips in among them. Seemingly their caution is only enough to register brief personal alarm. Individually anxious, the rabbits hastily hop aside from the path the quiet weasel is pursuing towards his selected victim. Crouched in hiding, they are still, heedless to the piteous death cry of their fellow. When the weasel has gone, the remaining rabbits soon present a tableau of contentment on the meadow, a pretty pastel in fawn and green.

I kept picturing the Germans of my own kind, people privileged to some education, as rabbits. My image would have been truer if I had seen the company of liberals the world over as rabbits of a clover field, myself among them.

But I did not see this. Despite the internationalism to which I had been led by careful educators, I had not drunk very seriously at that fountain. I still beheld the map of the earth as in the usual school geography — the land done in blobs of color to denote the nations, and responsibilities limited by national boundaries.

My scorn was a self-righteous scorn. It was none the less bitter because I had found in Germany a people of whom I can write unconditionally that they are the most generously kind, the quickest to sympathy, of any people I have yet known — a folk tireless in the practical things they will undertake and accomplish for one on the slightest acquaintance. This applies to all. No line can be drawn between the Nazi and the others across which one can point, saying, "This is white and that is black."

At that time, in Germany, there were plenty of front doors with this placard out: *Arzt für seelisches Leiden* (Doctor for Suffering of the Soul). On my mentioning these soul doctors people told me that there had been many more before Herr Hitler took charge of things. Now their clientèle was falling off. National Socialists explained that their movement gives joiners "spiritual release by self-forgetfulness in common effort" — "great moments of disciplined fury when souls rise and mingle in divine comradeship" — "exaltation to all who have been afraid of life and its insecurities" — "rejuvenation to men and women who have grown soft, covetous, mean, and timid."

The quack doctors would be outlawed by the Führer, so I was told, if this were necessary. He never wastes attention on things which will die of their own weakness. When the Reich is completely National-Socialized they will all be out of business simply because nobody will consult them. I have listened to the movement's Minister of Enlightenment and Culture broadcast: "National Socialism is humanity's greatest experience. It is man gloriously in search of his soul."

On the day of this broadcast I encountered National Socialism in three small shops. Radio talks usually last well over an hour, some continuing two or three, the Führer occasionally speaking nearer four — a physical feat no one else surpasses. While the Minister of Enlightenment and Culture's talk was going on I entered a chemist's shop to have a prescription made up. The radio was open full blast, in accord with the government order that those who speak for the Party shall be listened to in every shop, public square, factory, school, and home. The proprietor's wife served me, as usual when I went there.

"*Ach* — we drink a witch's brew," she exclaimed bitterly, waving her hand at the noise.

"Hush, Margo," whispered her husband, and I saw that another customer was coming into the shop where we had been alone. When he had been served and was gone, the husband admonished his wife again. "You never know where reporters are. The very walls have ears. If you are not more careful you will get us both taken into corrective custody."

She shrugged her Rhenish shoulders. "To think that I worked to help this party into power. Under the democracy I actually ran round persuading my friends to vote for them. They heralded their approach as deliverers and they stay as conquerors. A woman cannot speak her own mind any more. She cannot think her own thoughts. Libelous thoughts are punishable by death, and libel is everything which isn't a cheer."

"It isn't so bad as all that," said he. "Give them time. A great many have tried to get the German cart out of the mud since the defeat. This party are elected to do it for us and we must give them their head in a fair trial. You are only bitter because you have foolishly got yourself into trouble."

"Trouble! *Ach* — it is no trouble to me," she replied

with scorn, and then explained. She had met a friend on the street who had asked, "How is business?" and she had answered, "Bad — practically nonexistent." This conversation had been overheard by a boy of fifteen, son of her nearest neighbor. He had reported it at the next meeting of his Hitler Youth Group.

"They have a weekly confessional," she enlightened my puzzlement. "We have these confessionals in all our National Socialist Groups. The creed of this party teaches that loyalty to the state ranks above every other relationship. It comes before loyalty between husband and wife, parent and child, brothers and sisters, friend and friend.

"In our Groups it is the leader's duty to encourage confessional. The adult or child who is most diligent in protection of the state stands highest in favor. Have you not heard of the instruction sent out to us from the leaders of the National Socialist movement? 'They who stand in the way of the victory of the Reich will be crushed. Illegal action will lead to physical extermination. The German folk are no spies, but he who does not report observations makes himself guilty of the crime as if he had committed the error himself and will be so punished.' Every German of the Reich over fourteen years of age must know this instruction by heart. No excuse for ignorance of it is accepted.

"My neighbor's son meant me no harm. He did what he thought was right in repeating my words at his little group. 'Klagen und Klatchen verboten!' — grumbling and gossiping are forbidden. We had a two months' campaign of education on this in the spring. His report was forwarded to the Party official of this district. I am now being taught to remember not to grumble. My punishment is light, really, compared to what some of my friends have received for no greater civic disobedience.

"Every workday morning, for six weeks, I have to present myself at the ward office of the Party. I must be there promptly at eight o'clock and wait until the official is ready to receive me. He is a young man, about twenty-six, always sleekly groomed. I have to say 'Heil Hitler!' as I open the door into his private office, giving the Nazi salute as I go in. Then I must stand before his desk — he remains seated — and, raising my hand in the salute, hold it there while I repeat 'Heil Hitler! Business is good to-day!' "

From the chemist's I went on to a grocer's shop to leave my daily order.

"*Grüss Gott,*" I said absently as I went in.

"Don't use that greeting to me," exclaimed the grocer woman. "I may forget sometime and give the same reply."

"Suppose you did?"

"Yes — suppose I did. *Ach!* Who knows what would happen? We dare not greet God here any more. We must hail Hitler. I have three little children. Who is to protect my little children if I am taken away? I have got to be careful for their sake."

She showed me a communication which she had received through the morning post, a message mailed in a plain white envelope with no indication on its outside as to where it came from. Inside there was a sheet of paper with the Party letterhead. There was no writing — just a small newspaper clipping pinned to the centre of the clean page.

The clipping reported that various people resident in

various neighborhoods had been selected to send in a memorandum as to those who were using the "Heil Hitler!" greeting. Certain shops, various individuals, even some postmen, had been found negligent. Addressed "Heil Hitler!" everyone responded "Heil Hitler!" but tested with other greetings several had not given back the salute of loyalty. The report closed with a question, "Is this the right way for these people to show gratitude for the great work the Führer is doing for us?"

"I wouldn't be worried by it," I said, trying to give her comfort.

"It is not a thing to be careless about," she asserted. "The long arm of arrest reaches everywhere. Even if one is taken by the regular police and wins one's freedom by law in the courts, the secret police can arrest again as one walks from the prison door. There is no court of appeal from under their hand. It is seldom that relatives or friends can find out where the arrested is taken. It isn't that I would mind arrest so much for myself, but what is to happen to my children? More persons go into the concentration camps than come out. Those who get alarmed there and show rebellious temper never come back. I have a slow temper, uncontrollable when roused. I must be careful because of my children."

"Heil Hitler!" she said loudly as I left.

"Heil Hitler!" I responded to the convention of her country.

Going to the shoemaker to have some repairs done, I learned that he was away — indefinitely away. There had been a search for books. Such searches, so a twelve-year son told me, are periodic but not systematic. A Party person may descend on only one house in a block when he comes. The child told me that no one is allowed to possess a book written by a pacifist, a Communist, a Jew, a Mason, or any book about Masonry; any book on politics or political science other than National Socialism; any book of science which refutes the National Socialist theory of race and blood; or any novel or poems by an author who has in any writing whatsoever ridiculed the National Socialist Party members or their tenets; any printing which gives any account of the Christian Church strife in Germany excepting that allowed by the Third Reich; or any book dealing with the German post-war period from a democratic or liberal point of view.

The searchers, two armed men, had found a book by the Englishman, Bertrand Russell, behind the shoemaker's clock. The child said it was a book telling of paths which lead to peace.

"Does your father read English?" I asked.

"No, he cannot. The book belongs to a friend. We were keeping it for the friend."

"Has the friend been arrested, too?"

"He is not in the Rhineland now and Papa would not give his whereabouts or name."

"Isn't the responsibility your friend's?"

"We do not reason that way in our family. We believe that loyalty between friends is above submission to the imposed will of this usurper party. We are every one ready to die for that belief."

"We certainly are," his little sister seconded his remark.

"Ena is brave," he said, putting his arm around her young shoulders. "She is brave. But she is young. She is only seven. She has so many years to resist National Socialist teaching. It isn't their harsh methods which the young have to be so strong to resist. It is their soft ways of confusing good with evil which resolve the power to resist. She has fair hair and blue eyes, as I have. I know what is before her. She is the type this party want to win to their cause."

"Where is your mother?" I asked.

"She has gone to try to find out where our father has been taken and get permission to send him some soap and clean linen. There aren't any comforts in the concentration camps."

When I left, the boy was at his father's last, repairing my shoes.

"I will pay in advance," I said, and put ten marks on the table.

"That is too much," the children told me quickly. "Two marks sixty is the price."

In the weeks following I had two experiences of my own concerning books. First, one which, although it may appear out of place, must be put in because of the bearing it had later on my life in Germany.

One afternoon in the late autumn I went for a walk with my husband, and when we returned, Hilgers, the manservant, told me that a man had called to see me. Hilgers described him as a very secretive man who looked like the secret police and would not disclose his business. He would be back at nine o'clock next morning and left word that I was to be in.

He came next morning. By my husband's order he was

shown into my husband's room. I was told to wait. Finally I was called. He was a publisher. He had read my *House of Exile* in the American edition. He knew the number of countries in which it was published and had seemingly a more complete knowledge of how it was selling in the various languages than I had. He had written to Boston for my address and learned that I was in Germany.

He explained that in Germany, under the National Socialists, it is necessary to have a government permit to print a book. He had that permit for my book. He had sent me a letter here. I must have got it, as it was registered. There was a contract in it, and he had waited for an answer. When none arrived he considered telephoning, then thought it better to come down to Cologne to see me.

I had not replied because my feeling was such then that I did not care to publish my book in Germany. My husband and our visitor talked seriously with me concerning this attitude. When the publisher went away he had the signed contract in his pocket.

A woman brought up in the Quaker faith cannot long indulge comfortably in a scornful righteous indignation. Her conscience will begin to twinge.

To remember that in the name "Friend" the people called Quaker have an ideal set before them; to believe that if one will appeal without fear to the good inherent in every other there will be response; to address noble and commoner in plainness, and treat the occupant of palace and cottage on the same human level; to avoid running into words either in speech or with the pen; to form no hasty conclusions — these are precepts a Quaker child learns.

Prodigal to this gentle faith, too often I find myself away on strange paths. Then remembered precepts call me home. I now resolved to subdue my emotions and try to give more intelligent attention to these people among whom I must stay for an indefinite time.

We found a pretty house for us in a village upriver from Cologne, and I sent for my boxes of books to be forwarded from France. Sometime later I received a notification from the Customs that boxes addressed to me had arrived containing books forbidden entry to the Reich. I went over. A customs inspector handed me a "black list." I found it an illustrious rollcall.

Studying it from beginning to end, the thought occurred to me that a person wishing to read for culture might use this in purchasing a library, if life had kept him too preoccupied to acquire the necessary education to make his own selection. It was fairly complete, so far as the languages of Europe and America are concerned, but lacking in Oriental titles — in fact entirely devoid of them. The works of the liberal Persian poets and the pacifist Chinese political philosophers were not on it. Even German, French, and English translations of their books were allowed to come in.

I handed it back to the customs inspector. I unpacked and he checked. From among my books all of Balzac, Anatole France, Victor Hugo, André Malraux, and Romain Rolland had to be laid aside to send out of Germany. All of Norman Angell, Walter Lippmann, Sinclair Lewis, Spinoza, Maxim Gorky, and Edna St. Vincent Millay must be relinquished. To the growing heap I must add the poems of Heinrich Heine; Thomas Mann's *A Man and His*

Dog; a score of Mendelssohn's *Elijah;* and, lastly, Lessing's drama, *Nathan der Weise.*

I worked quietly, feeling bereft. Before leaving France I had selected carefully when preparing the boxes of books which were to follow me. A gypsy can carry but a limited library. These were my friends, companions chosen for my exile. Choking back self-pity, I was silent until I came to *Nathan der Weise.*

To part with that slim volume seemed more than I could bear without protest. It is a favorite of mine — one of the stories I like best of all the stories men have told.

Besides, it was given to me by a German who judged its tolerance good and true — as I could show in the comments he had written on the margins of its pages. It was a gift from a man who lies dead somewhere under the forest of black crosses which mark the graves of unnamed German soldiers fallen on the soil of France — a youth who gallantly flung his life away, as did thousands of others of his generation, fighting for what he believed was the right. In this telling I brought tears to the eyes of the sentimental German who as a customs inspector of that soldier's Fatherland was denying me the privilege of bringing home this book. But to no avail. *Nathan der Weise* was now under ban here. The book was on the black list. He could not let it enter.

The customs inspector, too, had liked the story of Nathan the father and his three sons. Until 1933 it had been possible to see it often on the stage. Now it was no longer played and to have the book was forbidden. He was sorry — very sorry — but if it was found out that I had it, and that he had let it in, then he would lose his job and his pension; he had a wife and children dependent on him; he could not run the risk.

He told me that there was no condemnation of Lessing and mentioned him as one of the writers celebrated by the National Socialists. I could have copies of all his other works. I could see his comedy *Minna von Barnhelm* and his *Emilia Galotti* on the stage this winter. The objection to the book I had was that Lessing had made the hero of this book a Jew.

I asked if he did not think that Lessing might be a better critic of what Germans should read than the men who compiled this black list.

"I do not meddle in politics," the inspector replied quickly. "I do my duty — and that has not been easy these twenty years I have served. Lessing may be wisest, but he has been dead more than a hundred years and the men who declared a ban on his book are in power. If I let the book in I may find myself in trouble."

I did not press him further. I laid my banned books into a box, fitting them so that their corners couldn't get broken, putting my favorite in a snug place. Then I sat down to rest on the box of books allowed to stay with me, feeling exhausted.

The servant of National Socialism brought a hammer and new nails, shining as silver, with which he fastened on the lid of the box that must leave the Reich. His steady, relentless blows shook me as if they closed a coffin, their fall beating a funeral dirge for the Germany whose matchless beauty Madame de Staël heralded in *De l'Allemagne*.

Is that Germany dead? Or does she lie as Snow White in a trance from eating a poisoned apple?

V

DINNER AT NIGHT

On right and left my dinner companions were Rhineland merchants — merchants "ruined" by post-war conditions, so they said. They told me of the loveliness of life here before the war, of peace suddenly broken in a beautiful summer — a summer when one had rooms at Le Zoute booked for August, and the other was on his honeymoon in the Baltic. They spoke of a Germany unprepared; of the closing in of a net by jealous encircling nations; of the bravery of their friends at the front; of the courage of German women.

It was a long dinner. They mentioned fourteen promises not kept by their foe; a forced democracy; a food blockade; invasion by black troops; inflation; Jews who got rich; disorder; immorality rampant; reparations; Bolshevism — on and on they talked to me, explaining why they needed their Führer and what a blessing his coming is to their race and nation.

But I was not there. On the rumble of their voices I rode far away until I stood on the deck of the *Empress of Asia*, docked at Yokohama, homeward bound. A neat little man in a brown kimono bowed before me. "Yes, Missy, long time I make the shirts for your Master. I know what Master want. I will have them finished when you come back from Pennsylvania. I will bring them on board."

Then he bowed his funny bows again, and, pride shining in the gaze he directed on the waterfront, he said: "Fine city we got — fine city Yokohama. Next time you please come to see my new home-and-shop. Master buy long time from me. Many years he is my customer. Maybe he like you to see my new place and tell him. Better light. Better air. Better everything. Thirty-five years I work and save. My son there too. And my little grandson, he just learn to walk."

"Yes," I promised. On my way back to China I would drink tea at his house and see his shop. His wife, daughter-in-law, son, and grandson would welcome me. It was all arranged. And I sailed out of Yokohama Harbor before the earthquake.

Autumn came. I was on the *Empress of Asia*, docked at Yokohama, bound for China. Holding Small Girl's hand, since she must stand on a chair to see, I stared at the place where a fine city had been — stared at a place where in one swift gesture the hand of Nature had wiped away man's life and possessions. I heard a voice behind me, "Pardon, Missy, I bring your Master's shirts."

"Yamamoto!"

The little man bowed his funny bows. "Yes, Missy, pardon, I bring Master's shirts."

"Yamamoto, you all right?"

"Thank you, Missy, I all right. I got courage."

"Your home-and-shop, your wife, your son's family, all right?"

"All gone, Missy. The gods take away. Yamamoto

get too rich. Get too happy. Get too proud. The gods take away — take away little grandson just learn to walk."

He undid his parcel. I must count the shirts. I must look at each one of them. He had promised twelve. I saw them — perfect to the last good buttonhole — my husband's every little specialty remembered. I heard him tell how he had been on board a ship seeing a customer when the earthquake struck. Now he had a tin-roofed hut where he lived and worked. He had got a secondhand sewing machine on credit from Kobe. A cloth factory trusted him, too. . . .

The deep German guttural of my right-hand neighbor's voice cut into my attention: "You are refusing everything. Surely you want some of this Bavarian cream. It is one of our best recipes — and you won't get cream desserts often."

My left-hand neighbor added: "You had best take some. There is a rumor that cream is to be stopped. We are short of milk and poor in fats."

They were kind. My refusal of the dish was inexcusably curt. But I was impatient to be away. Far away from Bavarian cream desserts. I wanted to be off to Yokohama to see again a little Japanese in a brown kimono, a man strong enough to take courage from disaster.

At another dinner party we were twelve at table. The cooking was excellent, the service unobtrusive, and the menu not too long.

We had asparagus soup; roast back of venison, chestnuts and Brussels sprouts, potato puffs, sliced orange, and a dry Bordeaux; then snowballs of ice cream in different flavors;

and coffee. The china was from Florence, the silver Danish, the glass Czechoslovakian; the guests, with the exception of ourselves, all German.

Talk was of many things, but principally of music and how music is similar and different in various lands. Then I drew attention to myself, uncomfortably, by my reply to a question from my host. He asked if I was finding opportunity to see and do the things I should like in Germany; and I answered that I should like to have gone to the All-German Harvest Festival in the Harz.

I knew about the festival because Rüdiger and Otto had written a long letter about it. "The Harvest" is celebrated as a school vacation in Germany, a break several days long, and they went to the National Socialist Thanksgiving in happy company with peasants from the farm of Otto's uncle. Tillers of the soil from every valley, plain, and hill in the Reich were invited. All were asked to come in native costume. Rüdiger and Otto wore the garb of peasants from the uncle's farm.

Our farmer from Eupen-Malmédy was there also. He sent us a picture postcard from Hameln, the town of the Pied Piper. He wrote on it that he was there because farmers of German blood from beyond the frontiers drawn by the Treaty of Versailles were especially wanted. He closed his greeting with the proud exclamation, "We Germans are one folk with one Leader!"

More than a million farmers had assembled, the majority bringing their wives and children. Trains and buses put them down at Hameln. From here they must walk up the long hills. From the summit of the granite Bückeberg a noted conductor and his orchestra called to them with music, playing well-known German tunes, thus helping them to climb.

In the purple and orange, green and blue and crimson, of their costumes they were a brilliant crowd, thronging up through the autumn-tinted trees to the gray boulders of the mountaintop. When they had gathered round as closely as possible, Herr Hitler spoke to them from the loftiest rock, his voice relayed to the farthest edges of the crowd through loud-speakers. "In years to come our government will stand as a rock of order and stability towering above the Red Flood" was in his speech. Then came magnificent fireworks. A thousand rockets scattered golden stars. The surrounding peaks smoked like volcanoes and burst into flame.

Hour after hour these flares of red light rose and fell, flickering gigantically against the night sky. There were food and drink in plenty for everyone. And on and on the enthusiastic conductor led the assembly in community singing. Songs known throughout the Fatherland were interspersed with folk songs which had been carefully gathered from the byways of the Reich. When the conductor introduced such a song just a few voices would join in; but if it had true German feeling it would belong to the vast throng before it had been repeated three times. Soon more than a million lusty voices would send it echoing down the valleys.

In description of the gathering, Rüdiger and Otto had used this expression: "*Er lebt. Der Volkstrom ist ein Geist. Er lebt*" — literally, "It is alive. The folkstream is a spirit. It lives."

This had seemed a marvelous festival when I read the

letter. Now, as I spoke of it, I was suddenly conscious that all other conversation round the table had stopped. There was a strange element in the silence.

Finally a man said, "You will certainly have a chance to go another time. The National Socialists have made this an annual gathering."

He dropped this into the vacuum — yet general conversation did not restart. I noticed several people crumbling their bread. At last a woman looked directly at me and held my gaze. She asked: "Have you read *Faust?*"

I hadn't.

"At least you have heard the opera?"

I had — several times.

"Don't you realize that the Bückeberg, this same granite summit from which Herr Hitler speaks annually to assembled multitudes, replaces, in our modern saga, the mountain to which Mephistopheles led Faust?" Her tone was hard, accusing; then it softened. "*Faust* is the story of a man who sold himself to the Devil — at first he was pleased and then he was sad. Goethe did not spin *Faust* from his imagination. Goethe — the greatest of our thinkers — made this drama of our folk legends. He carried the manuscript with him sixty years — working on it and reworking it. *Faust* is us — us in a way perhaps no foreigner can understand."

Another evening we were guests at a house where taste and wealth had combined to create a home into which it seemed right that art treasures from all over the world should be gathered.

Candles glowed on the table, their flame reflected on

the polished board; but the night was moonlit and the curtains had not been drawn. Generous windows gave a view of the mountainside sloping irregularly down to where the Rhine flowed, a silver river between silvered banks.

A Chinese Goddess of Mercy, a beautiful figure, stood in a niche of the dining-room wall. Bronze chrysanthemums had been laid at her feet.

Our host and hostess were friends of German friends of ours in China, and this was the first time we had met them. He is a noted scholar, a man who has devoted his life to the study of early man, with special emphasis on the Germanic race. Both are amateur musicians, as were nearly all who gathered round their table.

After dinner there was music, selections from composers before Bach. Nearly everyone played and sang. The set of songs I liked best were given by our hostess, songs similar to Elizabethan lyrics and sung to a harpsichord.

At the close of the evening we were asked to stay on a few minutes after the others had gone.

When we were alone with them our host said: "We had hoped that we should see much of you when you came to Germany. From the letters of our friends in China we feel we know you. But the way of our life has changed. I have been dismissed from my place at the university. I have been invited to the university at Madrid. Elfriede thinks we should go."

"We must go. We must get away from here. We must live where there is human freedom," Elfriede declared with quiet intensity.

"It might be best if we stayed here. I could work on

my researches here at home. I do not know if I ought to do it," said he. "My wife has always been wealthy. This house is hers, from her grandmother; her dowry supports it. She has always lived in luxury. She cannot understand what living on a professor's salary will mean."

"Helmut — that is not fair. I'm not a slave to materialism."

"No, *Liebling*, thou art not. Forgive me."

They seemed to have forgotten us, and we rose to go. But they wanted us to stay.

"It is like this," he explained. "I was a poor boy — a schoolmaster's son in a little village. My parents contrived and I contrived. I got through the university. I was a teacher. I studied; I wrote things. I never gave any attention to politics. We Germans have a deep sight, but not a broad sight. I looked only at my own subject. I did not work for the National Socialists. I did not work against them. I never thought about them except to be sad when my brother-in-law mixed in politics and was killed. I thought just of my own subject. The book I worked on for years was published a month ago. The last twelve years every thought I haven't given to the book I have spent on building up my department at the university. My department has a reputation — a reputation among scientists in Germany and beyond."

"The book is wonderful," put in his wife. "It is a big book with dozens of illustrations. People like it. It is a costly book, yet it has sold more than a thousand copies in a month. It has not been forbidden — it was on sale in town this morning."

"I got my dismissal in a letter from Berlin, which came

eight days ago. It says that I may no longer teach or lecture in the Reich. I took the letter to the head of the university. He had received no notification from Berlin; he said I had best go up to the Bureau of Education about it. I wrote for an appointment, but I got no answer. I went up. At first it seemed I should never get past the clerks. Each person encountered in the bureau said, 'It is not usual to question the decisions of the Reich.' Finally I did see the Minister. He said the same thing, and no more. I said, 'Then I presume all I can do is to say good-bye' — and he replied, 'That would be the wisest course.'"

"The wisest course is to leave Germany quickly," declared Elfriede.

"I think, think, think all the time — what can I have done to sweep away my work like this? I lectured that week in Düren. It was a lecture on the Goths — what could I have said that was not allowed? I spoke only of the eastern Goths, their movements, their disappearance — the sagas. Or was it something else — something I did — "

"It is futile to do that puzzling, Helmut. We are fortunate," added his wife, "that he had this invitation to lecture in Madrid just at this time. We can be off at once now."

"Can you pack in a week?" I asked.

She looked puzzled; then smiled, a sad smile that twisted at one's heart. "You do not understand, of course. We shan't be able to take many things. Germans who leave their Fatherland to-day cannot take much. We are under a shadow — we do not know why. But we do know one thing with certainty. If we leave we shall be listed as traitors — my fortune, forfeit to the state, will go into the coffers of National Socialism. It is not the loss of the money I shall mind; but strangers — such strangers — in my grandmother's house!"

In less than a week they were gone. I heard of their departure through a couple who had been our fellow guests at their house. They had gone quietly, without saying farewell even to relatives or their most intimate friends.

Sometime later these friends showed me a Berlin newspaper. It contained an article on "traitors against the Reich whose fortune is forfeit to the state" and gave a list of names. There were seventeen in the column, some of them world-famous. The names of our former host and hostess were on the list.

I was reminded that the professor had had a brother-in-law who had mixed in politics and was killed. I asked about this brother-in-law, and learned that during the Republic he was an outspoken Social Democrat. When President von Hindenburg appointed Herr Hitler Chancellor on January 30, 1933, this man issued a pamphlet warning citizens against the encroaching dangers of dictatorship. After the Reichstag fire on February 27, he stated without reserve his opinion that the National Socialists had done this themselves to unloose a wave of terror and ride to power on it.

He worked hard to oppose them in the March elections, and issued a pamphlet against the proclamation of the anti-Jewish boycott of April 1933. He tried to form a league of men and women organized to fight the "Law of April 7" when published, because he felt that its "reform of the organization of the Reich" simply meant the handing over of government to complete Nazi control. He issued a pamphlet telling Catholics that the Concordat signed between Hitler and the Vatican on July 8 would be betrayed by Hitler as soon as he had made what use he could of the Catholics.

On July 16, not quite six months after Hitler became Chancellor, a law was published forbidding all parties except the National Socialist Party. Shortly afterwards this man went for a walk one evening and did not return. At Christmas the wife shot their five-year-old son and herself "while of unsound mind." She had that morning received a package — a cigar box marked with a swastika and the word "traitor" before her husband's name. It contained ashes.

I was not yet used to things like that. I recovered consciousness to find the narrator splashing cold water on my face and neck. My friend was crying quietly, as she scolded me: "You have got to learn to steel yourself against shock. This thing isn't going to end in Germany — or in Europe."

Saint Martin's, Saint Barbara's, and Saint Nicholas' Days had passed.

On wreaths of *Tannenbaum* hung from the chandeliers in German homes the four candles of the four Advent Sundays had been lighted one by one until they glowed all together in glad announcement of the approach of Christ's birthday.

It was Christmas Eve. Marie was home from Switzerland for the holidays, Brenda spending hers with her grandmother in London. We had been invited to enjoy the festival with a family living some distance away. Ready before the others, I looked at the Christmas number of a magazine while waiting and, attracted by the ideal in it, read this: —

The Holy Night festival in German lands is not an invention of the Christian Church. It is an age-old custom handed down to us from our remote ancestors. The day of the Winter Solstice was sacred to them, and the period round it was a holy season. Down through the ages to the present day the true German gives himself to good deeds without the ulterior motive of expecting a reward from Heaven. For us the Christmas festival must be forever a festival of well-doing.

We were off. It was a long way, a winding way through town and countryside. The Christian markets were still open, but their stalls were nearly empty of dolls, toy furniture, engines, dappled horses, woolly lambs, colored balls, tinsel, gilded cones, candies, fruits, and nuts. Folk hurrying home had their arms full of parcels. Every cluster of houses, no matter how large or small, had its *Christbaum*, a tall evergreen tree standing in the open, its graceful branches decorated and ready to light at dusk, a star on its highest tip.

Each person we saw appeared engrossed with Christmas. A woman was busy setting a row of white candles in her front window. A man pulled a cart heaped with red-berried holly. Mistletoe in a great bunch swung on the back of a broad-shouldered youth in soldier uniform. A girl with Gretchen plaits herded geese through a roadside gate, hampered by a basket of bright apples in one hand and a basket of hazelnuts in the other. Axe in his belt, a handsome brown-bearded giant strode forward carrying a hemlock on his shoulder, whistling *"Stille Nacht, heilige Nacht."*

Warmly dressed, we opened the car windows. Crisp and cool the December air blew in. Up and up wound the way into a place of pointed firs. Snow had fallen. We saw the tracks of deer, and then a deer. These were the scenes of the old German Christmas cards — this the same little red-breasted bird balancing serenely on a twig, these the houses, the villages, the people. "He is almighty and strong who at Christmas was born," sang a farmer unharnessing his team in a barnyard shed.

On and on we went. My heart sang. I was happy — happy to have Marie, happy to be traveling through a German Christmas-card landscape to Christmas in a German home. A bunny scuttled across a field. We saw a little boy with red cap and red mittens. Smoke rose from house chimneys.

"Freue dich, O Israel. Bald kommt, bald kommt Emanuel . . ." (Jubilant, O Israel. Soon comes, soon comes Emanuel). Sweet and clear sounded the high voices of three rosy-cheeked country maids carrying pails of milk.

"There is Saint Nick's reindeer!" cried Marie, pointing to a wood. He stood at its edge, a handsome buck with finely antlered head.

The road dipped, leading into a valley threaded with villages — villages as charmingly built as the others we had passed, but strangely quiet. Dusk was gathering. Each had its *Christbaum;* yet not one was lit. At the entrance and exit of every village, and sometimes before houses, stood a sign against Jews.

"Juden dürfen hier nicht bleiben" (Jews may not stay here) — *"Wer die Juden unterstützt fördert den Kommunismus"* (Who helps the Jews helps Communism) — *"Juden unerwünscht"* (Jews not wanted) — *"Wer da naht mit platten Füssen, mit Haaren kraus und Nasen krumm, der soll nicht unser Land geniessen, der muss hinaus, der muss hinaus"* (This flat-footed stranger, with kinky hair and hooked nose, he shall not our land enjoy, he must leave, he must leave) — *"Deutschland! erwache aus deinem bösen Traum, gib fremden Juden in deinem Reich nicht Raum!"* (Germany! awake from thy bad dream, give stranger Jews in thy Reich no room) — *"Juda, entweiche aus unsrem deutschen Haus!"* (Jews, vacate our German house) — these were among the things we read. The writings before house doors were on white sheets stretched between two posts thrust into the ground and plainly lettered in black. They all had to do with women either married or engaged to men of Jewish blood. They were personal allusions to each girl or woman, and of a sexual vileness I would not have believed had I not seen them.

The signs continued, and there was one at the entrance of the village above which stands the *Schloss* of our host.

"Where," I thought, "where are the sons of those Saxons who put into their tribal laws the peace of Josephus?"

We arrived and were welcomed. We took off our things in the wing assigned to us, admired the big tiled stove in each of our rooms, went down to where the household were gathered. We had met our host and his wife but once, at a house in Coblenz, and they had generously invited us to see a real German Christmas. They introduced us to their children, other relatives, and friends.

A pleasant wine was served. We had conversation, and more conversation. Supper was expected. We had been told that it would be early so that there would be time for the singing of carols, the compulsory listening to the government broadcast, and the tree before going to midnight Mass. Supper did not come. I noticed that our hostess pulled a bell — pulled it again after a short interval. No one came. Then, outwardly composed, she pulled it steadily while taking part in the general conversation.

At last the man who had served the wine appeared.

"Is the food not yet ready?" she asked.

"The cooking is done," he replied, "but I cannot serve it. There is a Jewess among you."

"Frau von D. is a Catholic — three generations a Catholic. You have served her every Christmas Eve since you entered our service."

"I do not serve her any longer. I am a good German, a *Kerndeutscher*."

"You know well that she is a good German and that her husband was *Kerndeutsch* — he fell fighting for our country."

"I obey the Party. I do not hand food to a woman of Jewish blood ever again."

"Very well," our hostess answered. "The children will serve. You have been with us twenty-three years. You may pack your things and go."

"You cannot dismiss me. I belong to the Party. You can't put my wife and me out of our quarters."

"That will do," interposed the master of the house. "You may stay until after Christmas, but you will not appear abovestairs again."

"No," said the butler. "It won't do, and you had best not annoy me. I know too much about you, — international pacifist."

"Get out! I am master here!" Their eyes met and wills clashed.

The man who had been butler for twenty-three years dropped his gaze, thrust his head forward on a bull neck, and advanced a step with clenched fists. "I have a book with every illegal telephone call and visitor you have received listed in it — with hour and date. You read the London *Times* — you are often in the borderlands."

"Go!"

The butler turned and was gone. Then our host said gently: "It is Christmas Eve — please forgive my roughness, my friends."

We were a company of sixteen in the room, among us several middle-aged women, and I had not distinguished which one might be "of Jewish blood." Now a pretty woman announced, "I will leave. I should not have come."

"No — no, Rösel," exclaimed our hostess. "No — you are always here at Christmas. We love you."

"Aunt Rosa!" The children pressed round her. "Aunt Rosa, you can't go. You can't go when we are in trouble. You belong to us. You stayed when we had scarlet fever!"

"Richard, don't let her go," our hostess was crying.

"She is not leaving," promised our host. "Sit down, Rösel — you are one of us. We are all Germans — Germans in trouble — Germans caught in an *Alpdruck*." (An

Alpdruck is a nightmare in which the dreamer is tortured as by evil spirits.)

We went in to supper. The table was decked with a beautiful linen cloth and adorned with evergreen, gilded cones, and gay Christmas ribbon. I have no memory of what there was to eat. No one could eat, but all made a pretense. The children served, and then a man came and took the task away from them.

He was Erich, the chauffeur, and he said, "Cook and I are against the conduct of that fool — he is a poor deluded sleepwalker."

"*Wir sind ein schlafwandelndes Volk,*" replied our host.

Staring at them, I thought that perhaps this was the answer to German conduct, and said it over several times to myself: "We are a sleep-wandering people."

The parents seemed to have forgotten that they had children and that this was Christmas Eve. All we adults round the table were preoccupied with our thoughts, but Erich did not forget. He urged the little ones to partake of things he handed, he whispered to them, he brought smiles, he even hummed "*O Tannenbaum! O Tannenbaum! wie grün sind deine Blätter*" — reminding them that the Christmas tree followed supper.

Then our hostess roused herself. She told a German legend of Mary, the Mother of Christ. Mary, walking through a winter wood where snow and ice covered ground and trees, met a hungry child. Mary bent down to a frozen rosebush, pressing it against her breast. And while the child watched the frost melted, the bush became green; it put forth buds, and roses opened as by the kiss of a June sun — the most fragrant and beautiful roses ever seen. An apple tree that stood near saw this and broke from the grasp of winter, came into flower and leaf; little apples formed, grew, and ripened — all while the child watched. Mary gave the child to eat of the fruit and her hunger was fed. Mary filled the child's apron with fruit, loaded her arms with roses, and sent her home.

From the supper table we went to stand before the salon doors and sing. Our host had disappeared, but from inside his voice called for one song after another. The children and Rösel gave the verses and he sang the chorus. Not until his wife's voice was heard in the singing did he open the doors. Then the doors slid wide and there was a lovely hemlock soaring to the ceiling of the great room, a dark green tree lit with white candles.

Beneath the tree stood a *Krippe* — all the figures of the story of the night of the Christ child's birth, beautifully made. And on low tables on either side were the Christmas gifts. Then I saw that the helpers of the *Schloss* had joined us — but not the quarrelsome butler. Master and mistress, children, helpers, and guests joined hands; circling the tree, we sang carols of the Child born in Bethlehem.

After this the father, aided by his two sons, gave out the gifts. Happiness came now, as there were many surprises. Few gifts had been bought; nearly everything had been handmade by the donor, carefully hidden from sight during the past year whenever the one who was to get it came near.

Die Bescherung, or gift giving, was interrupted while the radio was turned on for the government's Christmas Eve broadcast. This was addressed "to all Germans, particu-

larly those beyond the present borders of the Reich."
Herr Hitler's deputy gave it, and there was announcement
that it would be repeated twice on Christmas Day. It
was: —

The world knows to-day, and politicians of other nations
have recognized this, that thanks are due to the Führer alone
that the peace of Europe was preserved during the past year
when it was often in grave danger. His prudent hand and
reassuring declarations have shown him to be a statesman of
world-wide capacity. Germans abroad need no longer be
ashamed of their Fatherland. They can be proud of it. No
doubt many other nations prefer that other Germany which
bowed to every foreign command no matter how humiliating
or deadly — the Germany of party strife, self-mutilation, economic decay, unemployment, Bolshevist disintegration. They
would have preferred Germany to yield up the *Reichswehr's*
last machine gun. Prowling foxes always prefer helpless mice
to prickly hedgehogs.

In the fable by Wilhelm Busch, the fox on meeting a hedgehog said to him, "Don't you know that peace has been declared,
and that it is a crime against the King's command to go armed?
Hand over your skin." And the hedgehog made reply: "First
have your teeth drawn, then we can talk" — thereupon he
curled himself into a ball with projected spikes and faced the
world armed but peaceful.

In spite of a promise given a once-confiding hedgehog, the
other nations have shown that they were not willing to have
their teeth drawn and so should not now take it amiss if the
hedgehog, grown wise, prefers to possess defensive spikes.
This is certainly safest for peace between fox and hedgehog.

When the radio was turned off no one in all the company said anything until a youth, who I learned later

was a stable hand, said grimly: "Well — I suppose that means conscription for army service is about on us."

"What makes you think so, Hein?" asked our host.

"That speech following on what I heard last week. I was at one of those compulsory meetings listening to a man from the South. Just at the end he pointed at a graybeard sitting by me and shouted: 'Grandfather, you won't have to wait long now to see your grandsons in the uniform you love.' "

Nobody spoke further, and the opening of gifts was continued. Hein was given the parcel for the butler and his wife.

We sat there enjoying our presents until time to go to midnight Mass.

I had never attended a Catholic Mass. We stayed for three. I found them very beautiful. In the gracious services of the Church every one of us seemed to have found reassurance about life. The lines of apprehension that had marked faces were gone, replaced by those of serenity. When we came out into the early morning air a few stars were still in the sky.

Rösel, walking beside me, said, "The Germans are a good people. This National Socialist Party is not representative. Its leaders are poor men sickened with longing for revenge on the defeat of 1918. They deserve our pity. I prayed God to forgive them, for they know not what they do."

A surprise awaited us. The children were up, in nightclothes and dressing gowns. Helped by Cook, they had prepared a breakfast table. Little angels, not three inches high, cut from wood and painted, marched down the centre of the long board and made a half circle at each place. The angels wore dresses of white, pale blue, or pink, and had golden wings. Each carried a tiny lighted candle.

"Angels are here," the youngest child said, "because we are thankful that Christ was born."

A fine damask covered the table. A low vase filled with *Primeln* stood on an embroidered doily in the centre. It was Sibylla's turn to have the Reading Circle, and our custom to meet for *Abendbrot*, or "evening bread." They had had a membership limited to five before they took me in. Now places were regularly laid for six. In rotation, meeting by meeting, one member read aloud while the others sewed or knitted, always for charity and usually for Germans abroad — the Sudeten in Czechoslovakia, the Siebenbürgen in Hungary, the poor folk of Austria, the Saarländer, and the Süd Tirolers. The book must be worth-while.

Just now we were having Theodor Storm's *Pole Poppenspäler*. The last reading had broken off where Paul and Lisei, separated since childhood, have recognized each other by the crucifix before the church. The others knew the end, but I did not; and it was a regulation of my admittance to their circle that I should never, privately, peer ahead into the story.

Helma had the turn to read. I was anxious that she should begin — begin before supper, or read at table.

"Certainly not. You cannot come here, *Ausländerin*, making rules. We eat first and then we read. That is our practice. Reading at table! Such manners! Have you no respect for Sibylla's food? We are here to enjoy eating as well as to read."

The eating was good. Sibylla had a four-compartment *Vorspeisen* dish holding *Sardinen, Appetitsilt, Geräucherten Aal,* and *Gemüsesalat;* also raw tomatoes, salt and pepper, butter and toast. These we ate on small plates placed on little lace doilies on large dinner plates. *Vorspeise* is the appetite rouser.

Little plates and doilies were removed and we took the next course on the large plates — hard-boiled eggs, Westphalian ham, slices of cold veal, *Kümmelsülze,* pumpernickel, and rye bread; cheese of three kinds, radishes, and butter; and a choice of draught beer, ice-cold, or hot tea.

When we had finished and helped her clear up — Sibylla keeps no servant — we got our work and Helma opened the book. She read of the glad reunion of Paul and Lisei, their love, marriage, and their life up to the place where Lisei's father, the old player living in luxury in Paul's house, longs to give again, just once more before he dies, his old puppet show — and wants his daughter, now the proud Paul's wife, to help.

At the point where the old man pleads for this wish, Sibylla's doorbell rang. The book was put down, and Sibylla went to the door. She stayed away. We sewed and knitted. Helma took up the cross-stitch work she was doing on a dress for an unknown child in the mountains of Czechoslovakia.

At last Sibylla returned, her face deathly white. "I may as well tell you now," she said. "Karl has lost his paper." (Karl is Sibylla's twin brother.) "He has lost his paper — but he is alive. They kept him five days. They took him last Monday — the family did not let me know. Ruth is here — she has been sent to tell me." (Ruth is Karl's daughter.) "They took him from the breakfast table — two young men in Party uniform. After five days they brought him home. He has signed a contract — sold the publishing business Grandfather and Father built up — given it in exchange for a farm."

"Is Karl all right, Sibylla? Normal?"

Ruth had come in. "Mother says he is like a man shell-shocked. Mother was a nurse in the war. She — she says he — he needs quiet."

The invitation to dinner was finely engraved on nice paper. I wrote an acceptance and went to post it. It was about ten o'clock of January 14, the morning after the Saar plebiscite. Asking for a stamp, I got one of a new issue, "The Saar Comes Home," picturing a pretty young mother receiving into her arms a bonny child.

"You had them ready in advance," I commented.

"We did," replied the clerk, handing me a tiny sponge on which to damp the glue. "The poor Saar folk! The poor Saar folk!"

"Now they are home, they will soon forget their exile," I consoled.

"Now they are Nazi property, their sugar feeding will stop and they will feel the heel and the whip like the rest of us." And then he jerked himself up. *"Mein Gott! What have I said!"*

"Nothing except that the weather is fine," I replied, and walked away.

If the reader should conclude that the Germany I saw in the winter of 1934–1935 gave the appearance of a sad and crushed land, then I shall have misled. Far from it. Music, dance, merriment, and enthusiasm were abundant in this world. My husband was in Germany for music. We went to opera several times a week, traveling here and there for it. Everywhere the opera houses were full. It was the same at concerts and theatres.

At the restaurants and amusement halls, — especially at the end of the month, which is pay day for many, — one could not get in if a little late in arriving. There seemed no end of balls celebrating various occasions. The Cologne populace is a carnival folk at heart. From November 11, Fool's Day, with its motto "Fool let fool pass," it makes use of every suggestion of an opportunity to throng the streets; merriment rises to a climax in the famed Cologne Carnival itself, until on the night before Lent one heard the boast, "Few in the city have slept for three nights past."

Dissatisfaction was met but accidentally, and tragedy apparent only when stumbled on.

Lecturers stumped the Rhine Valley continuously, extolling the virtues of National Socialism — unheckled and uncontradicted. Hoping thus to widen my vocabulary, I became an attender, taken along by this and that acquaintance. I learned new words and phrases from ardent orators scorning liberalism, and how to shout in a dozen ways that democracy is dead.

The theme "Germany must keep the key to her breadbox in her own pocket" was presented so often that when a speaker neglected any of the tenets of this belief I could have risen from my seat to prompt him. I listened more than once to the prediction that within five years of his acceptance of the Chancellorship Adolf Hitler would have the Treaty of Versailles torn to ribbons, and in ten the German legions would stand on the frontiers of the Treaty of Brest-Litovsk. I came to accept as usual the statement that in our lifetime we should see the Third Reich, an armed fortress, hold the peace of Europe secure.

I was often in company of massed crowds. They sang more easily than they cheered. When such ambitions as above were mentioned, they seemed unenthusiastic. Except when led into acclaim they were quiet.

One day I went to Renate's to give her some wool I had got from England. I found her in bed; not ill, just upset — upset over the continued arrests of Sisters of Mercy and their confinement in prisons under sentences of five and ten years of hard labor. She explained that these Catholic nuns had served their fellow Germans as true sisters of mercy during the war and the years that followed, nursing the sick and wounded, finding food and clothes for the hungry and cold.

She told how, when there was no more money in Germany for such use, they had gone to Holland, and succeeded in borrowing it. She emphasized that the German character is honest, and these Sisters are of the German people. They had given their word in Holland to repay, and they had been steadily repaying. Then, on October 1, an edict had suddenly been issued from Berlin forbidding any person to take more than ten marks over the frontier. They had tried to find some legal way to

pay their debts — tried to deal with Berlin about it —
and failed. Now brave Sisters volunteered to take it over,
and, if caught, to suffer what came.

"The Sisters are wonderful about it," Renate said.
"They do what they know is right and then bravely bear
what happens. It is terrible that these good women should
be treated so. No gratitude shown for what they did
in years not long past. And then the waste — the pitiful
waste of it. They are needed — needed now to nurse the
sick and tend the poor right here."

The evening of the dinner party arrived. Our host was
a National Socialist official. I sat on his left. He asked
me my opinion of conditions in Germany and I had his
attention for my replies. Others were drawn into the talk.
They were not rough people, or loud. They had the vigorous look of physical fitness which characterizes both
men and women of the Party, and quick frank ways of
speech. All seemed to be ardent believers that through
National Socialism leads a way to German salvation.

They were reassuring. I cannot explain how it was,
nor remember distinctly what they said. But I came
from that dinner reassured. I was won by earnestness
and good words. That evening I wrote in my diary,
"There are honest and intelligent people in the National
Socialist Party — people who deplore the same happenings as I do — people who strive to restrain the rough and
ignorant — strong and capable men and women who may
succeed."

VI

A NATION AT WORK

SPRING came on as beauteously as any spring I ever saw. Snowdrop gave place to violet. Windflower spread a white carpet round the gray boles of the budding beeches. Misty bluebell and dainty lily of the valley filled wooded glades. Forget-me-nots gave charm to banks, and wild iris stood in rows along marshy streams.

But before the first winds of spring shook perfume from the tight buds, Germany suffered a sad fortnight. It was said that Herr Hitler rested at his house in the Bavarian Alps communing with nature and consulting a noted reader of the stars who watched his horoscope. The propagandists of the Third Reich were quiet. We had no political speeches, parades, or rallies.

The local newspapers were peacefully busy reporting social discord in the neighboring nations of Europe and far-away Australia, India, and the United States; contrasting the sorry plight of people there with the accord in which the fortunate folk of Germany lived. In this fortnight I went twice to the cinema. Prior to a Greta Garbo feature I saw a strip depicting Bolshevik strife, rough and bloody, from which their Führer had saved Germans; and prior to Mickey Mouse a strip showing German soldiers of the old army embarking happily to war, cheered, embraced, and decorated with flowers by adoring womenfolk. In this latter strip the men were handsome, the women fair, the children sweet, and the photography lovely. It was attractive. I mentioned its charm to the stranger on my left. He muttered, "Propaganda."

During these days the National Socialist secret police made silent arrests. Late at night and early in the morning they took man after man from German homes. News of this was not published, but it traveled as if carried by the birds. Rumor gave the number of the taken at more than two hundred, whispering that all were of the cultured class. I knew three of the arrested. One of them was our host of Christmas Eve. They were taken without accusation and thrown into prison without trial.

As accurately as I could learn, this is how the arrests were made. The doorbell or knocker sounded. There stood two, or at most three, tall men with pairs of pistols in their belts — men between twenty-five and forty-five with the daily-dozen-followed-by-a-cold-shower look, the smoothly tailored uniform, the precise manner, the direct speech, which characterize the National Socialist Party. The chosen hour was one at which they would find the wanted man relaxed, surprising him at a meal or in bed. They asked for their victim and were admitted. He got together the things they allowed him to have and went away with them.

Other members of the household behaved as if hypnotized. They had no faith that he would have a chance to free himself by any legal means, no hope that the courts of justice would be open to his use. Their minds were filled with memories of what they knew of others who had been taken in this way — disappearing forever, returned in a closed coffin, or, if let out alive, coming back starved in body and crazed in mind. Yet they did nothing. Family and friends let their man go. They neither stayed the arrestors nor insisted that they be arrested with him. They did nothing.

"It would have been of no use. We should have been shot."

When he was gone they wept and made efforts to find out where he was kept so as to send him food, bedding, clean things. They pulled wires trying to get him released — getting somebody who knew somebody who knew somebody else with power to have him let out.

The man's church did not stand up in a body for his defense. The university where he had taken his degree made no move. Seemingly a German has no club or organization of any kind which looks to his protection. I had believed that the Student Corps were modeled on the principles of chivalry and supposed they would do something for their members in such cases, but learned that they do not.

So far as I was able to ascertain, there is no German group whatsoever to-day which publicly maintains that a German man should have an open trial in a German court, and that the judgment of that court is German justice. The persons I questioned told me that the present-day Germans have forgotten the use of the Saxon *thing*.

It seemed true. I saw and heard German men and women as yet unconnected with any such victim, as well as relatives and friends of a person so imprisoned, rest their heads in their hands and cry in despair, "We never had this in Germany before. It is not right. It is not right. But what can we do?" Many times I witnessed this.

There was much patient suffering.

Also, very frequently, I heard a hope expressed: "This terrible time will pass. It can't last. It will pass." By some miracle, with no civic effort on the wisher's part, a Santa Claus, a fairy godmother, a Prince Bismarck, would arrive on the scene of German history and make everything right again.

Others said, "Herr Hitler does not know what is done in his name. He is a good man. He will straighten it out when he knows."

On March 16, 1935, Herr Hitler's edict reintroducing compulsory military service was broadcast. The people in whose company I happened to be just then heard the announcement with alarm. Their concern centred in fear that France would reply with bombs.

In the succeeding hours I found this anxiety widespread. In street, home, and shop, people spoke of nothing but "Will France and England let this pass?" When bombs did not fall, there was general relief, and a return to laughter and song.

A man with whom we talked in an interval at the opera said, "This explains the recent raids of the secret police. Herr Hitler is shrewd. He has avoided any danger of German opposition to conscription by taking into the dreaded concentration camps a few men from every part of the Reich, thus striking terror into the hearts of pacifists in general. If we had the list of the arrested and the dossier of each, I imagine it would be found that every man had at some time or other in his life displayed an interest in pacifism."

In my presence no one spoke against conscription. Many expressed hope that it would help solve the unemployment problem, and more were firm in the idea that a year of military discipline would do every youth good.

And spring came on. Our house looked to the Rhine, across a meadow sloping to the water's edge. French windows opened to a paved terrace on the riverside. From the eastern end of this terrace stone steps led down to a garden, where lawn, trees, shrubs, flower beds, and fountain had been neglected.

Sitting on the low wall that protected the terrace, I told my husband how I would fix the garden "if I could." But his attention seemed entirely occupied in watching the sun set behind the dim spires of Cologne Cathedral, and lambs play a pretty game of run and dash on the meadow. I went away for a few days and returned after dark on Easter Eve. Easter morning I woke to find a note on my pillow telling me to seek my rabbit's basket out of doors. From my windows I discovered crocuses, daffodils, tulips, and pansies in bloom where no flowers had been coming on. As my Easter surprise he had had a local nursery trim, repair, and plant exactly to my desire.

The song and movements of birds added charm to the silence of flowers. Lark, thrush, blackbird, finch, robin, wren, and warbler sang their delight in the loveliness of spring, winging flights through orchards of flowering pears, apples, peaches, apricots, cherries, and plums, halting to swing in formal gardens on branches of magnolia, lilac, mock orange, and snowball. Spring was here. A family resident in a valley famous for its nightingales asked us to come to hear their chorus, and we heard nightingales sing the whole night through.

Life was marred only by the wickedness of man to man. Nature's Easter was spoiled by horrid anti-Jewish banners and splashes of nasty yellow paint. By now I knew that shopkeepers did not put up the anti-Jewish signs in their own windows, or villagers hang them in their villages. The signs were forced on them by an anti-Jewish bureau in the National Socialist Party.

"In such ways as this is the thorn of hate pressed into the German heart to fester a cancer there," a German woman, an "Aryan," declared.

Knowing of the cruel treatment of German Jews, and thinking of good men and women shut away in concentration camps, I had no happiness in the beauty I was free to enjoy. Many Germans were like me in this.

People often spoke of something Goethe wrote: "What our fathers have bequeathed to us we must earn, if we are to possess it." But among these people none seemed able to do more than regret what they had lost, and the Germans of the National Socialist Party had vigor. They kept up a steady flow of propaganda, primitive as a tom-tom rhythm, and perpetrated on their fellow Germans vandalisms almost beyond belief.

Our German relationship was fairly wide. We knew a number of Germans before we came here, and none neglected us. Without request from us, many resident abroad wrote their relatives and friends in the homeland asking them to be kind to us, and they were. Besides this, I cannot imagine any traveler, student, or sojourner in Germany being long without friends. The most casual meeting often leads to the suggestion, "Let us meet again." My husband's music drew many to us, and the publication of my book increased the number.

The book was issued during the spring of 1935. The translation was done by an American who had come to Germany just after the close of the war, not knowing one word of German when she entered. Busy as a housekeeper, with music as a hobby, she had never tried a translation before.

"*Du liebe Güte*," exclaimed German friends when they heard of the translation in progress. "Why didn't you make the publisher hire a well-known German translator?" "There isn't any hiring about it," I would say. "We are halving the results."

The publisher had faith. When the finished job was in his hands he was warm in its praise. As for me, that translation is just the way I would write German — if I could. Critics shared this enthusiasm when they read the book, many stating that it read as if originally written in German.

To this was added another satisfaction. The Vienna State Gallery gave permission to copy Moritz von Schwind's lovely "*Siesta in einer chinesischen Familie*" and reproduce it on the cover of my book — the first time a color reproduction had been made.

The House of Exile sounds too much like a detective story in German. We searched for another title until the translator's husband made us a gift of *Süsse Frucht bittre Frucht China*, meaning "Sweet and Bitter Fruit of China."

The German public liked the book and bought it. It is
not a cheap edition.   In fact, I thought that it had worked
out to be rather costly.   I had entered Germany with the
feeling that these people had no money for luxuries, and
I had not yet learned that among vast numbers of them
a book is not counted a luxury.   I never heard anyone
express surprise on learning that a person had gone without meals or material things to buy a book.

My book brought me a contact with the German people
which might have fallen to me from out their own *Volks-
märchen*.   It belongs, not to reality, but to the magic of
the *Gebrüder* Grimm, Bechstein, or Wilhelm Hauff.   I
liken it to the wand given the old Chinese doctor in the
German fairy tale, that he might look with it into the
human heart as through a window.

I have been told that it is not a German habit for readers
to write to authors.   They do to me.   Hundreds have
written, and letters continue to come.   The writers are
of many kinds: a maker of violins, a pagan preacher, a
Christian, a ship's captain, a forester, a railway signalman,
a banker, a schoolmistress, a farm family of eight who all
signed their names below the mother's, a man who dwells
in a self-made boat moving happily over the inland waterways of his Fatherland, a wife who lives in a gray stone
castle, Hitler Youth and Hitler Maids, factory laborers
and factory owners, young conscripts and seasoned army
officers, folk who I discover have disappeared for treason
against National Socialism since they wrote, and members
of the National Socialist Party who are the German government to-day.

Rich and poor, town and country, from up and down

the hills and dales of their Reich they have written to me — people of a land in dire revolution who write like poets, every one of them, and seem to look over what is at their feet into some wondrous garden.

A letter from a German address invariably brought a request to let my correspondent entertain us. My husband had come for music; he kept on the path of his intent. I had no reason for coming except that of keeping his house, and we had efficient German maids who quickly learned our ways. Soon they were competent in the same manner as our Chinese helpers, needing no further instruction from me, and by now I knew that I must widen my education to include as accurate a knowledge of the Germans as possible. A miracle had opened the way. I accepted the opportunity.

In the limit of my time it was not possible to go to all. I must choose carefully, hoping by meeting individuals of different walks in life and of varied opinions to come near to true understanding of German character. I gave first attention to avowed National Socialists.

Although I had now lived nearly a year among the Germans, my encounters with the Nazis had been purely accidental. I had attended some of their lectures, but only for language study. I had repeatedly stumbled on their evil deeds. I had been impressed by good words at a dinner table. This had been followed by the Nazi arrest of my host of Christmas and others.

In deliberately setting to work to look at the National Socialists my intent was not malicious. My purpose was not to spy out their wickedness. It was evident that they were ardently engaged on a programme of some kind in

the part of the world where I happened to have to live.
I hoped to find some good purpose behind their apparent
barbarism.

I have never reached toward acquaintance with a German — man, woman, or child — without response.   The National Socialists were the busiest of people, yet they had
time for me.   To the company of Rüdiger and Otto, the
young S.A. I had met through a sorority sister, and the
people we had met at dinner, I could soon add a score of
names.   One and all, they took care to answer my questions,
giving me the attention that earnest parents give to a child.
They were always willing, even eager, to show me the work
they had under way.

Submerged in music, my husband lived aloof from
politics, as did the majority of the Germans we met
through music.   Such people said they were "uninterested
in politics," but I had come to notice that they treated
people who were Nazi with a caution which could not
have been greater toward dynamite.   They did this even
though the Nazis were their own brothers, sisters, children, or parents.   When it was seen that I was spending
much of my time with avowed National Socialists, I was
several times warned that I played with fire.

I could give this no heed.   Neither could I explain
adequately.   A number of people who had been friendly
began to act as if they feared me.   I could not leave my
path although I lost acquaintances whom I had begun to
treasure.   I had to go on at whatever cost.

The creed I heard the Nazis proclaim resembled in no
way anything I had been taught or suspected about the

Germans. Some of the people round me were enthusiastic about their ideas. Others cried, "How are we to get out of this strait jacket?" The majority kept cautiously out of the Nazis' way, but lived, cheered, sang, and marched to their order. The Nazis were dominant over all Germans within the red and white frontier. Their flag with its red ground for socialism, its white circle for nationalism, and its *Hakenkreuz* for anti-Jewism, floated triumphantly above every head, my own included.

It had become imperative that I should know who were Nazi, and why. I needed also to know why they call their government the *Dritte Reich*, or Third Government, and just what their oft-seen posters, "*Hitler — Arbeit und Brot*," meant. I had to learn these things by actual acquaintance with National Socialists.

I would have escaped this if I could. An urge deep within me made it impossible for me to turn any other way. The calls of pretty blue titmice, the reeling melodies of golden-crests, and the deliberate notes of busy tree creepers, so much softer and higher pitched than the voice of the dunnock, tempted me to ornithology instead, whispering that watching the activities of birds is a happier occupation and quite as worth while as observing the ways of humans. Just in these very days I wanted to give full attention to spindle-legged larks, recently hatched, who ran along paths between fields of red clover now in bloom near our house.

But some force had hold of me firmly, making me cultivate every opportunity I had for acquaintance with the National Socialists of the Dritte Reich.

The term *Dritte Reich* was soon explained. Vaguely I remembered from history lessons that the Germans had a very long history, much too long to be encompassed under three periods of government. Those lessons belonged to the days when my grandfather was teacher; my new instructors treated the past differently. The Nazis call their period of government the Dritte Reich because they judge only three periods of German history to be of sufficient importance to count.

The first is the *Deutsche Reich*, generally known as the Holy Roman Empire, established by the Saxon, Otto the First. The tribal duchies were brought, not without some stiff fighting, to acknowledge Saxon authority. The submission of Bohemia was added to the combination. Next Otto reopened Charlemagne's *Ostmark* to German settlement. Leading the Germans forward under the victorious banner of Saint Michael, he put an end to the Hungarian thwart to German destiny.

A Pope refused him the Imperial Crown. Ten years later another Pope called him into Italy to quell an uprising. The task done, he entered Rome with his troops and his Queen to receive the jeweled circlet, the plain gold orb, and the sceptre and sword of imperial authority. From this day in 962 until Francis the Second lost it in 1806, the Germano-Roman peoples were united under an Imperial Crown worn by German kings.

The Second Reich is the one founded by Prince Otto von Bismarck, a Saxon, for the Hohenzollern Kings of Prussia. From 1862 until dismissed by the rashness of the last Kaiser, Bismarck took the lead in Prussian affairs. He met liberal and democratic ideas with resolute resistance, gifted the people with social insurances which bound them to the state, and increased prosperity by tariff protections. With adroit diplomacy and three short victorious wars against Denmark, Austria, and France he created a German Reich composed of twenty-five states with Prussia at the head, and this government endured until 1918.

The Dritte Reich, or third period of importance, is the National Socialist government, created by men who have never accepted defeat, have always looked on those who signed the Versailles Treaty in the name of Germany as traitors to their race, and who have never had any feeling but scorn for the Weimar Constitution.

My Nazi acquaintances were serious, earnest people, belonging to various classes. A part of their creed is the abolishment of class barriers. They were alike in physical fitness, enthusiasm, and possession of well-fitting uniforms. They were always able to get good cars to take me to look at Nazi works, and generous in giving their time to my education. Each seemed sincere in belief that the road on which Germany was now started was the right road.

Several of them assured me that their Führer is a man to whom voices speak as voices spoke to Joan of Arc. They explained his accent, which I had found peculiar, by telling me that it has a similarity to the speech of the Sudeten Germans. They took satisfaction in the fact that the one singled out by God to be their leader comes from the borderlands of Germany.

An S.S. (member of the *Schutz Staffel*, the black-uniformed Elite Guard of the Storm Troops) told me that it is by psychology more than by might that the nation has been conquered. I learned that, according to the National Socialist idea, the will of the Führer is the will of the German people, and that logically "he who does not stand with the Führer is no longer German."

German Jews he brushed aside as if of no importance. "Aryan" Germans who do not think as National Socialists must be converted if possible. Otherwise, if of sufficient importance to be a political danger, they must be eliminated. When the Nazis came into power they already possessed a fairly wide index of outstanding persons, and since then this has been enlarged to cover the country. No one is disturbed who is not a potential danger to the fulfillment of the Führer's laws when proclaimed, but it is necessary to have as complete a record as possible of everyone's past. So this card index has been compiled.

The system used in keeping down uprisings is never to annoy until it is possible absolutely to crush, separate, and then destroy, finding ways to confuse elements that might join so that there is no need to combat their united resistance. "A secret of National Socialist success," the serious youth explained, "is the accomplishment of a thing before others have any idea that there is intent to do it. Faced with the fact that it is already done, those who might oppose are put in a quandary."

All National Socialists are pledged to blind obedience. For instance, should it ever happen that an S.S. finds his father's name on the list of Germans he is to take to a concentration camp, he may not question or disobey. If, in such a time as the "cleanup" of June 1934, he should see his brother against the wall when he is in the firing squad, it is his duty to shoot when the command is given.

The S.S. take a Spartan oath, and on them rests the duty of maintaining internal order in the state. They wear black uniforms decorated with silver. They may use fire-arms at need, and they are closely connected with the secret police. Theirs is not a state-paid service, nor is that of the S.A. men; they hold jobs in offices and industry, but must be given leave with full pay when needed for a state duty.

After the death of President von Hindenburg, when Adolf Hitler accepted the position of full responsibility for the Dritte Reich, the army swore an oath of personal loyalty to him. In the weeks that followed, this same oath was asked from every branch of the many state serv-ices — church, school, railway, customs, postal, telegraph, telephone, police, tax bureaus, and so forth, until every person drawing state pay should be so pledged. All fell smoothly into line excepting the church and a few edu-cators. The church opposition was too large to be imme-diately squelched. The educators had the choice of con-centration camps or prompt exile.

None among those I met seemed to know with any cer-tainty how many German men or women were in concen-tration camps. The numbers mentioned varied from hundreds to thousands. They told me that earlier it had been said that such imprisonment was but a temporary measure during revolution, that there would be an amnesty and people would be let out as soon as National Socialism was established. But unfortunately people learned slowly, and certainly the number arrested was growing rather than getting smaller.

There was considerable talk of what should be done

with these people in case of war. It was said that the task of guarding them, combined with keeping internal state order, would be more than could be managed by the force which could be spared from the front. Some said they would have to be put to death to save food. Others were emphatic that they must be forced to work on munitions and in other essential industries, housed in the work place under guard. But, as with everything else, they had to wait for an expression of their Führer's will to know what would happen. Many were certain that at present all able hands in prison were kept at productive labor. "Since they have to be fed, any other system would be a waste."

I heard much of the "legality" of National Socialist actions during these days, but I never understood the reason for mention of this until I met a man versed in law. He said that Germans are very legal-minded and want things "legal." Excepting the present era, so far as he knew there had been no time in German history when laws were edicts, or a ruler occupied a position comparable to a Son of Heaven in China proclaiming the law and serving as the medium through which a God spoke his commands.

The early German tribes had no written language. Consequently they left no written records. But after the Germans became literate, in the Roman Catholic monasteries several devoted themselves to collecting and recording oral traditions of their tribe. These "mirrors," as they are called, are in the public libraries of present-day Germany open for anyone to consult. The laws of the Saxons were the first to appear. These were followed by an Imperial Code, "Acts relating to Public Peace," published at Mayence in 1235. Other sources of information on traditional German ways are the *De origine, situ, moribus et populis Germaniae* of Tacitus, the comments of Cæsar, the *Nibelungenlied*, and the *Waltharilied*.

History shows that through the centuries the German people built up a thoughtful system of law for the regulation of their affairs, aiming at the protection of the individual as well as the maintenance of order in the state. It was a German boast that their courts were above corruption, law a sacred calling, and that no peoples anywhere surpassed them in this. Germany was divided into many states, and regulations differed somewhat, but they had a common legal tradition. Minor things might be unlike, but there was much exchange of experience, and a desire far beyond their own borders for "German law."

They had such a vast accumulation of statutes that early in this present century a decision was reached to overhaul the legal system and revise the code. A group of German lawyers were appointed to make a survey of German, Austrian, and Swiss law. They began work in 1902, and in 1909 published a preliminary survey, followed by a more complete publication in 1913. Their work was interrupted by the war.

Immediately after the war the democratic governments of Austria and Germany agreed to revise their laws and make them exactly the same, basing their work on what had been done by the above commission. They reasoned thus: we are forbidden now to join together, but later, when we are united, our law will be in order and the unification of our affairs will be simple. So, without any public fuss, Austrian officials and lawyers came to Berlin and worked quietly on this with German officials and lawyers.

They made a joint plan, but, because of great political unrest in Germany and Austria during these years, it was never written into the Criminal Law Code as desired. Governments changed so frequently that it was practically impossible to get the bill passed. The legislators never got around to attending to it. Immediately the National Socialists came into power they set lawyers to work on this problem. In the fall of 1933 the Prussian Minister of Justice put out the first memorandum on their effort, and in 1934 the Academy for German Law published a further report.

Up to that time German law had held to the principle of no punishment without a law — *nulla poena sine lege.* The old book clearly stated, in the introductory remarks: *"Eine Handlung kann nur dann mit einer Strafe gesetzlich bestraft werden, wenn die Strafe gesetzlich bestimmt war, bevor die Handlung begangen wurde. Bei Verschiedenheit der Gesetze von der Zeit der begangenen Handlung bis zu deren Aburteilung ist das mildeste Gesetz anzuwenden."* (An act can be legally punished only when this punishment was legally established before the act was committed. In case of a change in the law between the date of committing the act and the date of conviction, the mildest law is to be applied.) The National Socialists have revised this to read: *"Bestraft wird, wer eine Tat begeht, die das Gesetz für strafbar erklärt oder die nach dem Grundgedanken eines Strafgesetzes und nach gesundem Volksempfinden Bestrafung verdient. Findet auf die*

Tat kein bestimmtes Strafgesetz unmittelbar Anwendung, so wird die Tat nach dem Gesetz bestraft, dessen Grundgedanke auf sie am besten zutrifft." (Whoever commits an act which the law declares punishable, or which deserves punishment according to the basic thought of a criminal law and in accordance with a healthy folk feeling, is to be punished. If no definite criminal law is directly applicable to the deed, then the deed is to be punished according to the law which in fundamental thought best applies.) *Nullum crimen sine poena* — no crime without a punishment.

Thus did they widen the power of the judge to a limitless authority, and also legalize their policy of bringing their fellow men and women into courts for deeds they did during the years before the National Socialists took charge of the Reich. For instance, a man who distributed pacifist literature in the twenties can be tried and convicted for that now; he may not be, but it hangs over his head like a sword on a hair — a warning to desist from anything which may call the attention of the authorities to his past conduct.

The new code also widens police power. In the words of Frederick the Great: "Police power means making necessary provision for the maintenance of peace and safety, and also for the prevention of dangers which threaten the whole public or any of its individual members." Now there is the simple statement: "The police have the task of putting into force the will of the Führer and can take all steps necessary for that end." *Hochverrat* and *Landesverrat* (high treason and treason against the state) are terms broadened to include anything which might upset or disturb the smooth working of National Socialism. The death sentence is given wide application.

In wider use, also, is a German form of punishment known as *Ehrverlust*, or loss of honor. It applies to political criminals in particular, but can be added to other sentences. A person so punished may no longer occupy public office. He is excluded from the National Socialist Party and all its suborganizations. He may not serve in the Labor Corps. He may not be a farmer, or an independent artisan. He must surrender all titles, orders, and medals he may have won in previous years of his life; he loses every right of German citizenship, including the right to serve as a guardian or custodian; he may lose control of his children.

Lawyers, judges, and courts function busily. Their machinery has not been disturbed, except that in a state run on the *Führerprinzip* the will of the Leader transcends every written law. If the judges "make a mistake" and free a criminal who should be held, the Gestapo are within the law when they rearrest and confine the one mistakenly freed.

"Hitler — Arbeit und Brot" I had seen prominently displayed ever since our first day in Germany. On request, the way was quickly opened for me to see what was being done about work and bread. From the outset I was told that the attitude of the National Socialists toward work is different from that of all others. Their emphasis is not on wages, but on the beauty of labor, the dignity of toil, the true happiness its successful performance brings.

My instructors said that a false shame has come into

civilization, an attitude of scorn for the calloused hand which has made people strive after the white-collar job. This has thrown society off its balance. I met lecturers and saw posters, pamphlets, and books prepared to emphasize the fact that all work honors the good workman. They aim at the ironing out of class barriers and envision a whole nation happy in working together under the will of one Führer, each person glad to put a hand to any task which needs doing.

The National Socialists want everyone in the Reich to have the experience of manual labor. *Arbeitsdienst* (labor service) is only now being made compulsory for girls, but from the beginning they were urged to volunteer for it. Many did; my daughter did. She went to a camp in which girls of her age from Cologne joined with the daughters of Essen factory workers. They got on well together. They had teacher-counselors. They rose early, had drill, camp housekeeping duties, and breakfast, and went off to land duty. I did not want her to go because I thought the task would be too hard. It *was* hard, and she liked it; she came back strong, brown, and enthusiastic. She had done her daily duty in a small farmhouse washing the overworked mother's floors, dishes, and children. Her companion worker had taken on outside tasks such as milking the cow, hoeing, and fence mending. It was all under careful management. They checked in and out for so many hours' toil, and they worked always under the control of a counselor. College girls whom I know volunteered to spend their summer vacations in factories; they worked without pay, and let the girls they replaced go on needed holidays.

Six months' labor service was made compulsory for every German boy; there are camps enough to take care of them all as they reach the age of eighteen. The camp directors are men who have gone through a course of training for labor-service leadership, which has been made a state career. I was given a card granting me permission to visit any such camp I might happen to pass anywhere in the Reich. In all I visited seven. The camps are scattered all over Germany; those I have seen are by water, near woods, in meadows, or in as nice a place as was available in the locality. New buildings have been put up in some places, but wherever possible empty castles, old manor houses, empty barracks, or sets of cottages have been used.

Each camp I visited was immaculately clean and tidy both in its surroundings and inside, and this cleanliness extended to the Labor Corps and their director. All had parade grounds, lecture hall, sleeping quarters, dining hall, and a surprisingly modern kitchen. The beds had good mattresses, white sheets, blankets, and neat blue and white checked gingham spreads. Every camp had flowers in its rooms. I ate in each camp, found the food plain but well cooked, and enjoyed the meal.

The camps are not of equal accommodation. Some are much better than others. I was told that the intent is to bring them all up to the level of the best as soon as possible, and I think this is a real intent. Germans like to have their equipment good and everything organized on a uniform basis.

The 40,000 "Soldiers of the Spade" who go to Nürnberg each year are, of course, a carefully picked group. They are not the average of each year's *Arbeitsdienst;* they are the cream. But the rest do not fall very far short of them in physical fitness, and it is amazing to see the stature and carriage improvement in a camp between the boys' time of entrance and the finish of their six months. Coming as they do from shop, factory, farm, and every sort of family, rich and poor, some are pale and some strong, some are bent and some straight, when they arrive. They all emerge brown and hard, holding their heads high and their backs flat.

When one visits a camp, all look contented; but the service is not done in pure contentment. Far and wide over Germany I have listened to considerable expression of dissatisfaction about it. I have heard farmers' sons lament the "gentlemen" in camp with them; and I have heard more gently bred boys grumble about having to mix with rough fellows. Besides this there is much complaint about having to take these six months and then two military years out of life for state service.

Some 250,000 come into camp each year. About a hundred are taken care of in each camp, the aim being to keep the groups small. The camp discipline is such as to make the boys slip easily into the discipline of their military service. Each boy is supplied with a work and a parade uniform, and each has two shovels — one for work and one kept unstained for drill. The days begin early and are strenuous. The boys have the task of camp housekeeping, which falls on them in rotation, drill, field work, and daily lectures in National Socialism.

It is the duty of the director to see that none of the boys overstrain themselves. Also care is taken that their labor does not disturb the paid labor market. They are assigned to tasks which would not otherwise get done, and toil at land improvements such as draining swamps, cutting needed canals, dredging choked waterways, reclaiming land along the coast, helping with harvests, or filling in any farm labor shortage. In the summer of 1938, many units were rushed to the French and Belgian borders, to speed the work of fortification.

"At first the criticism was raised that we should never be able to find enough work for them," said a Labor official who showed me around, "but we Nazis are not short of ideas. We can think of plenty of work to keep every person here busy."

After visiting seven Labor Corps camps I wanted to halt and learn what was done about the employment of people who need to earn money to support families. "Everything in its order," I was told. "We have grounded you on the principle that everyone must learn to find work natural and good; next you will have the definition of a National Socialist state."

A National Socialist state was defined as a state organized against poverty, discouragement, and enemy blockade. To achieve this result there must be overhead planning and a complete control of economic activities. In such a state the indifferent and the discontented have no rights which the patriotic will respect. The aim is to create and maintain a worthy standard of living in a powerful nation, which can be done by mathematical method and hard work. The battalions of science must be harnessed to the programme.

Before the war, economists had warned Germany that an overdependence on the rest of the world had developed, but she had to suffer a blockade before taking this seriously. People had managed to live through those years, but under such distress as need never be repeated. Now was the harsh time of readjustment. A self-sufficiency which placed the Reich on a safe basis must be achieved, and the balance between town and country work put straight. It must not be forgotten that agriculture is the first industry and manufacturing the second. Germany was rich in scientists and able workers. Wise men had made a plan. It must be ruthlessly executed whether everyone liked it or not, because it was right and good.

"None shall be denied the right to work here. Neither will any who can work be allowed to be lazy. The majority of people really like to work; the fundamental thing is to fan that desire and then find things to be done. The truth is that there is so much in need of being done that every hand can be busy. We shall soon have a labor shortage. Unemployment is an absurdity, a disease of modern so-called civilization."

The first step was to get an index of everyone able to work. The unemployed were only too willing to fill up forms telling all about themselves, and stating what they had done and what they would like to do. These answers were added to the forms filled in by people already employed. Soon the Dritte Reich possessed a file of 25,000,-000 people. Assigning them work was easy. The bureau of overhead administration needed thousands. Hundreds who knew languages were wanted for censorship work, as every tenth letter in the ordinary post must be examined and all the mail of people on the suspect list opened. Krupps and other rearmament factories needed thousands

of workers. Builders, masons, carpenters, cement workers, in numbers beyond count, were necessary to execute
the Führer's dreams for national rejuvenation — Berlin re-
done on a magnificent scale, Nürnberg made a fitting
place for rallies, assembly halls in every city, a swimming
bath for every village, a house and garden for every worker,
boulevards joining every part of the Reich, and such a stir
in manufacturing as "fairly took the breath away."

As to labor conditions I learned that both employer and
employee must be under close state control. Neither
strikes nor lockouts were allowed, and no excessive profit
on either side. The worker's wages could not be higher
than production warranted, and watch must be kept that
private wages did not coax men from government jobs.
Corporations may not distribute more than 6 per cent
interest on capital invested, any further profit being reserved for industrial improvement and expansion. "In
this way we shall soon have the finest industrial equipment
in the world."

Hours of work are "twenty-four if our Führer needs
twenty-four." No one can change a job without permission from the Labor Front. If a man's wages absolutely
are not enough for his family, he must turn to the various
services for state aid. Wages are settled by the Labor
Front. Some of them seemed microscopic to me, but I was
assured that this is a practical Reich with the sense not to
starve its workers to death. Its foundations rest not on a
gold standard, but on the strength of the producers.

The laborers had serious faces and a quiet mien. Visiting factories, I noticed how orderly and methodical they
were. Often I heard music coming from radios, and I was

told that men are quieter and work better with occasional music to do their work by. When I mentioned their paleness I was reminded that we had now reached midsummer, a time of trying heat, and was then told of the "Strength through Joy" holidays on which many would soon be going. These are excursions at reduced cost.

There is a scarcity of skilled workers, technicians, chemists, and inventors. Prizes are given to those who find ways to replace the raw materials Germany does not have, and those who show ability for laboratory investigation receive every possible help. There are too many people wanting professional and clerical jobs, and too many small shopkeepers. No one is supposed to have a business which is nonessential. If a person wants to be a hairdresser and there are enough hairdressers, he cannot be one. Boys and girls about to leave school have to state their preference for careers, but if that work is not needed they must take something else. The same with white-collar people; if there are no jobs of the kind they want, they must take what is offered. "It does a man who has only pushed a pen untold good to wield a shovel for a change." A person who refuses the work offered may not draw any relief.

Taken to see public works, I saw a vast number of buildings in the process of going up. Scaffolding seemed to strew the land in such a fever of construction as probably has not been known here since the era of Gothic architecture. The Nazi period is marked by straight lines, precise shapes, calculated spaces, and size. The man who took me on this tour led me to scenes of activity with shining eyes: "This will be bigger than the Great Pyramid"; "This is going to be greater than the Roman Colosseum"; "Has the Great Wall of China more masonry than this?" His enthusiasm was genuine. I, too, stood awed before the work of man's hands. Human beings are so small, yet can do this, I often thought. The places for mass gatherings were largest — not cathedrals to honor God in Heaven as in centuries past, but arenas for masses.

"Why do you want them?" I asked.

"To feel our greatness."

I remarked on the fine workmanship.

"We build for the future. Our Führer's orders are that all we build now must last at least a thousand years."

Next I saw airports, new factories, and new farmhouses of the resettlement plan. We traveled over wide stretches of the *Reichsautobahnen*, and stopped at a place where a road was under construction. These roads are entirely new roads — no making use of old bits.

The Germans build well. The roads are not ugly scars across their land; they are things of beauty, exciting in their charm. They are invisible a short distance off; then one comes on them — silver ribbons. No telegraph poles, advertisements, rows of refreshment stands, gasoline stations, or ugly houses line their banks. Grass strips separate the two ways of traffic, and these often divide around hills to meet and run side by side again. The roadsides are planted with shrubs and trees natural to the district; the bridges harmonize with the valleys they traverse.

None but motor traffic is allowed on them. In forest places, signs which light up at night ask one to be careful of the deer. Clear neat signs give the names of towns along the way, with a diagram showing how one must turn off to get to the town, and similar notices point out digressions to gasoline stations.

We stood now watching a machine from out of which a ribbon of road surface poured like paste from a tube. It lay there wet and smooth.

"We have beaten the rest of the Western world in road building," said my conductor. "We go forward at a cost of but three cents a square yard."

I am sure he believed what he told me, but estimates I was given later indicate that the finished road cost from ten to fifteen times his figure; perhaps he was speaking of the simple surfacing we were watching, while I was asking about the entire construction. At the time I did not question his estimate and inquired about wages; here there was no chance of misunderstanding and his information proved reliable.

"How much do the workers get?"

"Twenty-five marks for fifty-three hours' work. Five they give for various fees, and ten for their own keep; they are housed in temporary quarters put up along the way."

"How can you get men to work for that?"

"When road building is offered a man, he must take it." He turned to look back at the finished road. "It is beautiful, isn't it?"

"It is," I agreed.

"It is — with a reservation in your approval," he took me up quickly. "Now tell me what you really think about it."

"It is built with conscript labor."

"And so was the Grand Canal of China, and every stretch of world building that ever got done. Every man, woman, and child must be gathered up in a mighty sacrifice to one resolute will when great things are to be accomplished. We have organization, discipline, enthusiasm, unity, ingenuity, generalship, and absolute control of resources," he asserted quietly and firmly. "Our Führer's will is decisive for all Germans — our law and his will are one. The working strength of every man, woman, and child within his dominion is power concentrated in our Leader's fist. With that might he forges our destiny."

That evening I heard on the radio: "The methods by which a people forces its way upward are of no moment, but the goal which is reached is important."

VII

GRAPE HARVEST

WHENEVER I am gripped by despair, or roused to angry passion by anything that Germans do, I rest myself in thought of kindlier Germans. When rough and brutal voices shout, I can hear undaunted because I have heard better German voices. In an age when some Germans are testing out the might of threat and fear as weapons of state, and must batter ruthlessly before they can learn that they have chosen powerless weapons, it is encouraging to remember other Germans who conquer successfully all who come near to them.

Four years of living cannot be pressed into a book. Much must be left out for want of space. But I could not give a true picture of the Germany I love unless a certain family were in it.

Warm weather lingers late in the sheltered valley of the Ahr. "Old Wives' Summer" the autumn is often called here. But by the end of October there is frost in the air from the Eifel every night after sunset, and when I first came to visit in the home of Wolfgang and Anna Bender, in early November, 1934, even the tardiest of the plants had joined the more prudent in drawing down their precious green chlorophyll. Leafed in reds and gold, the trees and vines and grasses filled the valley with such beauty as sets the heart to dancing in delight.

Anna met me at the foot of the path that leads through terraced vines to her door. I saw her standing there before I got down from the postal bus — a slender woman in a fresh print dress, her brown hair worn in a coronet braid round her head, and eyes that are cornflower blue. When we were in her house, my wraps and valise put away, we had coffee seated by a broad window. Then she fetched her work, the ripping of her husband's overcoat. Supplied with a ripper, I helped.

Below us to the river sloped the vineyard of her dowry. Through an orchard on the west we could just see the roof of her parents' dwelling, which is set in a dell. Some distance beyond rose the steeple of the village church. The gray stone cottage in which we sat, with the grape terraces on three of its sides and a wood lot over the hill, is Wolfgang's inheritance from his father.

Anna led me to an east window to point out a sunny ridge, saying: "My man has chosen the best of all his land for a new vineyard. Our eldest daughter, Anna-Marie, is sixteen. The grapes are ready to bear next season. The harvest from these young vines will be hers to fill her hope chest, and when she weds the vineyard deeds go with her to her new home."

We took up our ripping again while Anna talked on about her children: "After us, the homestead will go to Hans, our second son. Ernst, our first-born, does not want a vineyard. Not all children born to farm families belong to the land. It is best for those who are not the land's own to follow the call which bids them be away. Ernst would be a physician. He has gone to learn. A vineyard keeper has gentle skill in his hands, endurance, intuition, and the power of quick decision. A vine-keeping ancestry may help our Ernst to be a wise physician."

Hans and his father came in from the wood lot, where they had been cutting grape supports. Greetings over, Wolfgang noticed our work.

"I am repairing this coat for the last time," Anna told him. "After next harvest you must buy a new one."

"It has been a good coat," he answered. "There is no weaving now like the wool cloth made before the war."

"The best of cloth does not last forever," she reminded him. "This is the third time I have turned this coat. The collar and cuffs are so worn that I must cut new ones from the length. Very short it will be!"

"Well — after next season's picking I'll get a coat," he promised.

Anna-Marie returned from helping with her grandmother's baking day, bringing a warm, fragrant currant loaf; and her mother promptly made her a witness to this overcoat agreement. Born in that dark winter of despair, 1918, she is her father's pride. "My sunshine" and "my light" he calls her in his sentimental German way.

"If you find any fault in her you must not blame her," Wolfgang will often say. "If she is spoiled, then I am at fault for spoiling her."

Soft of voice and quick of wit, yet with no barb in her words to hurt those against whom her humor is directed, she has inherited her mother's lithe figure and her father's red-gold hair.

Suse and Otto, aged nine and ten, slipped in. They had

loitered on the way from school. Each gave me a grubby hand and made me a deep bow. They were scolded and kissed by both mother and father and sent to wash. They soon returned, shiny-clean, to stand leaning against their big brother Hans, one on either side of his chair.

Everyone in the Bender family has his or her duties. There is no discussion as to who shall do what in the daily tasks. On the evening of my first arrival, before the family scattered to tend the animals, gather the eggs, milk the cows, and prepare a beautiful supper, Wolfgang played Beethoven's Sixth Symphony on his gramophone.

"Some day I hope to own the Ninth," he declared as he put the records carefully away in their case.

During my visit Anna cleaned and pressed the cloth of his overcoat, and puzzled out its remaking to the best advantage. Sewing on the buttons, the morning of my departure, she assured everyone within hearing, "This is the last winter he can wear this coat." And as he tried it on, thrice turned and now shortened by the necessity of replacing its frayed collar and cuffs from the length, Wolfgang affirmed, "Yes — next autumn, if there is profit in the harvest, I'll get a new coat."

While the vine sleeps the toil of the vineyard keeper goes on. "Grape growers who would prosper must water their vines with sweat every month in the year," according to Anna's father.

Men of prudence firm their terraces as soon as the harvest is cut, putting back any stones that have fallen from the walls which hold them to the hill, and replace rotted vine supports with new posts. Their womenfolk go through the vineyards lifting each vine that has been pulled down by the weight of fruit and retying it securely to its supporting post with binders of reed.

Time is then taken from the care of the vineyards to make the homesteads and the places of community meeting snug against the coming cold. Roofs are mended and storm doors put up on house and stable. The kitchen shed is filled with fuel. Tender garden plants are bedded with leaves and mats. Men join in tightening their churches, neighborhood halls, and schoolhouses. Indoors the women make ready for winter by closing every crack that might let frost into the cellars where food is laid by for the season when nothing grows, looking over the family's warm clothing, airing the feather quilts, and refilling with fresh earth the pots of ivy geranium, begonia, and oxalis that bloom by the windows.

"Men should be ready for their wood-lot work when the leaves turn," young Suse informed me.

"When the leaves yellow, the trees are drawing their life fluid down into their roots for winter storage," Wolfgang explained. "Vine supports are strongest if hewn when this life fluid is passing through the tree's trunk."

Wood should season a year before it is set in the earth, so the vineyard keeper hews his vine posts the autumn before he needs them. Oak is best. Oak properly cured will hold a vine through all weathers for twenty years. Therefore in his wood lot it is the oaks that Wolfgang pampers by clearing out other growth to give them plenty of air and light. Helping the acorns to sprout abundantly, he picks up handfuls that have fallen in the shade and scatters them in open glades. Often he transplants oak saplings to better places than those where they have started. Hewing his vine supports, he bears in mind the generations to come after him, and takes no more than he must each year.

The Benders stack their roughly hewn posts in an open-ended shed, leaving the trimming and shaping to be done on days when weather makes it impossible to work out of doors. The posts hauled in, the next job of the year is the carrying up of manure from the cow stables to enrich the terraced earth. This is the hardest of all a vine keeper's work. It occupies much of the winter. Hods are used, similar in shape to those masons have, but larger, and Hans says there is no way to carry them but on a man's back. A man in the prime of his strength can make fifteen trips a day to a height of six hundred feet, carrying a hundred-weight each time.

I enjoyed my first visit in Anna's house, and as I left she bid me come again freely whenever I wanted to. I have gone often, finding peace there from the stress of my own city life.

While the vines are dormant it is the women's task to prune them back, leaving only one branch of last season's growth, which is to bear next summer's grapes, and to clean all twigs and grippers from the stalk. Trimmed while they sleep, the vines do not bleed. In open weather Anna and Anna-Marie kept at this job, as it takes many months to attend to all their vineyards. On rough days they were occupied inside, preparing the coils of rye straw and reed twine used for binding the grapes to their supports. Both the straw and the reeds are soaked in water, then worked until pliable.

Snow fell on Christmas Eve. All through January the valley of the Ahr was mantled in white. There were three days of vacation for Christ's Feast. Then the Benders went on with their work. Except when there was rough wind or blinding snowfall, Wolfgang and Hans continued to carry their hods up into the vineyards. The grape growers of this place unload their fertilizer in evenly spaced heaps and do not spread it until certain there is enough for all the vines. Otherwise a vine keeper might find that he had none for the last terrace.

When they are doing this work Anna will not let her menfolk into the house until they have washed and changed. She puts warm water and fresh clothes in the shed for them.

In February we enjoyed a false spring in a sudden thaw and a spell of weather so warm that it was comfortable without a coat. The air was laden with the promise of summer. I went down to Anna's to find young Otto sunning himself on the doorstep in company with Tiger, the cat.

"*Liegt die Katze in Februar in der Sonne, liegt sie in März hinterm Ofen mit Wonne,*" the boy sang out as I approached.

The others were all up in the vineyards. He had been left to tend the home chores and was sitting with Tiger until milking time. On one of the terraces I found Anna, Anna-Marie, and Suse busy with their pruning shears. They all agreed that the weather was lovely, but hoped that the mildness would soon end, lest the vines be wakened.

Wolfgang and Hans were hastily hoeing the manure into the thawed ground to save it from the winds which might blow it away in March. The soil here is filled with slate. They all believe that the slate gives their grapes an iron which builds up strength in those who drink the wine such as is not found in the juice of fruit grown elsewhere. Slate makes the earth hard to till. Wolfgang and Hans were tearing the ground open with hoes resembling miners' picks, digging the fertilizer well in. The more the earth is tilled, the better vines thrive. All the year, whenever they can find time from other tasks and the ground is not frozen, they work through their vineyards terrace by terrace. The end reached, they turn back to start again where they commenced to hoe.

"Twenty times round each vine is the least number of hoeings any sensible tiller gives," according to Hans. Otto is too young yet to do a day's work with the hoe, but he is often made to do a hand's turn that he may grow into understanding of the patience that a man needs.

The weather did soon turn colder, as the Benders wished, but with a greater fierceness than they desired. Otto's prophecy, quoted from his grandfather, came true. March arrived with a blast that drove the cat behind the stove. The earth was frozen hard, and cracked open. The heaving frosts split vineyards asunder. Stones from the supporting walls were tumbled from terrace to terrace. Ragged gashes were torn across the ground — looking into them, one could see the exposed vine roots. Men hastened into the bitter weather to mend as best they could the damage done by the cruel strength of the cold, stuffing sacking, newspapers, and old quilts in to cover the roots.

The changeable weather brought the valley an epidemic of influenza. Anna's own hardy family escaped the sickness. She joined a corps of neighborhood women quickly organized to nurse the suffering. The local doctor was away when the epidemic began, answering a summons for having turned a radio off when Adolf Hitler was speaking. When he returned he praised the women highly for having used just the right remedies in his absence.

There was great rejoicing at his return. Reported by a malicious person as disrespectful to the Führer, he had taken his case directly to Berlin. He had turned the radio off because while it was on he could not hear the heartbeat of a sick child whom he was tending. Pleading his own case, without a lawyer's aid, he had won release and pardon. He had been away less than a fortnight.

"There is justice in our Fatherland," he told patients as he went his rounds.

The true spring came with Easter. The Eifel whitened as with drifted snow under the blossoms of the wild cherry and the blackthorn. Grass sprang up. Primroses unfolded their petals. Violets lifted their heads. Iris thrust clean blades through the soil in Anna's garden. Yet the grapevines slept on, heedless of the perfumed call of growing things.

After April's second gentle rain, Anna's Cousin Beckhaus, a near neighbor, set out a new vineyard, moving his plants before they wakened. Each little vine was shaded with a slate to keep the sun from pulling too hard on it during its first summer on the terrace. Vines are started from slips, usually in the kitchen garden, as his were. For three years after transplanting they are pruned back to drive their growth into the root, and in the fourth year vines are allowed to bear their first grapes. The crop comes strong and healthy.

There is a Portuguese grape grown here sometimes which bears for a hundred years, but unfortunately its taste is not a favorite. People of the Ahr prefer varieties of red and white French grapes which have to be replanted about every twenty years. The roots go down forty feet and more, and they must be pulled out with chains when the vineyard ceases to bear. The land has then to rest for three or four years while the soil is cleaned by growing vegetables in it. The clever among experienced vineyard keepers are wise concerning the crops that are best for reviving the ground so that vines will thrive in it again.

In the Ahr a man may not plant just what he will in his land. He has to carry every slip he desires to grow to a communal examination before he can put it in the earth. There are many grape diseases and this common law is a safeguard for the valley. If disease does get into a vineyard, the vines are destroyed and the plot fenced and sealed by the mayor until the earth is cured. The American wild grape has been found marvelously free from the danger of root trouble and Ahr growers like to use it as a stock, grafting on their favorite variety.

In recent years government regulations forbidding the sending of money out of Germany have made it difficult to secure these roots, but some families have a relative living in the States who will express them and wait for payment until international economics are untangled. Wolfgang got American roots for Anna-Marie's vineyard, and the vines for Cousin Beckhaus's planting were grown from slips which she gave him.

During the fair days of spring the men hoed diligently in their vineyards, letting air and light in round the grape roots. Anna and Anna-Marie bent the single branch which they had left on each vine, when they pruned, into a hoop, binding it into shape with the rye-straw twine; then fastened the hoop to the vine's post with a knot of reed.

Through a diligent bustle and stir all down the valley the vines continued quiet. The swallows had long returned; the blackbird had finished his courting song; the larks were nesting before the grapes cautiously stretched out leaf buds clad in mittens of fuzzy wool.

"*Bodenständig* should only be used in reference to folk who stand firmly on the earth," spoke Anna, correcting me. "Like the noun 'farmer,' it is a word that no family has a right to until it has proved its steadiness by more than one generation of successful living on the land."

A vineyard keeper worthy of this title has his wood lot for poles, his field for potatoes, his orchard of fruit trees, his stabled cows, his dwelling house, and his vines. He eats bread of his wife's making which is baked in the village oven, where each family has its allotted day and the fire is banked over Sunday. His laundry is rubbed clean at home, rinsed in the clear waters of the Ahr, and bleached on the grass. He walks without arrogance but with self-respecting dignity. And, Protestant or Catholic, he brings his children up to earn their keep, pay their debts, revere God, and love the Fatherland.

When such a man marries, in the valley of the Ahr, he needs four thousand vines to support himself and his wife in decency. As his family increases he requires more. A healthy man and his wife can tend up to eight thousand vines without undue strain, but if they increase their vine-

yards beyond this number they should employ help —
unless they have grown sons and daughters. Casual labor
does nothing except harm in a vineyard. Vines thrive best
when tended by persons who have grown up in the vineyards. It is the custom here for young folk who do not
yet own enough grapes to occupy them entirely to hire
themselves out to neighbors; and it is the recognized duty
of a son, or a son-in-law, to tend the vineyards of parents
who have lost their strength.

Along the lovely green waters of the Ahr, since Napoleon
passed, the vines have been the property of working vine-
yarders. This arrangement differs from conditions on the
banks of the Rhine and the Moselle, where many of the
vineyards are owned by absentee landlords and a goodly
number of the best terraces are held by the Prussian State.
Charlemagne planted the first grapes to grow in German
soil. According to legend, he sent his servant Kunrat to
Orléans for the vines and set them in the earth with his
own hand. When the first wine harvest was ready he
journeyed from Aix-la-Chapelle, in regal procession, to
taste the beverage. Draining his golden goblet, he declared
the German wine to be a drink which gave back his youth.

After this success, many vineyards were planted along
the Rhine and the Rhine's tributaries. Graf von Hoch-
staden, Count of Altenahr, who held the land on both banks
of the Ahr by feudal right, ordered it terraced and set with
vines. When he died, his valley of vineyards was inherited by his brother, a Catholic bishop. The bishop bequeathed it to the Cathedral of Cologne.

When Napoleon came he took the valley of the Ahr
from the Church and sold it out in small lots. Many

families here speak with pride of their deed from Napoleon. Folk who stand firmly on the earth, they have held to the opportunity which the Corsican gave them through all the decades since.

Under the hot sun of May the woolly knobs on the grape-vines pushed out farther and farther. Now that the vines were waking, the vineyard keepers feared a frost. May the eleventh, the thirteenth, and the fifteenth are called "The Three Ice Saints."

"This is the time when icebergs floating down from the far North bring cold to Germany," the village cobbler told me when I took my country shoes to be soled.

Visiting at Anna's, I found the family saying prayers daily in church, as their neighbors were. Thermometers had been hung in all the vineyards and men kept guard at night, reading the temperature every half hour. The "Saints" passed safely, but the watchmen stayed on, neighbors taking turns, as the air held frost.

On the night of the sixteenth an alarm was given which set the church bells ringing from village to village, calling out the vineyard keepers and their families. Cannons barked the order for fires to be lit. The people knew where to set their fires and how many to put alight by the way the cannons were fired. They worked in corps, each with a leader whom they obeyed without question or delay.

The village was wrapped in a blanket of protecting smoke made by burning coal tar. The greatest danger is on the clearest nights, and the lower parts of the vineyards are in gravest peril because the cold intensifies by its own weight. The peril is in the sudden thawing under the morning sun, when the life drips out of fruit buds. Wrapping them in smoke prevents this thawing.

Such a frost is a nuisance to the German housewife, who likes her house kept spotlessly clean, but for the sake of the vines, which are the valley's livelihood, the valley must be filled with coal-tar smoke. Black gets in everywhere. Still, everyone is glad to have the grapes saved.

After dawn the buds were officially examined and in every village along the Ahr the *Bürgermeister* pronounced the grapes unhurt. Bells and cannon carried the glad tidings. Laughing and singing in their relief, the people of the Ahr filed into their churches to thank God for His mercy.

Then the women hurried home. By noon the smoke had settled. At suppertime Anna had fresh curtains up, snowy linen on the beds, the doorsteps scoured, and the garden flowers rinsed off. Rain at the end of the week washed the valley, cleaning away the last traces of tar smoke.

The vines put forth branches. The leaf buds broke their sheaths and slowly unfolded their tucks, spreading their greenness shiny and moist to the sun. Under the protection of the leaves the flower buds opened their tiny petals, and the bright June weather was sweet with the blossoming of the grape.

I sat by the riverbank watching swallows teach their young to feed on the wing. Four round little birds, steel-blue, squatted on the swaying branches of a riverside willow. Scolding and coaxing, turning and twisting in flights of easy grace, the mother and father, their cheeks pouched with insects, circled over their children. One by one the birdlings would venture out to have their mouths filled, then flutter back to a perch.

But Wolfgang and Anna, hurrying by, gave no heed to this. In June the attention of vineyard keepers centres on their vines. She carried her scissors. He had a spraying tank swung over his shoulder.

Bright June weather brings on the first real surety of harvest — the tiny green grapes, a few days after the blossoms fall. It also brings on the danger of mildew and hatches out the hay moth. Wolfgang fights mildew with sprays of sulphur and copper vitriol thinned with chalked milk. Every leaf on every vine must be noticed; those on which the spray is blown take on a gray-blue color. Mildew must be watched out for so long as the leaves are growing, well into September.

Anna's concern was with the hay moth. The first had been seen fluttering over the house arbor. She was on her way to the village hall, where women were gathering to make the hay-moth banners. So I went along. These banners consist of a light stick with an oblong framework at one end over which white muslin is tacked. At the time of use, the muslin is smeared with a sticky substance prepared by the village committee and distributed at cost.

After school the children were sent into the vineyards with the banners. The catcher was cleaned and freshly smeared each day. Suse and Otto and their young neighbors had to carry on this chase every evening until the last hay moth had disappeared from the valley.

"My children, I thank you," Wolfgang said on the last evening of the moth chase as Otto and Suse, reluctant to leave the twilight, came in to bed at Anna's call. "You have saved my winter overcoat."

He spoke too soon. In August, after a long spell of hot dry weather, came the wasps, a plague of them, endangering a vintage which promised to be exceptionally good in both quality and quantity. The insects settled on the half-grown grapes, sucking the juice and bringing in their wake flies and earwigs.

Working in groups with a leader, as in the smoke column, the vineyard keepers fought the wasps. They sought out nests, burned sulphur under them, and, when the wasps were stupefied, poured on boiling water. They hung bottles of sweetened water in the vines throughout the vineyards, emptying them systematically of drowned insects morning and evening. Still the menace persisted.

Finally the advice of the village cobbler was heeded. He contended that what the wasps needed was a drink, and that if trickles of fresh water were arranged, from slightly opened taps, at which the insects could quench their thirst, they wouldn't destroy the grapes. This was done. The plague ceased.

On the last day of August, the schoolmaster's eldest son, now an official in brown uniform, came to remind Hans that this year all men born in 1915 must do their Labor Service. Questioning him, Wolfgang asked if Hans's work in the vineyards did not count as labor for his country. The man in brown explained that the purpose of the Labor Corps is not work in the ordinary sense, but a bringing together of all classes from different parts of Germany in the comradeship of activity.

"You do not intend to object to your son going?"

"Certainly not," Wolfgang replied. "We of Ahr are a peaceful, law-abiding people who obey new regulations as soon as explained to us."

It was arranged that Hans should go into camp after harvest for his six months' service.

Through the summer, while the grapes grew, women were as busy in the vineyards with their pruning scissors as the men with their hoes. All barren growth, except shoots for next season's bending, were kept snipped off. Every useless tendril on a vine takes of its strength, reducing the size of the grapes.

When the grapes took on color the vineyards were officially closed. The notice was given by a boy walking through the village ringing a bell. It was also printed in the local paper.

The *Bürgermeister* decided the day. (This is not a state law, but a custom.) Everyone had to close off his vineyards. Thorns and brush were piled up at the foot of the paths. Not even the owner could go in. This is the time of waiting for the harvest. The vine keepers have done all in their power to help the vines; now the vines are left in undisturbed peace to finish the grapes.

The men rested, loitering about the village or lounging through the sunny afternoons on the banks of the river. The women spent their freedom from outdoor work in making their homes fine. There was a tremendous scrubbing and cleaning; then a great cooking and baking. The shelves of storeroom and cellar were filled with pies, cakes, puddings, boiled hams, spiced sausages, roasted chickens, and a variety of pressed meats. Anna and Anna-Marie, who has a deft hand with yeast sponge, made innumerable loaves of bread, buns, and coffee twists.

The harvest is the crown of the vine keepers' work. A good harvest is celebrated as a joyous festival. The schools were closed. Relatives and friends came from far and near. The women guests fetched hampers of their cooking, gifts to add to all the hostess had made ready. As the women arrived they fell in with the final preparations, turning a hand to the churn or the whipping of bowls of cream.

The *Bürgermeister*, himself a vine grower, proclaimed the grapes ripe. The boy crier ran through the village with his bell to spread the tidings, and the vine growers all gathered at their village hall. With ceremony and song the brush was thrown aside, and the harvesters went in with baskets and scissors.

As filled, the baskets were emptied into a wicker carrier. Each time this was full a strong man lifted it on to his back, carrying it down to a handcart below the vineyard. As loaded, the carts were taken to the owner's cellar or, if the family were members, as Wolfgang and Anna are, to the *Winzer-Verein*.

Before this coöperative idea was established every man made his wine in his own cellar. But the best vintners are often the poorest salesmen. Buyers took advantage of this. Frequently they stirred growers to bid against each other so as to get the wine cheaply. As a result many vine keepers were continually poor, some actually in debt after a good harvest.

Some few, of course, were clever. So it came to be that the ability to bargain gave a man more reward than skill with vine and vat. This was wrong. Finally the vineyard keepers drew together. At Mayschoss in the Ahr, sixty years ago, the first *Winzer-Verein* in all Germany was formed.

To-day every grape-growing neighborhood in Germany has its coöperative society. Of course in each district some men stay independent. Under the *Winzer-Verein* system the members take their harvest directly from the vineyard to the society's cellar. Here a machine picks the fruit from the branches and grinds it through a crusher. Then the pulp is weighed with an invention which measures the sugar content.

The result is written in an open book, into which any member can look whenever he likes. Each family has a credit according to what it has brought in. The wine is made together and the vats are under the care of the best wine makers. The selling is done by those who are best at business. By coöperation, Wolfgang believes, a neighbor lives better than when every man's hand is out just for his own house.

The year had swung round in its circle. Frost, sharp in warning of winter's approach, was in the air again. Wolfgang and Anna came up to Cologne to light candles in the Cathedral, and to buy Wolfgang's overcoat. By letter we arranged that I should meet them in town, bringing them out to stay a night with us. At five o'clock we met at the appointed place, the Cathedral steps.

They had arrived before me and were waiting. A stiff wind blew across the Cathedral square. Seeking no shelter, they stood staunch against its blast, her hand in his. Under his arm he held a brown paper parcel.

Greetings over, I asked, "Did you get a nice coat?"

"We have spent our money," answered Anna, then added, her eyes twinkling, "I know what you will think. You will think, 'Those crazy Huns!'"

"No, no, Nänchen," admonished Wolfgang, tucking a wisp of her hair back under her hat with a gentle index finger. "No, no, my little dear. Our foreign friend is an American. The Americans are intelligent people. An American would know that there is more warmth in Beethoven's Ninth Symphony than in eleven overcoats."

VIII

MARRIAGE

MAI-DA'S[1] mother has an intense interest in the history of marriage. From the House of Exile she wrote asking me to collect information on customs among the Germans so that she could compare their practices with those of the Chinese.

She wanted this to begin in tribal times and to be divided into three epochs: the pagan; the encounter with Christianity; and the National Socialist era, in which I was now living. She desired to know the age at which engagements were arranged and marriages consummated; who arranged marriage; what were the property rights in marriage; the regulations concerning divorce; and if remarriage was permitted to widows, widowers, and the divorced.

It seemed more than I could accomplish. I turned east and west for help. In a dozen scholarly quarters I was told that this was a subject requiring a lifetime of research, a subject to give lifelong occupation to a learned professor. When I wrote to Mai-da's mother, she did not reply; but I got a commanding line from my mother-by-affection: "Proceed without further evasion." I did so, aided by such assistance as I could enlist. Beginning with reluctance, I

[1] Mai-da is my foster sister in China, as described in *The House of Exile*.

became interested and chose from the vast store of data as well as I had wisdom to do.

The early Germans had no written language, but each tribe had its code of laws which were passed orally from generation to generation. These, as later collected, display no neglect to legislate on marriage.

Despite diligent search we could find no ruling on the age for legal engagement or marriage in either the Swabian or the Saxon Mirror, or any other collection of tribal laws. We came on a statement, not a direct quotation, that the Franks and the Saxons both allowed marriage at twelve years; yet all the pictures we found of ancient betrothal showed brides and grooms of mature growth, and the legal age for marriage in Germany to-day is twenty-one. Couples can marry sooner, but only with parental consent. Reading the saga *Dietrichs Flucht*, we judged poetic its declaration that until the time of its hero neither man nor woman wed younger than thirty years.

Turning to the Romans, we discovered that on coming into contact with the Germans they were struck by the fecundity of these monogamous forest people and amazed at the lateness at which they mated. Cæsar tells that the education of German youth put great emphasis on bodily strength, encouraged the living of a hard life, and that there was high praise among them for those who kept chaste until they had their full strength. Tacitus, writing about 98 A.D., says that until the age of twenty the German men did not pay much attention to women, and remarks that the girls also did not hasten marriage.

In all the tribes marriage appears to have been counted a matter of serious concern, not only to the couple about to wed but to their kin. The girl must have the consent of her relatives, and the man's people must be willing to receive her. In case the girl's father was dead, her mother, unless she had left the father's family by remarriage, spoke the last word on the betrothal. Otherwise the girl's uncle, her brother, or whoever stood before the law as her guardian, was responsible.

If a guardian knew of a ward's intent to break a marriage law and did not do all in his or her power to stop the girl, then guardian and ward were equally guilty. When any person knew reason why a betrothal or marriage should not take place and withheld this knowledge, that person must be judged exactly as if he or she had married illegally. This accords with a ruling contained in the *Sachsenspiegel:* [1] "Anyone who knows of a crime contemplated or committed and does not report it shall be treated as one who has done it."

As a safeguard against wrongful mating, betrothal among the Germans had to be a public ceremony, taking place not at night but in clear daylight in the presence of at least twelve persons. The company made a circle round the pair, and the girl's nearest male kin must ask first the man and then the maid if each wanted the other. The answers had to be plainly heard. The marriage must then take place publicly within a year after the betrothal — unless the maid be disabled by serious illness, the man unavoidably held away by war, or testators had shown reason why this contemplated union was unlawful.

A picture of an eighth-century betrothal shows a hand-

---

[1] "Mirror of the Saxons," the oldest code of law in the German language.

some man offering his promised bride a ring on the point of his sword. Rüdlieb, the singer, commemorates this as a custom in the tenth century. Lines spoken by the man at such a service were: *"Nun sollt auch ihr den meinen nehmen. Gott gönne mir, dass ihr lange gesund seid, denn alle meine Freude liegt an euch."* (Now you shall take my ring. May God give you long life, for all my joy lies in you.) An account of a marriage among the *Schwaben* relates that the guardian gave the bride to her bridegroom with these words: "I give my ward to you in faith and I ask you to be a good and just husband to her." The bridegroom then took her under his protection, promising his life to her with a golden ring.

Regarding property rights we found innumerable regulations, multiplying in their complexity as time advanced.

It early became the right of the daughter to receive a *Mitgift*, or dowry, at marriage in accord with the wealth of her family. She could soon go to a court of law to obtain this if necessary. This dowry was her own property, not the property of her husband. He had the right of administration over it, but if she wanted to sell any part of it her family had to be consulted. If children were born to her they inherited the dowry. In case the marriage was childless the dowry fell back to the woman's family.

The *Ostgothische Recht* gave two situations in which a husband could spend his wife's dowry: first, in time of famine, when he had already used all his own property; second, when his wife had been taken as a hostage, as sometimes happened in war, and he possessed nothing else with which to rescue her.

This dowry, any other property a woman had from her kin, and her morning gift, presented by her husband on the morning after marriage, were her fortune. Article 31, Book I, of the *Sachsenspiegel* declares: "When a man takes a wife he takes her under his protection and becomes the rightful guardian of all her goods. No woman may give her husband a present from her belongings as this would take it from her rightful heir. The man has no other right in the property of his wife than the right of guardianship."

Regulations concerning the property accumulated by a man and a woman during their marriage differed in various places. The laws of the *Ostfalen* and *Engern* allowed the woman nothing beyond what she had in her own right when she wed, and the morning gift. Other codes gave her as much as a half of all they had achieved together.

As the property of a married couple, though administered by the husband, was separate, it was easy to divide their estates according to law when either of them died. Neither had rights longer than lifetime. Property must pass according to law and was not disposed of by private gift or by will. When a woman died before her husband the inheritance of a mother's property by her children appears to have been generally accepted among the tribes. Their father, as guardian, administered their property for them until they were of age. When the man died before his wife, the widow, if she had no children, had to leave the house of her husband within three months unless her husband's heirs allowed her to stay. If she had children she had the right to live on with them in the house of their father.

As regards remarriage, the law appears to have been fairly similar everywhere. As stated in the *Sachsenspiegel*: "Because a man does not want to live without a wife he can take three and four wives one after the other, no matter how many die before him. A wife can do the same and bear legal children to each new husband just as if he were her first. Children inherit from their own parents."

Divorce was permitted wherever it could be shown that the parents' separation would bring no disadvantage to the children. No obstacles were put in the way of remarriage after divorce. As marriage was a public ceremony, divorce had to be a public ceremony, the couple loosening their bonds in the presence of witnesses.

When a couple divorced, the woman took away with her what she had brought and her morning gift. Even should the man be willing, she could carry off nothing else, since his heirs had a claim to what was not rightfully hers. Buildings which she had erected on his land must be left standing. They could neither be moved nor torn down in spite. When the man had lived on her land, the same regulations applied at his leave-taking.

When encountered in strength capable of challenging Germanic customs, the Christian faith and Latin civilization were a dual force embodied in the Roman Catholic Church. The principal conflicts of opinion were as regards who shall marry whom, where the wedding ceremony shall take place, divorce, and celibacy.

History shows the Germans holding fast to their own language and keeping a grip on their native habits, even when eager to receive the gifts the Church offers; and the Church, heiress to the astuteness of the Roman Empire, giving her gifts and allowing the pagans to keep such of their native ways as she cannot get them to drop.

The Church ruling on divorce, however, was consistently absolute: marriage is an everlasting union. This may be why it was so difficult to get the pagans to marry in church no matter how beautiful the wedding service was made. There is a district near Salzburg to-day, many centuries under Catholic rule, where the couples do not come into the church until the woman is seven months along with child. These people are farmer folk desirous of families, and by the right of tradition the man may take his be-trothed maid, and they do not marry in church until certain that the bride can give him children.

The pagan Germans had no tribal experience of celibacy. There was no group of men or women in their society set apart from the others by lifelong vows of chastity. A fecund and child-loving people, when the priesthood was opened to them they appear to have found it foolish, as well as difficult, never to marry. There are pages filled with the drama of the Roman Church's struggle with a German priesthood which would marry and have families. Many of these men were not even penitent. They argued that marriage is good and that it is right to have children. This although the Church reasons be clearly explained, among these reasons being the one that a celibate priest-hood guards the democracy of the Church, preventing the growing up of a priestly class, and making it necessary in every generation for priests to come from lay families.

Then came the Reformation. The Protestants saw no harm in marriage. Saint Paul himself had given advice sanctioning it for the followers of Christ. The testaments of Christ's disciples gave the Catholic Church no authority for its ruling on celibacy. The Protestant clergy could marry.

Concerning divorce, Luther said that marriage *"ist ein äusserlich, weltlich Ding, weltlicher Obrigkeit unterworfen"* — an outward, worldly thing and under temporal authority. The Catholics had the judgment of the Council of Trent: "Marriage is a sacrament of the church." Regarding marriage as an institution of God, eternal and inseparable, the Catholic Church could not sanction divorce. Separation could only be obtained by proving nullity of marriage. Under Protestant rulers divorce came to be written into the civil law.

From a judge I heard that in modern times, as under tribal regulations, care must be taken that no damage be done the children by the divorce. Their happiness and their good were emphasized as more important than anything concerning their parents, two people who had made a mess of life. In granting the divorce, due consideration must be taken of the fact that a man and woman at odds make a wretched home centre for children.

It had become the custom for marriages and births to be recorded by the church. Then in the last quarter of the eighteenth century and on into the nineteenth century the German kingdoms, principalities, and dukedoms, one after the other, enacted laws compelling civil registration. These civil codes ruled that a marriage which had simply been concluded and recorded in church was not legal. Furthermore, they decreed that it was not necessary for a

church service to be performed.   Couples could be united
by a state official.

As regards property, women retained their pagan right
to claim a dowry at marriage, they continued to possess as
private fortune whatever came to them by the old fashion
of inheritance from kin or the new fashion of will, and the
custom went on of a morning gift from husband to bride.
Romantically, it appears to have been usual through a long
period of this epoch for the man to protect his wife by
taking complete charge of her fortune for her, doling out
"pin money."   Woman had her legal rights, but society
frowned on such boldness as going to court to maintain
them, and few dared.   Tears were considered more civilized than the old tribal method of appealing to the *thing*,
or judicial assembly.

Oral arrangement came to be no longer sufficient for
the settlement of a couple's money affairs.   When they
married they must have a statement drawn up by a notary
and signed in the presence of witnesses.   They had to
decide whether they would hold their property jointly;
have a complete separation of their estates, the husband or
other guardian managing the wife's for her unless she was
over twenty years of age and desired to manage it herself;
or whether they would have a special agreement dealing as
they chose with what each had brought into the marriage
and whatever might come into the possession of either of
them during the years of their life together.

In all cases the man had to pay for the wife's living and
that of their children, maintaining them in accord with his
means.   He must settle any debts she incurred at shops,
for running his house and for dresses.   Shopkeepers could

sue the husband for the wife's bills, unless she was extravagant and he had given public notice that he would not pay, by advertisement in a newspaper on a date earlier than that on which the credit was given. A husband had no right to publish his wife's name except when she repeatedly spent more than a just proportion of his money.

The Protestants appear to have had no church ruling on remarriage after divorce or death. Civil laws put no stays on remarriage for Catholic, Protestant, or nonbeliever, but the opinion of society, high and low, did. Children, so I have been told, were always given serious consideration when second marriage was contemplated: and the marriage of a father to his wife's sister, for the sake of the little ones, was not unusual.

Prior to the Dritte Reich the Germans had a loose federation and research into their habits is hampered by their independencies. From tribal times up, they have been a folk of many opinions stoutly maintained, and on every ruling there is certain to have been a little duchy or tiny town which refused to conform. Even the German Empire founded by Bismarck was a union in which states and cities held on to their separate rights; and while the Weimar Republic had a constitution for all Germans within the boundary drawn by the Treaty of Versailles, it gave rather than restricted liberties. Consequently all general statements on marriage up to this time must be qualified by remembrance that practices differed and ways quite contrary often flourished side by side.

In the Dritte Reich concern with marriage centres on who shall and who shall not beget children to inherit citizenry; and since men and women have given up their independence, vesting power in a Führer, or leader with supreme authority, edicts apply to everyone within the present frontiers and in whatever territory may be joined on. New laws aim to cleanse the bloodstream of mixture judged unsafe, stamp out hereditary disease, and achieve a return to the healthy fecundity celebrated in history.

Condemned to detention in the fortress of Landesberg am Lech by a decision of the National Court of Justice at Munich on April 1, 1924, Adolf Hilter used the leisure and liberty which he possessed as a citizen of the Weimar Republic, even when under arrest, to write down the principles of the movement he led, in his book *Mein Kampf* — "My Struggle." Among the seven hundred pages there are a number giving his view on marriage. His view is concentrated on eugenics.

When Aryan blood, so Hitler argues, has been mixed with that of an inferior race the result has been the end of the culture-sustaining race. . . . North America, the population of which is for the most part Germanic, has interbred very little with inferior colored nations and displays a humanity and culture decidedly different from that of Central and South America, in which the settlers, mostly of Latin origin, have mingled their blood freely with the aborigines. Each time foreign blood has been introduced into our nationals, its sad result has been the breaking up of our national character.

A few paragraphs further on Hitler states that nations, or rather races, gifted with cultural talent have this latent in them even though circumstances unfavorable at the moment prohibit their development. Therefore to represent the Germanic peoples of the pre-Christian era as cul-

tureless barbarians is outrageous. They never were. The
harsh climate of their northern home forced them to exist
under conditions which prevented their creative qualities
from developing. If there had been no classic antique
world, and if they had come to the more favorable
southern lands, and had there taken to themselves the employment of the inferior races who were the earliest tech-
nical aids to progress, the capacity for creative culture
which slept in them would have produced a flowering just
as splendid as that which happened in the case of the
Hellenes.

For this reason, he contends, the conservation of the
ancient racial qualities, which, given opportunity, create
the beauty and the dignity of a higher humanity, should be
the chief concern of a national state. . . . Unfortunately
the kernel of our German nation is no longer racially homo-
geneous. . . . On the contrary, the poisoning through the
blood from which our national body has suffered ever since
the Thirty Years' War has not only upset our blood but
disturbed our soul. . . . Germans are without the herd in-
stinct which arises when all are of one blood and which
protects nations from ruin, especially at moments when
danger threatens. This fact has done us untold harm. . . .
It has robbed the German nation of its rights of mastery.
. . . The Reich must gather all Germans to itself. It must
not only choose the best of the original racial elements and
conserve them, but slowly and surely raise them to a position of dominance. The world's history is made by
minorities. . . . The pledge of success lies in the selection
of the best.

Then comes a clarion call: "The first duty of the national state is to lift marriage up from a perpetual disgrace to the race and to consecrate it as an institution dedicated to reproduce the Lord's image, not monstrous beings, half man, half monkey."

This is followed by a criticism of society which allows any corrupt degenerate to reproduce himself and permits the sale in every chemist's shop of the means by which the healthy stop birth. He protests against the lack of honor and morals in "this brave world of bourgeois" where forced prevention of fecundity in sufferers from syphilis, tuberculosis, hereditary disabilities, in cripples and the insane, is counted a crime; whereas the prevention of fecundity by millions of the best people is not regarded as a sin.

Continuing, Hitler writes that it is the duty of the national state to put race in a more important position and to see to it that the race is kept pure. Childhood must be made the most precious possession of a nation. Only the healthy must beget children. It is disgraceful of persons diseased or with inheritable disabilities to send children into the world, and an honorable action for them to refrain from parenthood. The state must declare unfit to beget offspring all who are diseased or have hereditary disabilities. It must also make provision that the fruitfulness of the healthy shall not be blocked. State action on this matter should go forward, unaffected by consideration as to whether the work is understood or misunderstood, popular or unpopular.

Hitler came into power as *Reichskanzler* on January 31, 1933, about nine years after his imprisonment. A sterilization law was added to the German statute on January 1,

1934. *Erbgesundheitsgerichte* in the form of appellate courts and a supreme court deal with cases under this law. The entire Reich is organized for the stamping out of hereditary defects as rapidly as possible, and a network of doctors serve this idea under state appointment and political oversight. A local doctor who shows himself negligent or careless in supplying information loses his right to be a doctor.

Individuals may apply for sterilization, or it may be asked for by their legal guardians, proposed by medical officers or by the governors of penal establishments. Persons who feel that they have been unrightfully listed for sterilization must appear before a hereditary health court and show cause why it should not be done to them. The usual court of decision is composed of a magistrate, the local doctor, and a physician whose special province is the study of hereditary hygiene.

Persons judged dangerous sexual criminals are castrated. Where the defects are hereditary and no criminality is involved, sterilization must be done in such a way as to cause as little mental and physical suffering as possible. Privacy must be observed and there are severe penalties for ridiculing the sterilized or spreading gossip. It is impressed on young and old that those who have disabilities which must be cleansed from the race got them through no fault of their own. In pity for the sterilized young, special schools have been established where they may have free education under teachers chosen to help them.

The healthy may not ask for sterilization. Any doctor performing such an operation, or a doctor, midwife, or any person aiding the healthy in birth control in any way, including the passing of information, commits a serious state crime.

Under the new laws for the protection of the family the spread of venereal disease is punishable by prison sentence in addition to sterilization; whoever refuses aid and help to any expectant mother, thus endangering mother and child, shall receive a prison sentence; and any man who maliciously, or out of selfishness, squanders family possessions and thus endangers the support of his wife and children can be disciplined by a prison sentence of two years.

A license is necessary for marriage. Applicants must bring a health certificate; and the healthy can wed only the healthy. Marriage between German and Jew is not permitted. I made inquiry at several Registry Offices and of two lawyers and did not learn of any other legal taboo based on race. One Registrar volunteered the information that Herr Hitler himself had said that the offspring of German and Pole are good; and elsewhere I was told at length of the splendidness of Italian wives who bring with them something of the warm South.

Marriages made before the law against Jews may be dissolved without any need to present to the court cause other than union to a Jew, which the petitioner now repents, and under date of May 8, 1935, I read in a newspaper that the text had been published of the supreme court's ruling that the utterance of insulting remarks about the Führer by a married woman can be grounds for divorce if the abuse does injury to the feelings of her husband.

No check has been put on the remarriage of widows, widowers, or divorcées, so this continues as before.

So far as I can ascertain the government is not concerned with making any change in the legal age of marriage, which stands at twenty-one years for both bride and groom, allowing younger marriage when the parents have given consent. I have not noticed any haste to marry younger or seen any signs of government pressure in that direction.

Young men have their six months' duty in a labor camp and two years of army service. Even were it economically possible for a husband to leave his bride alone during his state service, when he has few and brief holidays, the National Socialist state does not encourage marriage until after these state duties have been completed. The young man is not considered prepared for the wise rearing of a family until he has undergone his training and assimilated its teaching.

Men who go directly from their state service to the bench, the shop, or the plough can marry at once. Those who choose a profession have years of study before they can earn a living, and unless possessed of a private fortune cannot marry until twenty-five or later. In the Dritte Reich men who are started on their careers, if of the stock it is desired to continue, are expected to have established families by the age of twenty-six.

Propaganda, social pressure, government grants of money, homesteads for those who need them, reduction of taxes for the married and for each child, cheaper railway tickets, advantageous holidays, and other aids encourage marriage. While there is as yet no compulsory law on this, one frequently hears of industrialists and other employers, as well as government departmental heads, who have issued a warning to the men under them that at twenty-six a bachelor has reached the place where he can expect no further advancement in position or wages until he has shown himself capable of assuming responsibility by taking his place in German society as a husband and a father.

German girls are expected to be capable housewives when they marry. After they leave school, those who can do so take a finishing course in household management. Others are trained at home by their mothers just as carefully as if taking a course. This takes time. Also, although not compulsory, it is considered good for a girl to have done six months of labor or social service. Like Tacitus, I have noticed that they do not hasten marriage and are usually the legal age or a little older.

In token of betrothal the man and the girl of the present day exchange plain gold rings with the date of the promise and both their names inscribed in them. These rings are worn on the fourth finger of the left hand until marriage, when they are changed over to the same finger on the right hand, and the wedding date put in. It is not customary now to have any elaborate engagement ceremony, but there is often a party for its announcement to which family and friends are invited. The schoolchildren come if the bride has been a teacher.

The custom of the *Polterabend* appears to be universal with all kinds of people. The dowry right continues. A girl can still go to the law for a dowry in just proportion to the wealth of her parents, but I never heard of this being necessary. All the Germans I know are devoted to their children and are exceedingly generous with them.

The marriage ceremony can be Catholic, Protestant, Registry Office, or take any form wished. Every marriage must be civically registered. The Germans delight in pageantry, and marriage, counted the most important event in life, is made lovely. The custom of the morning gift from the husband to his bride is usual.

Wedding anniversaries are festival days observed by the couple giving each other some remembrance, and family and friends sending them gifts, most often flowers. The silver wedding, after twenty-five years, and the golden wedding, after fifty years, are notable events.

I attended a golden-wedding celebration where the table was decorated with orchids, food and wine were of the choicest, and one of the most noted string quartettes in Germany played the wife's favorite selections. When guests commented on how beautiful it all was, the husband said simply: "I did not want this day to be less than the day on which she married me."

Traveling through the country one sees the homes of simple folk decorated with hemlock and gold, a sign that fifty years of marriage is celebrated there. The first time I saw this was in Ahrweiler, a little town on the river Ahr. The evergreen was shaped in an arch over the door and twisted at the top to form a bell. The cottage curtains were of cloth dyed gold. A kindly-wrinkled man sat at the window working on a shoemaker's last, looking like Hans Sachs.

IX

IN STEADFAST FAITH

Wie der Ring den Finger fest umschliesst,
So gelobe ich Dich in fester Treue zu umschliessen.[1]

(As the ring surrounds the finger,
So I promise to embrace thee in steadfast faith.)

THESE are a people of warm hospitality, and I have had pleasure in many a home on high hilltop, broad plain, or snug in folded valley.

It was in the heart of Hessen. The farmstead is a lower Saxon farmhouse shaded by kingly beeches, set in rolling acres that have been tilled in direct descent through son or daughter, according to Kälb family testimony, since the seventeenth century. The present Farmer Kälb and his wife have but two daughters and no son.

The sisters had been betrothed to the sons of neighbors for nearly a year. Herta, the younger, was wed first. Käthe's husband would enter the farmstead as heir to its mastership. For this reason it was thought best to clear the settlement, by the younger's taking her dowry from the sister's joint inheritance prior to his arrival.

The wedding days were chosen with care. It is important to watch the stand of the moon when fixing the day; a rising moon promises good fortune to the couple, while a moon on the wane carries their luck away. And

[1] From a German betrothal ceremony of the tenth century.

there are other considerations. The date selected must not fall in a season when the press of work is so urgent that neither the households of the bridal pair nor their relatives and neighbors have leisure for wholehearted celebration of the marriage. Wednesdays and Fridays are reserved for widows or widowers who wish to remarry. Sunday may be used, but the devout of this neighborhood do not like such frivolity as feasting, drinking, and dancing on the Lord's Day. Sunday choice is vetoed by the local pastor except when he is convinced that no other day is possible.

Herta was married on a Saturday in June, in a lull which followed the haymaking. Because the exact date was dependent on the hay, invitations could not be issued long in advance; but dowry and trousseau were ready at home and relatives and friends knew the season she had chosen, so they were prepared to accept when the *Brautwerber* rode around on horseback to invite them.

He wore flowers tied with ribbon in his buttonhole and carried a staff adorned with flowers. At each house, as is the custom, he was asked in to have cake and a glass of wine. He had so many invitations to deliver that on reaching home he had to be lifted down from his horse.

The marriage eve was called *Polterabend*. The wedding party gathered at the bride's home for a supper followed by music and dancing. Herta was queen of this evening, crowned with a wreath of myrtle placed on her fair head by her sister Käthe. Evil spirits were chased away from the betrothed pair by the breaking of plates and cups on the threshing floor.

The early morning of the wedding day was occupied with a byplay. The bridegroom sent four of his men friends, mounted on mud-splashed plough horses, to demand the bride. They pounded at the house door for entrance until an old woman servant called out: "What is it you want?"

"We have come for the promised wife."

Thereupon she replied, "There is no bride for you in this house," and after some further parley they departed.

Next, one of Herta's girl friends, dressed in her Sunday clothes, was taken over to the groom's farm in a Kälb wagon. She was offered to him as wife, but he refused to accept her. He declared his chosen to be more beautiful, more humble, better educated, and in every way more capable of suiting him than was any other maid in the wide world. So the substitute returned.

In a short while, the groom sent his bride a gift. When opened, the basket was found to contain coarse bread, rancid butter, and skimmed milk. It was sent back with the message that unless he had better to offer he must give up the idea of marrying her.

And now he came over himself, riding on a fine white horse. He was dressed in good wedding clothes and accompanied by eleven *Kränzelherren* all handsomely garbed and riding their best horses. His horse was adorned with pink roses and the horses of his company with white. He carried his bride a pretty blue basket holding flowers just picked for her in his own garden. Under the basket were found a sweet cake iced in white with her name on it in pink, a loaf of white bread, a roll of fresh butter, and a package of fragrant spices. He and his company were invited in to breakfast.

The young couple were side by side at the table. They

ate from the same plate and drank from the same cup, thus signifying their harmony. A trumpet blew! At the first note of warning to prepare for the church Herta rushed away, closely followed up the stairs by her mother and her *Brautschmückerin*, the married woman who had the duty of helping her into her marriage dress. When the time allotted for dressing the bride had passed, trumpeters blew the signal for the church procession to form.

Herta rode to church in her father's hay wagon, which her bridesmaids had turned into a bridal coach by covering it with myrtle and white roses, winding even the spokes of the wheels, the wagon tongue, and every inch of the rigging with the flowers and vines. Four brown horses harnessed in white and garlanded with roses and myrtle drew the coach. The eleven *Kränzeljungfrauen* sat round her on cushions lower than the seat they had prepared for her.

The groom's parents and the bride's parents, each pair in their own horse-drawn carriage, led the way; then came the bridal coach escorted by the bridegroom and his eleven attendants, and behind them came the wedding guests. Since Herta was leaving her father's house, the carts carrying her wedding gifts followed after her, each cart decorated with hemlock.

The procession stopped when the bridal coach reached the crest of the hill that the bride might have a long last look, as a maid, at her girlhood home. There below her, across the swaying fields of ripening grain, stood the solid, comfortable, well-kept farmhouse where she had always lived. Standing in her bridal coach, Herta sang farewell: —

"So leb' denn wohl, du stilles Haus,
Ich zieh' betrübt von dir hinaus;
Ich zieh' betrübt und traurig fort,
Noch unbekannt an welchen Ort."

(So fare thee well, thou quiet house,
Grieving I leave thee;
Grieving and sad I go forth,
Not yet knowing whither.)

At the Protestant Church the young couple were pronounced man and wife in a religious ceremony during which the gold rings that they had worn on the fourth finger of their left hands for their engagement were changed over to the fourth finger on the right hand — the hand on which all Germans wear the wedding ring.

From the church the wedding party, now accompanied by the pastor and his family, went on to the home of the bridegroom, where dinner was ready and musicians played the wife's welcome. She received spices and flax and money as she crossed the threshold of her new home, and a gilded horseshoe to throw behind her, thus attaching fortune to her reign in the house. Then the bridegroom drank with his bride from a glass which he smashed so that it could never be used again. The drinking of wine together symbolized their final agreement to hold each other in steadfast faith forever.

Summer sped by. Käthe, the elder sister, chose the last Saturday in October, when the rush of the harvest was over, for her marriage.

Saturday is considered a satisfactory day because guests can linger on in the house of the wedding, or with folk on neighboring farms, visiting through the day of rest without a twinge of conscience about neglected work at home. Women who live so far apart that they seldom see each other can go to church together, and also have an opportunity to exchange recipes and patterns. Men can learn each other's methods of planting and feeding and even make profitable business deals. And, too, given this lengthened opportunity, many a courtship is furthered.

It is quite usual for some of the *Kränzelherren* and *Kränzeljungfrauen* to lose their hearts to each other. These eleven groomsmen and eleven bridesmaids are the outer festival frame for the bridal couple, and at the same time their symbolic guard against evil. They arrive first at the wedding festivities and leave last. They are the leaders in the work and in the pleasure attendant on the celebration of marriage, and are selected by the bride and groom from among their favorite young relatives and friends.

Käthe is fond of amusement. At her *Polterabend* the dancing continued late. She was made to rest in bed next morning until the hour when she must rise for the bridal breakfast. Her mother, her bridesmaids, and others of the household were up and bustling round at dawn. All disarray caused by the china breaking was swept from the threshing floor and everything in the house and its surroundings put in perfect order.

The bridal coach was made ready. Chrysanthemums and bright autumn leaves were prepared for decorating the team. Käthe refused to have white paper roses. Final arrangement was given to the wedding presents on display in a room at the back of the house, special care taken that the name of the donor was on each gift, and a chair placed for the elderly friend who would sit there knitting. Wreaths and garlands had been hung in rooms and hall, for the *Polterabend*. Quick hands now replaced those that were not so fresh as they had been yesterday.

Men swept the entrance court where on rainy days they thresh their corn, beat peas or flax, or mend tools and harness. Then they carpeted the court with fragrant hemlock boughs. Trestles were put up and long boards laid across them. The busy bridesmaids spread the improvised tables with snowy linen cloths, setting china, silver, and glass ready for the wedding feast.

In the big old-fashioned kitchen, fires roared in two enormous stoves, oven and saucepan giving off delicious odors. Mother Kälb and a corps of her helpers lent attention to what was cooking, talked with the women who would stay home to watch the dinner, and checked over the certainty that larder and springhouse held plenty for all the expected company.

And, just as I have seen in China, through the early morning hours servants and children kept arriving with gifts of food from near-by relatives and friends, and each porter was given a coin. These gifts were generous loaves of warm bread, freshly churned butter, foaming pails of new milk, baskets of eggs, roasted geese, pickles and marmalades, pies, and every sort of nice cakes.

Father and Mother Kälb had been anxious that neither of their daughters should fare better than the other at marriage. Since Käthe was to be the future mistress of the homestead and Herta to go to a new home, they had spent themselves in care that Herta's dowry should equal but not exceed what her elder sister was receiving. The sisters had trousseaus which were exactly alike, including identical wedding dresses.

Käthe lingered mischievously over her bridal breakfast, refusing to leave the table to dress for church until the trumpeters had blown a complete *Ständchen*. She had to be hurried into her marriage clothes. When she was got up to her mother's room for the dressing, her matron of honor soon fastened round her slim waist a fire-red skirt of finest wool, trimmed with bands of blue and black velvet ribbon and embroidered at the hem in a wide gay floral pattern. It was smoothed neatly over her many starched petticoats.

She slipped her arms into a blue jacket with sleeves embroidered to match the skirt. A black silk apron, adorned with garlands of fine blue flowers that had taken her mother many hours to stitch, was tied in place. This was followed by the adjustment of a shoulder shawl called a *Flittertuch*. It was of black silk embroidered in blue flowers to match the apron and heavy with gold beads sewn on in an elaborate pattern. Laughing, the bride whirled on dancing feet so that everyone gathered in the room to watch her dressed might enjoy the costume's full glory.

Pretending to be cross, her attendants brought her to a standstill and her mother gave her a slap followed by a hearty hug and kiss. Her dress was tidied and the work of her adornment went on. She had a necklace of large amber beads fastened under her chin with a huge silver clasp, and silver breast shields pinned to her jacket. Clasp and shields had the same ornamentation: a flaming heart, two doves, the bride's initials, and the date of her wedding. As is the custom, the mother fitted the wedding crown on the bride's head. This crowning is symbolic and it is the girl's mother who puts on her the dignity and responsibility of her new position in life — that of a married woman.

The wedding crown was made of many-colored glass beads, red and orange predominating, and worked in a design of grapes, heads of grain, and fruit — the symbols of fertility. Little mirrors were set all around in the crown to ward off evil spirits. The wedding veil, which was arranged on the crown and fell over the bride's dress, was of yellow lace and had similar little mirrors sewn to it.

Käthe's veil was not yet arranged when the trumpeters in the yard below blew the signal for her wedding procession to start to church. The bridal coach came round and waited. The other conveyances were drawn up. The wedding guests collected ready to go.

Seen from the window of her mother's bedroom, the company below made a pretty pageant. Some of the men were in the black coats and high hats that Germans in town wear to weddings. A few women had on store clothes. But the majority of the wedding party were dressed in the colorful local costume. The younger married people, who had not yet grown too stout to get into them, had on their own wedding garments. The man's dress is a round flat hat often set at a rakish angle, a white linen coat fitted tightly at the waist, and dark trousers. Eight handsome silver buttons fasten the coat in front and two matching silver buttons are set at the head of deep pleats in the coattail. There are ornamental breast pockets and a pocket in the coattail from which a bright silk handkerchief floats as the pleats spring open.

Many of the women had white embroidered collars starched so hard that they stood out like wheels. All their skirts were fire-red. They had their accessories in many hues, but everyone conformed to the fashion that the ribbon on the skirt must correspond to the color of the jacket, and the apron must match the shoulder shawl. Apron and shawl are often a gift from the farmer to his wife. They cost according to the value of the gold beads. From twenty-five dollars to a hundred can be spent on them. Girls usually receive fairly simple ones at marriage, unless it happens that a maid is given an heirloom set by her husband's family.

The little girls wore embroidered white dresses over many ruffled petticoats; their long hair had been unplaited and hung in waves from under little crocheted crowns of blue and pink flowers. Young boys were in tight black trousers and blouses with starched collars. Every man and boy had a buttonhole bouquet of flowers tied with ribbon. The children in this district are fair.

The wedding party went to church and returned. On the way back Käthe's bridegroom began to sing a happy song to her. She answered. The groomsmen and bridesmaids joined in. Soon young and old of the wedding party were singing. When the first carriages reached the homestead door the colorful procession was a chorus strung out along the winding country road.

Just as if she had been a newcomer, Käthe was welcomed into her house with spices, flax, and money, and she threw the gilded horseshoe behind her to attach luck to her door. The bridal couple drank the wine of steadfast faith. The husband smashed the glass.

Then the wedding party would have started dancing at once, but Mother Kälb would not have it. She appealed to Father Kälb, who was already wheeling right about and left about with a pretty niece. He brought the company to order. The dinner was ready. It must be eaten now or the hot dishes would be spoilt.

At last all were seated. Grace was said; plates and glasses filled. After a toast to the bridal couple the feast started. There were so many good things to eat and drink that the dinner went on for hours. Children who fell asleep at the tables were carried upstairs to be tucked away in the big red and white beds.

When no one could eat any more, the wedding party rested — the women on chairs or upstairs in the beds with their children, the men by taking a stroll in the fields and having a look at the stock in the barns.

At six o'clock a horn called the party together. The debris of dinner had been cleared away and coffee was ready. This meal over, floors were prepared for the dance. An orchestra of local talent tuned up. The folk music here has a rhythm equal to rousing a throb in the most sluggish pulse and the figures of the dance are executed with vigorous stamp and swing. At a *Bauernhochzeit* the bride must dance with every male guest, the groom with every maid and woman.

It was enough even for the lively Käthe. When she had finished her duty dancing she sank exhausted on a bench. Now came a lull in the music. A little girl brought a dish filled with grain and fruit, and a little boy a pretty box from which he took a wooden stork and a *Kinder-mann*. Before they put the gifts in the bride's lap, the boy recited a poem expressing the hope that she be blessed with many lovely and intelligent children. Then dancing went on.

When midnight struck, Saturday was done, the Lord's Day about to start. The orchestra put away their instruments. Last drinks were offered round. Excepting those persons invited to stay the night, the company drove off calling *"Auf Wiedersehen — auf Wiedersehen"* across the widening distance. A Sunday quiet descended over the farmstead.

With Monday, life settled into the prudent routine followed on every successful farm. Käthe, ever a good worker, was occupied with establishing her position as a married woman in the house and dairy where she had grown from childhood. Her husband was busy learning the way things are done on this *Erbhof* where he would later be full master.

Life's routine was pleasantly interrupted by visits to and from Herta, when the most amazing excitement occurred. A youngish man in government uniform called. In that strange way in which news travels in these times a report of the sisters' weddings had reached the capital; and, more strange still, the government was interested.

The representative wanted to see the bridal clothes. He paid many compliments, emphasizing the fact that in all Germany there are no people so admirable as those closely connected with the soil, and none who have been able to guard the ancient customs and ideals as well as they. He explained that it is important that everyone else in the Third Reich shall know about them and their worthiness.

"What our Hitler wants," he said, "is that each group within our country shall understand about all other groups and folk come to be proud of each other. He does not want to break down district traditions in this strenuous work now going on to make us Germans one united people. He wants to foster the use of local costumes and tribal customs by letting everyone see how fine they are."

As he talked Mother and Father Kälb looked hard at him to probe his worth. They did not make his task easier by adding a word to the one-sided conversation. The youngish man from the capital kept on until he had made the point that the Reich invited the two couples to visit Hamburg and Berlin to show their beautiful clothes. There would be no expense. Everything was to be given them. They would be shown a wonderful time. All that the young couples had to do was to wear their wedding garments and answer questions about *Niedersachsen* habits.

Mother Kälb's anger was straight. She thoroughly disapproved of people making a show of themselves and it was particularly unseemly that young brides should do so. Thank you very much, her daughters would stay at home. Father Kälb put his pipe down quietly and said that from its outward aspect the idea did not seem a good one. Käthe's husband kept his eyes on his own boots.

The youngish man was neither annoyed nor put off by their response to his offer. He was a pleasant fellow. He asked if he might stay through the afternoon, going about with Father Kälb as he did work on the farm. Father Kälb had no objection.

The visitor took an intelligent interest in everything. He was quick to lend a useful hand. Since he was there at *Abendbrot*, he was invited to the meal. He was not pushing or rude in the way in which he frequently mentioned facts as to why it is wise for all Germans to draw close together in these days.

As it happened, Herta and her husband drove over to get some eggs she wanted for a brooding hen while the man from the government was still there. While they were out choosing the setting of eggs, Käthe was able to tell Herta in private the reason for his visit. The sisters knew that their young husbands would enjoy the trip if it could be taken advantage of. They did not need to discuss the arrangement that Herta should try to persuade their mother while Käthe attended to father. This is the way they have always done things.

The end was that these four young people who had never been beyond their own market town made the trip. They visited Hamburg and Berlin as guests of their government. Feted and handsomely entertained, they saw the sights at each place, and they attended a gathering of young couples in native costume from widely separated parts of the Reich. There they saw purple petticoats, every manner of headdress, high-topped boots, blue linen smocks, fitted bodices, very short leather breeches, even lace gloves and silver shoe buckles. Listening to the conversations of strangers, they were amused by queer dialects and funny expressions of speech; and they flocked into a hall with all the colorful company to hear a speech made by a man from Berlin who lauded the worth of farmers and explained their duty to the state.

Everywhere they went they were treated as people of importance. At Hamburg they were invited aboard an ocean-going steamer and saw in what comfort travelers go across the seas. At the capital they had seats at the opera to hear *Die Meistersinger;* and were taken in the interval to shake hands with Herr Hitler. He was not distant and haughty: he was simple and friendly. Everywhere they went they met people. Germans different from the folks at home — yet every one of them pleasant and kind.

"It was fine," declared Käthe after they were back. "I enjoyed it. I appreciate what I have been given. It was marvelous we had it. However, what I find is that the best part of travel is getting home again."

X

AN ARCH OF EVERGREEN

"COME and visit us and the trees," read the letter from Wiegersen.

In the autumn we sighted the red wall topped by four towers. Gates swung open to let us in. Rounding the curved road, we stood before the *Schloss*. Smooth lawns sloped to forest borders.

Katerlieschen and her family came down the steps to greet us. We were welcomed in under the arch of evergreen which by tradition spans the entrance door when a master of Wiegersen is in residence. Thus for the first time in my life I stayed on an estate devoted to the nurture of trees.

My room looked into a beech, my favorite of all the trees that grow. Leaning out of a window, I saw the noble tip reaching for the sky, lifted on a straight bole, and thought of roots going down into the earth deep as the tip is high. Not a rotten branch had the tree. Clean boughs curved gently up from the trunk to droop lower than the points of their take-off. *In ingentem evadit amplitudinem.* What better than to dwell beside the wild live spirit of a glorious beech?

Here at Wiegersen, a paradise on earth, my troubled mind renewed its courage. Generation after generation the heirs of these broad acres have kept their land sacred to trees. Through the ups and downs of fortune, timber has never been sacrificed to the exigencies of the times. Lovely and beloved, the trees grow here from seedlings to maturity, the life span of many far longer than the life of man.

In the company of our host and hostess and little Katerlieschen, my doubting heart leapt up to faith in Germans. Amid their trees I remembered a thought Mencius has left us: "Through pain men grow." Walking forest ways, I recalled how the Chinese had to pass through the terrible era of Ch'in, when the unripe among them spent sixteen years in destroying their scholars, burning their books, scorning the precepts their forefathers had built up for the conduct of man to man, vesting right in might, drilling children to follow one fanatical will; and how this had passed and the Chinese had been able to make for themselves the era of Han, a period of enlightened living the like of which this earth has seldom witnessed.

Close to the eternity of nature, I felt how ephemeral are the mistakes of men. In the voice of the wood I seemed to hear a promise that this era in which Germans are living is but a purgatory through which they will pass. Under the forest sky I heard an eternal melody of which a German poet has written: —

Über der Wipfel Hin-und Wiederschweben
Wie's Atem holt und voller wogt und braust
Und weiter zieht . . .
                    und stille wird . . .
                                        und saust. . . .
Über der Wipfel Hin-und Wiederschweben
Hoch droben steht ein ernster Ton
Dem lauschen tausend Jahre schon
Und werden tausand Jahre lauschen.

(Over the treetops swaying to and fro
Hark! it takes breath and blows more full and roars
And passes on . . .
            and dies away . . .
                   and sighs. . . .
Over the treetops swaying to and fro
Lofty sounds a solemn melody
To which a thousand years have listened
And thousands more will listen.)

Somehow that serene rustle sang me a song of hope.

These are the forests of the German fairy tales.
Through them move woodsmen dressed in uniforms so soft
in their gray-green color as to be almost unnoticed among
the trees. Light shines in shafts of gold through the conifers and cuts bars of silver across the trunks of oak and
beech. Woodsmen fell and trim and plant in an unhur-
ried quietness which seems scarcely to disturb the wild
creatures. Under the trees, each hour of day and night
has its ever-changing charm. I could never decide at
Wiegersen whether I liked best dawn, noon, evening twilight, or the dark of the forest night.

The family at Wiegersen live long quiet days. The
pace of their time seems tempered to the growth of trees.
Our host is a man of mild temperament, loving simple joys,
and our hostess gifted with kindness and the arts of a natural hospitality. Our days were filled with many small
pleasures.

Breakfast was eaten all together at a table out of doors.
It began at eight o'clock, a hearty meal for a family long
up: brown bread and butter, boiled eggs, fresh tomatoes,
slices cut from a ham, smoked sausage of several kinds,
cheese, honey and jam, and a great pot of delicious coffee

frequently refilled. Our breakfast plates were the country breakfast plates of Hannover — smooth, flat pieces of white wood on which one lays bread to spread it with butter and anything else to taste, then cuts the bread into squares for eating.

Eating was leisurely and accompanied by leisurely talk. In these hours I learned much of German forests in general, as well as of this one in particular. Perhaps most important of all, I grew to love a German family and have respect for them.

In such ways only will humanity get past the false barriers of nationalism which have so corrupted human society. Individually we must come to appreciate the truth our liberal forefathers glimpsed — that the nature of man and the operations of his mind are fundamentally the same in all places.

Life here was in the woods, the *Schloss* truly a forester's home; and the trees seemed somehow more important than men. They were beautiful trees. And the season was autumn, a time when nature helps one to quiet thought. Pathways, called *Pirschwege*, led through the forests; these are aisles where, year by year, pine needles are piled to sink down into a cushion of springy softness on which footfall makes no sound. Many ladders led up to platforms where one could sit behind a screen of hemlock boughs, put on to protect the perch, and from there watch the fox, badger, deer, and other animals.

It is good to see them so, intent on their own affairs. A black buck roves these ways. He is the master of Wiegersen's pride, a handsome fellow no gun is allowed to touch. These lines that might have come from the brush of a

Chinese are from a German poet, Georg Trakl, born in
1914: —

> *Stille begegnet am Saum des Waldes*
> *Ein dunkles Wild.*
> *Am Hügel endet leise der Abendwind,*
> *Verstummt die Klage der Amsel,*
> *Und die sanften Flöten des Herbstes*
> *Schweigen im Rohr.*

> (Quietness meets at the edge of the wood
> A dark deer.
> At the hill the evening wind halts,
> Stilled the plaint of the blackbird,
> And the soft flutes of autumn
> Are silent in the reed.)

For Katerlieschen the German forest would not be the
German forest without the deer; and now that I have known
woods where they live, every grove will be strangely
empty without their shy presence.

At Wiegersen there are sheltered racks where food is
put out for the deer in severe weather, and tables where
dinner is laid for the birds. Deer get hay, unthreshed
sheaves of oats, turnips, and sometimes corn, and they are
provided the year round with salt to lick. Partridges like
malt, bunches of mistletoe, and ripe apples, while pheasants
favor roughly broken dried cod.

Often we walked with our host and his head forester and
heard forestry lore. There have always been two schools
of thought about tree planting. One favors mixed groves;
the other, stretches of wood all of one kind. Both methods
are practised at Wiegersen. The nineteenth century was

an age of internationalism, and this shows in the forests here, as men then prided themselves on having as many kinds of trees in their soil as possible.   In National Socialist times the rule is German trees on German lands, and only native trees may be set where new planting is needed.   The self-important jay is himself a planter.   He is fond of carrying seeds and acorns and putting them in where he will.   Beech especially he strews through groves where the forester did not intend to have them.

"Well-managed woodlands are a source of profit to the owner, provide healthy employment for many men, are of great material value to the nation — and they have their spiritual value too," said the forester as he told of trees. "The spiritual value is something beyond reckoning, but I doubt if any German could long be happy in a place where he could not enjoy the rest and comfort of trees."

Willow, poplar, and birch reach the peak of their development at about fifty years; ash and maple have their best period near eighty; fir and larch can safely stand until two hundred; beech, elm, and silver fir keep in good heart longer, although at one hundred they are already noble trees. The oak, with its roots reaching into damp gray clay, will keep up a healthy growth well past three centuries.   But it is not usual to let a forest have its full growth, and even the longest-lived are often hewn before one hundred and twenty.

The conifers grow to greatest height, then the oak, chestnut, beech, elm, lime, and ash.   Irrigation and manure are a help to trees, aiding them to grow a fine wood.   Failure to thin growing plantations, and failure to fell when at maturity, soon ruin a forest.   Intelligent thinning, felling, and replanting enhance the landscape, according to my taste. Every day has its task where a wood is kept in good condition, but wood folk never appear to hurry.

Beech is usually felled in November and December and left to bleach, oak thrown in January and February, ash and elm any time during the winter. Firs and pine may be hewn without need for such great care about the time. In order to allow of extraction during the period between the close of shooting and the beginning of nesting it is wise to have finished selecting and marking the trees before the end of autumn.

Wood sawn up and arranged in neat piles, each holding so many cords, stands in the forest to season. Crooked and faulty pieces, butts and tops, are cut into firewood. Plantations of spruce are grown for the Christmas-tree market; they are cut at four to ten feet. The tender bark from young oaks twelve to fifteen years old is the most desired by tanneries. Yew is in demand for gateposts and other places where strength and endurance are needed. The cuttings from willow find a ready sale for basketry and other twisted work. The collieries are a big market for timber, which is also wanted for building, for paper, and now for the making of cloth. Nothing is wasted.

Sometimes we went to the *Kindergarten*, a nursery for trees set in a sheltered place deep in the forest. The German system of rotary tree culture creates a need for baby trees each year, and it is the custom for each forest to nurture the majority of the trees that are to grow there. The care of these is an important part of the forester's duty. Started from seed, they are kept in clean straight rows in a plot safely fenced against rabbits and deer. I liked the *Kinder-*

garten. It whispered of a hopeful German future — each tree growing up toward light. Quite a foolish idea. But the little trees gave it to me.

Daily we went to the lake nature has provided as a swimming pool for Wiegersen. The water has the same look and feel as the water of the Rancocas in New Jersey — cool and warm in patches, with a clear brownness.

There was time for Katerlieschen to enchant me with the charm of her native tongue when used by poets. Beginning with Goethe's *Wandrers Nachtlied*, she read aloud her favorites from his native verses. *"Wer hat dich, du schöner Wald, aufgebaut, so hoch da droben . . ."* she quoted to introduce me to Josef von Eichendorff. (Who has built thee, thou beautiful wood, so high there above?) As lovers of the forest she made me acquainted with Achim von Arnim, Hoffmann, and Clemens Brentano.

Then she brought forward Lessing as a writer of animal fables, followed by Wilhelm Busch telling tales of Isegrim the Wolf and Reynard the Fox. In *Im tiefen Forst* we wandered with Erich Kloss deep into his wood.

During the last century a fire raged through the *Schloss.* Such treasures were rescued as there was time to save, but first attention was given to the protection of the surrounding woods. When the fire was conquered it was judged of less importance that the home had been destroyed than that no live trees had been lost.

When the rebuilt *Schloss* was ready, King George, the last to rule Hannover as an independent state, honored the housewarming with his presence. His signature is the first in the "new" guestbook, the one we signed. Wiegersen was then a forest estate in the royal kingdom of Hannover.

Below the signatures of guests at that dinner, the Countess, then mistress of Wiegersen, recorded the menu and the programme of music provided for their entertainment, items interesting to read now.

At Wiegersen one saw many things of rare charm: a spread of Venetian lace lying across a couch, cupboards and chests made when hands cherished tools, exquisite needlework on fine linen, beauty definitely German, and treasures from far places. But the beauty most often in mind is that of the forests. Leaves do spread a pattern across the heavens exquisite as the finest Venetian lace.

Without visits such as this I should have lost faith in all Germans; but following every period of doubt it was my fortune to be allowed to know people who gave me re-assurance. By these friendships I am bound to Germany forever, one with that country in triumph and failure.

As we were leaving, our host said, "We in our generation are shaken by hard winds. Wind but settles the roots of strong trees. It should be the same with men."

Wiegersen in Hannover is but a part of a vast system of forestation which holds sacred to trees a quarter of all land within the German frontiers. Living here, we had the pleasure of never going far out of sight of woodlands no matter where we traveled. I found this a happy contrast to the barrenness of those parts of China where centuries ago forests were sacrificed to the need of a time which has left in its wake drought, flood, and ever-recurrent famine.

All the trees of the temperate zone are native to this soil. The elm and the ash, the maple and the chestnut, the poplar and the pine, share place with an abundance of wild fruit and nut trees. The oak is widespread in its habitation. The finest oaks I have seen anywhere grow in forests westward of the Elbe. The beech is at its loveliest in southern Hannover and Schleswig-Holstein. The linden, dear to Schubert and to Heine, is charmingly present nearly everywhere. Silver firs mirror their frosty grace in the blue lakes of East Prussia; and, league on league, conifers march the hill ranges from the Harz to the Alps.

The present-day Germans are the children of people who worshiped their gods in groves. On forest walks one meets folk who speak of the beech as Wotan's tree and mention the oak as belonging to the god of thunder. Once when I was out in a storm a woodman's old wife opened her door and shouted at me to come in. I was glad to sit by her fire and while away the hours of the tempest listening to tales such as that of a raven whose duty it is to fly through the trees warning creatures and human beings by making a storm, which lets them know that the gods are about to ride past and they should go into their homes and not try to spy on holy secrets.

In a forest in the Deister I was shown a rocky place called *Teufelstanzplatz*, or Devil's Dancing Ground, by the German who showed it to me. My attention was drawn to a large flat stone with a groove chiseled in it. According to legend, this stone is one formerly used for heathen sacrifices. The stained groove was a gutter for blood. My guide called the stone *Taufstein*, or christening stone. She explained that when the first Christian priests came here they took the stone from its pagan use and used it in the service at which they baptized their converts.

One night, after the stone had long been in Christian

hands, the heathens got possession of it again. They decided to sacrifice a Christian virgin on it and baptize pagans
with her blood. Everything was prepared. The virgin
was killed. But not a drop of her blood would run out
over the stone.

Forest wandering is one of the joys of Germany, and
Hans Schmidt introduced us to this pastime on our first
Sunday. Then came the Wiegersen visit. Later I had
beautiful weeks with the American who translated my
book, wandering in Thuringia, "the green heart" of Germany. She invited me to a house that had been lent her
in a forest village. During our strolls she shared generously
with me from the store of blossoms she has gathered out of
German literature. The habit grew on me of going for
forest walks alone, as many Germans do.

"Here is a present," said Hans Schmidt one day, dropping
a parcel on the table beside my sewing. "I've joined the
league to divert you from politics."

It contained a *Fusswanderkarte* for every forest in Germany, maps showing which kind of trees grow in various
districts, and this bit of weather wisdom: —

> *Blüht die Eiche vor der Esche*
> *Gibt's im Sommer grosse Wäsche.*
> *Grünt die Esche vor der Eiche*
> *Gibt's im Sommer grosse Bleiche.*

> (Buds the oak before the ash,
> There will be a great washing in summer.
> Green the ash before the oak,
> There will be a great bleaching in summer.)

All the afternoon while my husband and his friends
played and sang in the adjoining room I wandered through

the woods of imagination. I had the maps at hand ready for use whenever I felt the need of the quietness of forest strolls.

Paths are clearly marked. At crossways, signs explain the turnings. There are resthouses scattered through the forests ready to provide meals and shelter, and woodmen's families have license to sell to wanderers, much as if they were innkeepers. A nice thing about this forest wandering is that every German is a delightful person when encountered in the woods. Even people who have seemed crude when known only in town are gentle when amid the trees. This is a folk over whom nature has power for good.

Except when out shooting, I have never seen a German hurt an animal. This seems queer when one compares it with the cruelties the rough among the Germans inflict on their fellow men, women, and children just because they will not quickly adopt the tenets of National Socialism. But it is true that they are not unkind to animals. Birds especially have such confidence that they fly easily to the hand to feed, and deer are often seen quite close.

The elk, the red deer, the fallow deer, and the roe deer inhabit the various German woods. There are chamois in Bavaria, Baden, and Hohenzollern. Moufflon dwell in some of the mountainous forests. Other animals here are the boar, the fox, the badger, the hare, the marten, and the squirrel. Hazel grouse, ptarmigan, and wild geese live along the northern coast. Wild ducks people the lakes. Mountain cock, heath cock, partridge, pheasant, woodcock, sparrow hawk, goshawk, buzzard, heron, and snipe are widely spread. Birds and animals that are rare are protected. The seasons for killing those that may be taken are strictly limited.

The German men are nearly all fond of hunting. They make a social affair of the chase and go to it gayly garbed. German hunting is usually done on foot, with the help of one or two dogs. The favorite chase is that of the deer and the boar. The favorite shooting is pheasant, partridge, and snipe.

Hunters often gather for the chase at the home of a forest owner. Many men have hunting lodges. These are most popular. They are rough-built of fir logs, the chinks filled with moss and mortar. The roofs have a long slant and extend well over the walls so that the snow slides off them a distance away. They are furnished with hewn tables and chairs, skins, and leather cushions. A shelf runs round the room to hold mugs and glasses, some very brightly colored, and the tin dinner plates stand here between meals. *Jagdtrophäen* are all about — the antlers of buck, the heads of wild boar, the heads of elk, and anything the owner has been proud to kill. The person who bags the most game at a hunt is the *Jagdkönig*, or Hunt King, of the day. The host must never achieve this position, but leave it to one of his guests.

Where Germans are gathered there is sure to be much eating, drinking, and singing, and here is a song typical of the fancies one finds lurking in the roughest Germans. *"Der Himmel da oben, der freut mich sehr . . ."* it opens. In English prose this is its theme: The heaven above delights the singer. Well would he like to venture up. But until now no angel has turned the lock opening the door to him. So he seeks on earth an open door, finding one and then another. He enters a forest house in the valley and goes in and out of its doors daily, greeting many thousand times the heaven which is the valley. He decides that *"Der Himmel da oben"* (the heaven above) is too high for him; it is very beautiful but its brilliance is far too bright, and when the sun sinks down the dark night comes there at once. *"Zu dunkel ist mir die schwarze Nacht"* — too dark for him is the black night — he has pleasure in the green night, the forest night. In the forest night he has happiness and joy — *"da bin ich genossen von allem Leid, in grüner Nacht."* (There am I recovered from all sorrow, in the green night.)

The German on whom civilization has not yet put a clear rational outlook has these vague inner sorrows. Through his poetry and his music runs a continuous search for a healing balm. Even the hunter eating and drinking after the chase sings of the forest greenness soothing his pain.

The chase occupies but a small part of the forester's year. One meets many woodmen who say that they are glad when the hunting is over and the forest left in peace. Such men like other times better than the days of killing, when deer run hither and yon seeking the right to live, and frightened birds fly through the copse.

When deer, boar, or other game destroy a farmer's property he is not permitted to shoot them. He must write a complaint, asking reimbursement for the damage done. The right to hunt game, even if ruining the fields, is reserved to the forest owner.

There is an oft-played operetta on this subject. In it the peasants of a small dukedom are bothered by wild boar raiding their potato fields. They petition repeatedly, but the old Duke gives them no attention. Finally they act for themselves. They have a chase and they kill the boar. Since they dare not sell any of the meat, as this would disclose their deed, they decide to have a week of feasting. They enjoy their week. All is well. Nobody from the Duke's household even suspects what they have done. A year passes. The old Duke is dead and a young Duke succeeds to the property. On taking over the estate papers he finds the unanswered petitions from the bothered peasants. He is very sorry for them. He resolves to help them at once.

He orders his *Oberhofjägermeister* to arrange a boar hunt. The news reaches the peasants, who know that every boar has been dispatched. What can they do? It is a crime to kill game. The whole village seeks to find a way to avoid prison or a heavy fine. The glorious idea of painting their own pigs black and chasing them into the forest for the Duke and his hunters to kill occurs to them. It is done. The complications which arise so amuse the young Duke that in the end he pardons the peasants for their offense.

At the time the Germans were changing from nomadic to pastoral habits, they cleared away virgin trees to enlarge their meadows and secure greater space for tillage than nature had provided. A whole period of their history is engrossed with a desperate struggle with the forests. The many place names ending in *metz* and *hau, rode, schwand, brand,* and *hagen* bear eloquent testimony to the hewing, rooting up, burning, and fencing accomplished. Enormous areas of land were stripped.

As in other lands, the ardor of the people overreached its purpose. Trouble such as they had never known descended on them. Instead of an increase in the food supply, they had less. Seasons of flood and seasons of drought were successive. Wind blew away soil and seed. Even the rain changed its behavior. Clouds floated by without dropping their moisture, or else let it down in torrents to run away as fast as it fell.

Famine tested their endurance. They began to speculate on the cause, and to seek ways of balancing the extremes of water surplus and water shortage. Their food supply, key to man's life, depended on a comprehension of the reason for these troubles and their remedy. Among them the romantic idea, common to many peoples, that droughts and floods are a duel between the elemental forces of nature and the heroic endurance of man soon gave way to a realization that trees have power over the incidence of rain and might to control water after its fall.

Way back in tribal history they came to know that when clouds drift above a bare track of country overheated by the summer sun they balloon upwards and pass without giving their rain. And when they float above the cool forest they let it down in a gentle fall. After the rain had fallen on the forest the Germans noticed that the trees held the water back so that it could not rush away, releasing it leisurely into the springs which in turn fed the rivers in manageable volume so that they did not burst their banks when there was a heavy fall, or dry up when the rains held off.

Once these German tribesfolk knew their fault, they manifested no spirit of evasion or disposition to laziness.

They set to work to restore forests as ardently as they had destroyed them. The deeper I look into the German past, the more cause I find for admiration for Germans, the more faith I have that they are of importance in the community of men, the more certain that they will return to political sanity and strive to repair what they have lost to themselves in recent years.

In regard to the forests, when they recognized the harm they had done they did not merely lament their loss. They replanted the trees. From then on they kept strictly to laws which they made for forest protection. German settlers, as they pressed into new lands, carried their forestry wisdom along. The preservation of a sensible balance between forest and cleared land became a fixed habit in every part of the world where Germans lived. They practised this for the sake of their water supply long before they had need to conserve or grow timber. The wood came in handy later. So far in German history, no matter how pressing the need was believed to be, no German ruler has ever yet sacrificed the forests to any state emergency.

The tribal community made the laws for the protection of the wood in the early days, and later each state had its forestry department. When the National Socialists came into power in 1933, control was centralized in Berlin. The states of the German federation are now provinces of the Dritte Reich, and copies of their forestry codes have been called in so that a national code may be devised. Forty-seven per cent of the forests are held in private families; 33 per cent are state lands; and 20 per cent belong to towns, charitable organizations, and various associations. Whatever the form of ownership, it has always been the custom for the woods to stand under government protection. Only foresters approved by the state may be employed in the care of woodlands.

I find the forestry codes interesting. Here are three extracts from "The Forest Law of the Grand Duchy of Baden," published in 1934: —

Trees must be so trained that the outermost branches of one meet those of another. They shall be kept in this manner to allow the natural seeding of the entire woodlands. Among leaf and needle trees, with the exception of the white fir, small openings are to be made to permit the entry of light. . . .

The charcoal maker is in duty bound to notify the forester before he starts his fire. After the fire is started he may not leave his pit by day or by night, and at all times he must have sufficient water at hand to prevent the danger of spreading fire. In windy weather he must erect a break to keep off the wind, and during such weather he may not remove the cover from his pit or draw out charcoal. . . .

The catching or disturbing of titmice and other forest birds and creatures is forbidden, with the exception of those coming under the list which hunters may shoot on the dates allowed. It is also forbidden to disturb the birds' nests. . . .

"The Forest Law of the Kingdom of Prussia" had this provision: —

Poor people living by the forest are permitted to gather and carry off dead branches. They may take only what lies on the ground and nothing is to be harmed. This may be arranged without charge, but if they are able the people shall pay a small sum.

The formation of a national code is simplified by the fact that the Germans have held their forestry lore as a common heritage. Although they might war over other things the tribes passed this knowledge from one to another generously, and later state agendas that worked well were open to copyists from other states. Private family ownership of woods has long been fostered because it has been thought that trees thrived best when kept in families who grew wiser generation by generation.

The National Socialist programme is both national and socialist. It favors the small landowner and also state ownership of resources. Formerly, estates such as Wiegersen were entailed. Now large estates have been freed of entail. The heir to a large estate may sell off acreage. If it be forested the Reich is a ready purchaser. But so far the owners of broad acres who keep their woods well have been encouraged to remain on them. General Hermann Göring holds the office at the head of the new national bureau, and he uses his influence more on the side of national efficiency than towards socialism.

The forestry service is a service employing a vast number of men. Statistics from Prussia show that in that province alone there were more than four thousand foresters in 1935. Everywhere among Germans education for the service has progressed along similar lines. Until the eighteenth century a man was ranked an adequately educated forester if he possessed a letter signed by a credited forester stating that he was learned in the care of trees and *wehrhaft und Hirschfänger* — that is, able to handle a gun and hunting knife.

For a long time the teaching-masters were just foresters

willing to take on pupils. Then these men began to found schools. Soon it came to be that such simple preparation as above was not enough, and now to rise to the higher positions in the service a man must have a full university course in forestry and further combined book learning and practical work. Those who go directly from the folk school into forest work cannot rise above a position as an underforester.

The care of the forest is systematized in an organization which links the forestry chief, called the *Reichsjägermeister*, or national huntsmaster, to the lowliest woodman. Each man in the woods is under the control of the one above him. In turn the man above is responsible for those below him. The forested land is divided into districts, their size depending on local conditions, and each district has a superintendent.

These superintendencies are official posts open only to university- or academy-trained foresters after years of forestry service. When a man achieves such a position he must immediately make himself thoroughly familiar with what is entrusted to his care. Without delay he must get in touch with every forester of his district, study the map of ownership so as to be familiar with the boundaries, look into the condition of the trees and the game, and inspect the books. Throughout the term of his service daily visits and tours of inspection are a part of his duty.

He must aid his foresters in the preparation of annual plans for the hewing and stocking of the woodlands under them, give counsel regarding the laying out of roads and the management of labor, watch over the utilization of forest products to guard against waste, attend to the district bookkeeping, and write detailed reports for head-quarters.

The forester has direct charge of the woodland where he is employed. His first duty is to keep his forest in good heart, neglecting nothing which would benefit its trees, animals, birds, flowers, and wild fruits. He must protect his woods against unlawful uses, thefts, and injuries, reporting immediately every breach of the forest police or hunting laws even though the culprit be the owner himself.

He must carry out the directions of the district superintendent regarding the hewing and the planting of trees. He must personally mark each tree that is to be felled, and attend to the measuring and numbering of wood cut. He must guard against waste. He must fulfill orders promptly, giving the needs of the government first attention; and he must not give any forest product over to anyone without first reading his permit.

He has to watch over every laborer, attending to the woodcutters, the makers of charcoal, the collectors of pitch. He gives out the privileges for pasturing and swine feeding, gathering of fruit and mushrooms, picking up dead firewood. He may ask the business of anyone who walks through his forest and order him off should he be seen doing harm to anything that grows there. From the day of his appointment until its end he must keep account and memorandum books, and these must be open to the inspection of his superiors in the service. Therein he must record wood taken from the forest, the labor used, and a statement of costs and receipts. He must keep a record of plantings and the results of methods of culture used, a record of game killed and the yield from it. He must also list every breach of the law.

Despite all these regulations, foresters look like contented men. Every one I have seen has had a fine face, lean, weather-tanned, and wrinkled if old. There is an unhurriedness about them, a peacefulness like that of the trees.

They live in *Forsthäusern*, usually very beautifully situated. Sometimes these houses are set on the outskirts of the forest. Often they are deep in the heart of the wood. In addition to his salary every forest official has free quarters and free fuel. He also has the right to sell refreshments to travelers.

Foresters have free doctor's care in time of sickness, state support if injured at their work, and pensions at retirement. For these benefits they have to give a percentage from their earned income, as is the case with all workers in Germany. There has been no fixed age at which men must retire, but there is much talk now of setting it at sixty years so as to give the younger men more opportunity for advancement. But foresters are reluctant to retire and leave a forest home where they have grown old amongst the tranquil trees.

The toy train stopped for me to get down at a wayside station and puffed off. This was a pleasant valley fragrant with the smell of newly sawn wood. The rutted track ran northeast through a grove of acacia, maple, and birch. At the sawmill I crossed a creek, and not far beyond this the way plunged into the darkness of pine forest. The only sounds were the scamper of a squirrel, twigs snapping under my feet, and the cackle of a cock pheasant who curled up on the wind trailing a handsome tail. Then, suddenly, I came out to oaks. Soon I saw the friendly lights of Doctor Z.'s house.

A curtain was drawn aside, and I saw him look out. He vanished, to reappear at the opened door. The moon had risen behind me. Its radiance shone full on him, and to my glad surprise it revealed Doctor Z. as the very sort of professor I had expected the Germans to have. Life had etched his face and whitened a halo of unruly hair. Arthritis forced him to walk with two sticks. But I could plainly see that in youth he had been the German professor I had always pictured as Jo's dear man in *Little Women*. Even before he spoke I knew that life had made of him just what must have pleased exacting Jo March.

Abendbrot had been kept waiting for my arrival. When the meal was over and the table cleared, he asked his housekeeper to fetch from another room the manuscript which I had sent to him with a request for help. At the time I entered Germany I had been near the end of a book about the originator of the Great Wall of China. My story of the "Ten Thousand Li of Stone" which Ch'in Shih Huang-ti ordered to be placed across his country's northern frontier had been announced for publication.

Into the writing I had put legends gathered through twelve years, and material collected by research through every source of enlightenment on the subject that I could discover. Late one night I put a last word on a final page of the chapters still to be sent. To-morrow this part could be posted. But when that morrow came I could not send it. I did not know why, yet I could not let this manuscript be published as I had written it. More than a year passed in indecision and through all this time my American editor encouraged me to complete the revision. I couldn't do it. These were months in which I wrote nothing. Startled, emotionalized by life in Germany, my mind was barren just as it had been during the last year of the war and the time that followed until I went to China. I sought every possible scholarly help. That is why I had written to Doctor Z. He had responded to my questions by suggesting that I send him my manuscript. Then he had written me no criticism; he had asked me to come.

My manuscript lay on his table. We sat in chairs before his fire. In compliance with his request, I fetched a book on Chinese philosophies from a shelf and opened it at the section relating to Yang Shang, whose theories influenced Ch'in Shih Huang-ti, the Great Wall's builder. Then he dialed his radio until he picked up the broadcast of a National Socialist orator. I moved my chair so that I could look over his shoulder as, phrase by phrase, he traced on the printed page statements identical with those made by the speaker.

After a little while he turned off the radio. From a corner cupboard I got him a folder holding things he had copied from the broadcasts made by the Führer. He read aloud alternately excerpts from the book relating to life in China in the third century before Christ and sentences from the folder relating to life in Germany in the twentieth century.

"Had you noticed this similarity?" he asked.

I said that I had. Then he talked about my manuscript. When it arrived he had started to read it because of interest in the amount of research I had done. He told me that it was not in research that I needed aid. He had sent for me because he thought he might help me to diagnose my trouble over it. Brought up a Quaker, and influenced by the wisdom of Confucius and his school of followers, I had in this manuscript spent my talent making a romantic hero out of a man of mighty force. All had gone too happily at the beginning, but fortunately, before I finished, the fates had moved me into Germany, where just such history as that of which I was writing was in the progress of making.

"It is easy," he said, "for two incompatible ideas to slumber side by side in the subconscious regions of the intellect, one condemning the brutalities of force and the other glorifying the achievements of might. You have written a thrilling narrative in words of amber and jade. I sat up all night to read it. But you must not publish this. You must not call it finished until your mind is mature. An author has power to influence others — and power to confuse others. Words must be used with care.

"Before you issue this book you must know whether you believe in force or not. If you do not believe in it, then you cannot glorify a Napoleon or a Ch'in Shih Huang-ti."

He was right. I acknowledged this, and we sat in a silence which was broken by the patter of little feet. The door was pushed open, and two sleep-tousled boys came in, the elder, about seven, carrying the baby one pickaback.

"We couldn't sleep. You promised we could see the Chinese lady. Granddaddy, you forgot."

They were sweet children, the elder serious, the younger merry. They stayed awhile; I went up to tuck them in when they had to go. After I came down the Doctor told me about them.   The mother had died at the birth of the little one.   Their father, who had never seen this child, had been in a concentration camp since the spring of 1933.   He is my host's younger son, the only one remaining.   The elder son was lost in the battle of the Marne.

"My son is thirty-two.   He was christened Johann, but now I think of him as Florestan.   Florestan, the hero of Beethoven's opera *Fidelio*, symbolizes truth held captive by evil."

"I am sorry he was taken," I said.

"And I am proud," answered this old German.   "Truth crushed to earth shall rise again.   I am proud that my son lies in chains for her.   These boys and girls so imprisoned are the heroes of my Fatherland — their courage will echo down the ages."

"What did he do to get himself arrested?"

"He refused to withdraw a remark he had made to the effect that the Versailles Treaty is less unjust than the treaty which would have been imposed on men in the name of Germany had our side won after four years of bitter struggle."

I stared at this German professor and asked: "Do you think your son right in saying that?"

"I do.   Right in saying it, and right in sticking to his statement."

"Well — of course he would go to prison for lack of patriotism."

"Patriotism, nationalism — absurdities.   The sooner we get rid of those foolish terms 'patriotism' and 'nationalism,' the quicker we shall arrive at an era of civilized living."

The next morning when I left, the little boys got permission to come to the station with me, and my host hobbled out a short way among the oaks.

"Trees give peace to the souls of men," was the last thing I heard him say. He stood with his back against the shaggy trunk of a magnificent tree.

XI

INTO AUSTRIA

My husband studied music in the Rhineland with a man living there who took a few pupils, not from need, but for the joy of teaching those who love the German harmonies. A day came when this teacher said that he must bid a sad farewell to this pleasure. He had received notice of a ruling: no professor could teach music in the Fatherland any more unless he secured a permit from a Bureau of Enlightenment at Berlin.

He explained that he was an old man too set in the concepts of an earlier generation to comply with a request that he present his credentials at a bureau in Berlin and trace his family tree back to 1800. He belonged to another era — a time when men believed that art knows no barriers of race, color, or creed. He could not apply for the certificate, although his reluctance covered no anxiety lest Jewish blood should be discovered in his veins. His inheritance was that accepted, even heralded, as "Aryan," Nordic, purely German. But he could not go back on his belief that civilization rests on a foundation built of many different stones, each contributory to the upward soaring of art.

Neither could he flaunt his opinion in the face of youth. Another generation possesses the world. He would offer

no resistance to this decree; he would not put it to the test
by continuing to teach without obtaining a permit. He
was tired and old. He said that truth is not easy to find.
Youth must find its own way to truth — stumble blindly,
if need be. He liked to teach, but he bade his pupils
"*Auf Wiedersehen*" with a melancholy resignation, saying, "I do not live in this world. I live in memory with
men who are gone."

I was shaken by this incident, and suffered an inner panic
from it. I do not know why it disturbed me so much. It
may be that one who has lived with Quakers and Chinese
unreasonably expects leadership from the aged everywhere,
and too surely feels that it is the duty of the old to light
the path for youth.

I was disconcerted beyond anything that my words have
power to explain each time I encountered shifting sands
beneath the feet of the German cultured. The more I
came to know of their great music and great literature, the
more seriously was I disturbed by such happenings, large
and small. These are a people unto whom much light has
been given, a people who have been favored again and again
by the birth among them of men empowered to hold a
candle up to truth.

I was led to a decision I had been trying to avoid. For
some time I had been uneasy about having my daughter
grow up in Europe. She ought to be in Pennsylvania,
where she could have the things which I had been privileged
to have. I do not like to be without her, but now I wrote,
and had prompt assurance that she would be welcome. We
all spent a few weeks in the United States. Too soon she
was settled, and we sailed away, landing at Hamburg and

motoring across Germany. Our next sojourn among the Germans was to be at Vienna.

Up from Munich over *Reichsautobahnen* we traveled to Austria. Designed to conform to the landscape, and built by the Dritte Reich to endure a thousand years, these handsome roads provide for those in haste an opportunity for speed with safety, and give to the leisured a glorious panorama of views through the magnificent Bavarian Alps. The day was the last of October in 1936.

We passed a river valley where three seasons had met. Summer was by the water, grass green and flowers in bloom. A buzzing *Bombus* flew boisterously into our car; invited out again, the bumblebee showed no concern about the season, but wandered from blossom to blossom in a honey-foraging. Autumn stood above summer on the steep sides of this deep vale, leafed trees and shrubs making a wide band of red and gold. Higher still the snows of winter glistened on conifers; and frigid mountain peaks, their white unmarred, seemed to touch the blue sky.

Leaving the river, our road ascended decisively, rounding rugged ways until we arrived at heights where snow was falling. We were glad then of the windshield warmer which we had got in Berlin, on German advice, to keep our vision clear. We came, at Berchtesgaden, to weather suddenly fair.

In his *Holy Roman Empire*, in the section on Frederick Barbarossa, Lord Bryce has written: "To the southwest of the green plain that girdles in the rock of Salzburg, the gigantic mass of Untersberg frowns over the road which winds up a long defile to the glen and lake of Berchtesgaden.

There, far up among its limestone crags, in a spot scarcely accessible to human foot, the peasants of the valley point out to the traveler the black mouth of a cavern, and tell him that within the red-bearded Emperor lies amid his knights in an enchanted sleep, waiting the hour when the ravens shall cease to hover round the peak, and the pear tree blossom in the valley, to descend with his crusaders and bring back to Germany the golden age of peace and strength and unity."

During the years that I had lived among the Germans I had heard frequent acclaim of Frederick Barbarossa, a red-bearded, blue-eyed knight-errant of their mediæval times. I had listened to celebration of his superb health and sound common sense, his courage in support of justice, his truth and honor, his joy in righteousness. Whether or not history could confirm all these attributes was un-important to me. For me it was enough that Germans of my day found good the virtues they proclaimed as his.

Because they did, I carried a wreath of laurel to Berchtesgaden. I found mountain peasants who assured me that the English nobleman's report is correct, and led me to the cavern. I put my tribute there, from whence, so simple folk trust, a knight of these virtues shall come forth supported by his crusaders.

In this same glen of Berchtesgaden a man named Adolf Hitler has his house in our time. He was born at Braunau on the river Inn, across the Austrian frontier, but not far off as the crow flies. From the romantic glen of Barbarossa's legendary resting place he now bugles a call of race to Germans in every part of the world.

"Do you think that the Führer of your Dritte Reich

might be your blond knight risen in another guise?" I
queried.

The burly Bavarians who had brought me here exchanged
quick glances. One of the two spoke. This was the only
reply I could get from them: "Time will give the answer."

A short way on, we encountered the red and white pole of
the German frontier. "Heil Hitler!" exclaimed the guard;
and, when formalities for exit were completed, "Heil
Hitler! — *Auf Wiedersehen!*"

"*Grüss Gott,*" said the guard on the Austrian side, wearing a uniform much less natty than those we had left. The
national colors here were red-white-red, and this was called
the land of the Fatherland Front. Evidently it was easier
to get past "Greet God" than to go by "Hail Hitler"
guards. The formalities were quickly done, and my husband was back in the car.

We should find life in Austria, so Rhinelanders had told
us, German "*durch Schlamperei gemildert.*" I wondered
about this now. Would life here be milder? And would
it be through slovenliness that it was mild?

As we drove into the country, Austria appeared poverty-
stricken. The first house we passed needed the roof
mended, and its paint was long since washed off, if ever it
had any. The road was not as in Germany. It was rough
and there were potholes. Those who lived on this side
could look over to the fine new boulevard, the smart uniforms, and all the shining polish of the Dritte Reich.

But the people we passed carried themselves with a non-
chalance, as if well content with their own side of the
boundary. We saw them in broken shoes, gray capes worn
and drab, looking not in the least crushed by circumstance,

but wearing the patina of poverty with a fine air. The scenery here was softer than that of the Bavarian Alps. Less grand. *Eine liebliche Landschaft*, a darling landscape, seen in a drizzle of rain which soon set in.

We asked a man we overtook if he would like a lift. He was going to Salzburg. So were we.

"You have come from the Devil's Reich?" he asked when settled.

Turning in my seat, I probably stared outlandishly. My husband, who never enters into political discussions in foreign countries, drove steadily on. The guest in our back seat threw up his head and laughed; then sobered and said, "A man must laugh while he can. The calamity our brethren across the way suffer is about due to roll over us."

I reminded him of the agreement made in the past July wherein, according to what I had read in newspapers, the Austrian government had received full and satisfactory assurance of the German intention strictly to respect Austrian independence. He hadn't the least faith in this agreement. He declared that it only provided more cover for sly underground propaganda issued from Berlin, designed to rouse a cry for union from this side of the boundary. This, he stated, had been intensified since the signing of the agreement.

"Do you think that this propaganda will succeed?"

He spoke slowly, sadly, each word clear: "Self-pity comes so naturally to all of us that the most solid happiness can often be shaken by well-spoken words delivered with no intent for good. And in Austria our happiness is not the most solid. We have many grievances which make us vulnerable. When people are told in sugared words that

they have been disfranchised of their world rights by the
enemy who defeated them in an unfair war forced upon
them, and are invited in the name of right to throw off
native leaders who are said to be the pawn of those enemy
states and take their forbidden but lawful place beside
their kinfolk in a rightabout-face against that wrong —
then, no matter how conservative the people thus addressed
may be, the appeal will confuse and eventually stir them."

He objected to National Socialism because the principle
of Germans' submitting in blind obedience to the absolute
will of one of their number was repugnant to him. "I
would denounce this idea even if I were permitted to be that
Führer. It is absolutely wrong. The Renaissance was
the dawn of the truth that we are individuals. The Nazi
theory leads back into the Dark Ages." Suddenly he
smiled, a charming smile. "Enough of politics. Here before us is Salzburg, a little town of the Italian Renaissance
that ran away north to tell us Germans of the light about
to come from sunnier lands."

Salzburg would be lovely seen at any time, but I am
glad I saw this town first in silver rain. Hermann Bahr
described the feeling that the place gave to me better than
my own words can do when he said, "Salzburg is nature
turned to stone and stone turned to spirit."

Here one finds beauty, spiritual beauty, with a sense of
gayety and humor. Perhaps these stones do hold more
than their geological elements, and something more too
than the touch of the hands that placed and carved them.
Our passenger said that this town of the Renaissance stood
as an island of peace while the bitter passions of the Thirty
Years' War, starting in Bohemia, surged over German

lands; and the culture that survived, kept safe in Salzburg, spread far and wide when that war was over.

He loved Salzburg and treasured the historic memories of its greatness as a centre of art and music. He told how, during the year 1916, people founded the Salzburg Festival community, its members pledged to keep immortal values alive.

Later, in a book called *This Salzburg,* I happened on an extract from the proclamation they issued then: "Mists surround the world, and there seems to be no end to the cruelest of wars. Nobody knows what the next hour is going to bring. All the same, we dare to express the thought of a Salzburg festival dedicated to peace, art, and joy. We call upon those who believe in the might of art, upon those who believe the works and values of art to be the only stable things in the eternal changes of time, to join us and to help us establish a refuge in the name of Mozart, where art lovers of all countries may unite in festive delight once the dark clouds of this world catastrophe have passed."

We put our passenger down at his request by an arch which bears an inscription recording the fact that in 1920 two thirds of Salzburg's population voted to be joined to Germany. The Treaty of St. Germain did not allow it, however. Before the man left he spoke of that. Standing undaunted in the rain, he called it "one of the mistakes of our time." In his opinion, if the Austrians and the Germans of Bohemia could have united with the democratic régime in Germany before it went under, perhaps their joint wisdom might have been strong enough to avoid the generation of National Socialism all will have to suffer.

He ended: "But don't for a wink of the eye think that

I am one who puts the blame for the present-day ills on the Versailles and St. Germain treaties. I know that the men who wrote those treaties did the best they could according to the light they possessed. Faith, hope, and idealism were in their treaty making. I'm too intelligent not to realize that fate gave victory to the safer side in 1918. We were all rushed into that war by an unclear set of circumstances. By the time we had fought each other with every means of science for four years, folk everywhere were quite crazy. Had our side won, the treaty making would have been done by General von Ludendorff and his kind. The 'peace by victory' they wanted would have put a definite end to what was left of the Renaissance."

I watched him and my husband exchange deep glances and shake hands. Then he asked where we were stopping in Salzburg, that he might direct us. When told, his face lit up. "Give them my warmest greetings," he said, and was off.

We had a nice stay in this town, where Renaissance and her child and grandchild, Baroque and Rococo, are present at their loveliest. There was music in the home where we were guests. We met charming people. It was pleasant to stroll through streets thinking that Mozart was once here. We attended a service at the Cathedral. We looked at the *Kollegienkirche*, St. Peter's, and the church of the Holy Trinity. I accompanied my hostess when she did house-hold marketing in the Universitätsplatz, and we went on to join our men at Tomaselli's, where they drank coffee and read newspapers.

We saw many houses with courtyards, loggias, and balconies; attractive wrought-iron tradesmen's signs swinging outside doors; several bathing places for horses, the finest the *Pferdeschwemme* where archbishops' steeds had their wash in the generations before motorcars. We passed No. 7 Getreidegasse, where Mozart was born, and from Kapuzinerberg we had a view of the town, plain, and snow-capped Alps just as he did when he wrote his *Magic Flute* from this height.

When we delivered the greeting from the man whom we had picked up along the road, the family of our host agreed among themselves at once: "That would be our good friend X." They said he should not go about speaking of the Dritte Reich in the way he did, but it was no use trying to stop him. An Austrian seldom took advice, and all over here had the characteristic, very different from other Germans, of personal independence. They resented the church whenever there was an attempt to extend influence beyond matters purely spiritual, and in politics had strong wills about the right of each to speak his own mind.

"Especially in these Alpine districts round Salzburg we are an independent folk," remarked a son of the house. "We have the historic memory that we stood our ground even against Napoleon."

He was for a union of all Germans. He was sure that Germans of the fallen Hapsburg Empire could join the Dritte Reich yet keep their own characteristics. These people were not ignorant of conditions on the other side of the frontier. They knew full well the harshness of discipline there, and recounted many incidents of brutality. Among these they told of a young friend who had married and gone to live there. She had written home that she did not like it, complaining of many things. Her letter was opened by the authorities and she was taken to a concentration camp. Despite every effort to get her out, she was kept imprisoned many months and gave birth to her child while there. She was never allowed a chair; her bed was a heap of straw.

The second daughter of our host stated that north Germany is by nature Sparta, but Austria is Athens. In her opinion, Austria's going into the Dritte Reich would exert a cultural, civilizing influence. Her uncle reminded her that she might be romantically thinking of Austria wrapped in the greatness which was the Hapsburg Empire, and forgetting that Austria could bring into this melting pot of Germans but seven small provinces and the city of Vienna, a mere six million people to add to a volume already sixty-eight million strong.

No one here avoided politics. On the contrary, throughout our stay in Austria we found politics a subject of almost continuous discussion. My hostess gave me three books in which Austrian authors have put forward a view that unity of language and race is not the best principle on which to base political union. They are by a liberal, Rudolf Sieghart; a Catholic, Ignaz Seipel; and a socialist, Karl Renner. She told me to read them because they would help me to a realization of the truth that the national communities of Europe should be merged in a pan-European government, but not to make the mistake of presuming that these views exerted any powerful influence on the present-day trend among Germans. Union with the Third Reich she accepted as inevitable, and very soon to occur.

When I asked if she thought the majority in Austria wanted to join the Dritte Reich she would give no judg-

ment. Many of her friends were decidedly against it.
Some thought Austria should remain independent and return to truly republican ways, reopening the closed Parliament.   Others hoped for a Hapsburg return in which young
Otto would be crowned, and a kingdom similar to that in
England.   Numbers of their children, like two of her own
five, longed ardently for a union with greater Germany and
believed that National Socialism here would be different
from that across the way.

She had heard it said that the National Socialist movement in Austria had its greatest strength among clerks and
shopkeepers, but it happened that not one of the people with
whom she dealt favored it.   She believed that the peasantry
wavered.   They had always been loyal to the Hapsburgs,
who had treated them well.   They did not like the present
régime because they did not like the way the priests were
taking part in government affairs.   Certainly they were
being told by Nazi propagandists of the benefits given
farmers in the Dritte Reich.

But she did not think any of these things really important.   The Führer of the Dritte Reich would bring his
native land into the German union.   He now had the
strength of sixty-eight million with which to win six
million.   It was only a matter of his finding a way through
the international hindrances.   Her mind was fixed on something no higher than my own would have been in a similar
situation.   She was concerned that when it did occur none
of her family should be involved in tragedies such as she
knew had happened in families in Germany.   She wanted
them loyal to each other no matter how things should turn.

She had thought much on the subject of nationalism and

read many books. Her father and her grandfather had been interested in movements to lead the Germans of the Hapsburg Empire out of this fold of many nationalities into that of greater Germany. She said that talking about it helped to clarify her thought. I liked to listen. These are some of the things I learned: —

The present-day nationalism in Europe began centuries ago in a rising of the masses against the unfairness of the rulers who held them in base subjection. The time when rulers were leaders of their own folk had passed. Chieftains and their relations had become kings and aristocrats. They intermarried widely, traveled, spoke several languages. Maids possessed lands and the people on them as dowry. Power over human beings was autocratic and passed as a chattel of inheritance, frequently going to heirs who had no connection but a property right. Their subjects began to form units of strength, and naturally these groups were made up of persons speaking a common tongue and living near together. Ideas seeped across Europe from one group to another, even swept across in great tides of common feeling, but only in national units could the people gather power to throw off the force that would hold them under.

The Reformation, so cruelly put down in the Hapsburg Empire, was a strong forward flow of this ocean of demand which was everywhere the cry of awakening peoples asking for the right to self-expression. The French Revolution was one of its manifestations. It has taken many turns — even the fanatical denial to others of the liberties gained for self.

The tide for liberties was strong among the Germans. Energetic rulers tried to keep it down. Then came

Napoleon's invasions of German lands and his setting up of French rule, including the creation of the Kingdom of Westphalia, with his brother Jerome on the throne. He held the Rhineland. He crushed Prussia to the earth. His troops were in Austria, in Baden, in Bavaria, in Saxony — they were everywhere. In the surge against French invasion and the fear of French return which continued after they had gone, the passion of the German people became a patriotic nationalism. In this wave of feeling began that sacrifice of individual liberties on the altar of united German strength which has continued generation by generation to the present day.

After Waterloo, England arranged that Prussia, a small state which had given invaluable help in the battle, should hold the Rhinelands secure against the French. This was an attempt to achieve peace on the continent, and thereby safety for England. Until then Prussia had been counted among Germans as insignificant — a rough, backward land of far less importance than Bavaria, Saxony, Hannover, or even little Weimar. True, Prussia had been coming up, but not in very cultured ways. The district was ruled by the Hohenzollerns, one of whom had changed his title from Elector of Brandenburg to King of Prussia. They had built up an army prepared for conquests and seized part of Silesia; but Austria — or rather the Hapsburg Empire, of which Austria was part — had dominated German affairs for centuries.

When German nationalism became the heartthrob of German patriots in every German land, Austria could not lead in a national movement. She was the property of the most international family in Europe, a family whose policy it was to discourage nationalism. German patriots looked to this Prussia on which England had showered favor. There they saw opportunity. The state was young, virile, and without the entanglement of any non-German population. Men from all over German lands offered their services to this state.

Many were accepted. Talented administrators, poets, philosophers, educators, and plain businessmen contributed to the building of that Prussia which the anti-liberal Prussian King asked Prince Otto von Bismarck to manage when the liberalism therein became too much for him. Bismarck made different use of the power he found in Prussia than many of its creators had planned. A part of his activity was the expulsion of the German provinces of the Hapsburg Empire from the German Confederation after Prussia had defeated Austria in 1866 at Königgrätz, in Bohemia, in a war he provoked.

When this occurred many German nationalists of the Hapsburg Empire wanted to leave that empire and be joined in the German Confederation. But it was no part of Bismarck's plan to have them in. They were too filled with liberal ideals and too Catholic for him to want them. Besides, they would bring with them the habit of speaking loudly on German affairs. The Frankfurt Convention of a few years earlier, of which Bismarck had refused to allow the Prussian King to take notice, had been led by Austrian German patriots whose ideas on the trend German history should take were quite contrary to his own. Consequently now, after Königgrätz, the Austrian and Bohemian Germans were cleverly advised that they could best serve the German cause by staying in the Hapsburg Empire and keeping that empire predominantly German in its expression on European affairs, a thing they could not do if they left. Not all Austrians were content with this device, but it worked.

It worked. The Hapsburg Empire stood with Prussia when Prussia invaded France in 1870. Long after Bismarck was gone this magic continued to work. Prussia, now the docile state of Hohenzollern rule, contrived that it was the Hapsburg Empire that declared an ultimatum in 1914 and thereby started what had long been pending — a European war. Prussia had the rôle of good friend supporting Austria in a Nibelungen loyalty. Austria bore the brunt of the defeat.

The Germans of the North German Confederation and the Germans of the Hapsburg Empire got different treatment. The Treaty of Versailles did not hinder the union of all the states and duchies of that confederation into a Reich sixty-five million strong with wide lands undivided by customs barriers. But thus were the Germans of the Hapsburg Empire dispersed: two hundred and thirty thousand passed under Italian rule to satisfy Italy's desire for a frontier running to the crest of the Alps; those of Bohemia and Moravia were incorporated in a new state called Czechoslovakia; six million were left to form a Republic of Austria — six million of whom more than half belonged to industrial districts permanently bankrupt because the fierce nationalism of new states made a Danube Customs Union with them impossible, and both the Treaty of Versailles and that of St. Germain forbade this Austria an *Anschluss* with the great Reich, except by unanimous consent of the League of Nations.

On the afternoon when these things were said we sat comfortably indoors, rain beating against the windows, both of us knitting. My instructress came to the end of a row, studied the pattern she was following, which was one I had brought her from America, and counted stitches. Then she voiced a sentiment I was to hear often from Austrians: "You must not think I blame the men who made those treaties for a single thing. After such warfare men are too heartsore and mind-weary for such tasks as they had to undertake."

She recalled the terms of the treaties of Brest-Litovsk and Bucharest, imposed when her side was winning. She had a vivid imagination regarding what the Treaty of Versailles would have been had a victorious Kaiser Wilhelm of Prussia and his General von Ludendorff reached Paris as they expected to do.

She told me something which was news to me: it was that throughout the war there had been hanging after hanging in Austria, man after man put to death for treason, suspected of disloyalty to the cause. There had been no united patriotic will to win there. Some men did their duty. Others did not, and went to their death on the scaffold. The Czechs had not been the only Hapsburg deserters. The Hapsburg Empire was breaking up, she assured me, and would have fallen into national states each racially jealous of the other even had the Great War, which accelerated this happening, not occurred.

She went back in memory to her youth. She had been her father's favorite; he had always wanted her near him. Playing in his room when very young, she had often heard talk which made her think that the world was about to shake apart into "racial sections." As she grew older she was very conscious of the struggle going on between Germans and non-Germans. In Bohemia they had to contest for place and position with the clever Czechs, whom it was thought the emperor encouraged too much. In Styria it was with the Slavs, and the danger from them was that they had too many children in comparison with Germans.

And there was the struggle with the Jews. In a belated effort to establish a "bourgeoisie," that their empire might catch up with northern Germany, France, and England in administrative, commercial, and industrial ways, the Hapsburgs had offered a ladder to the Jews. Jews from all over the empire rushed into Vienna. Glad of this chance, and being no part of any of the troublesome jealous national groups, Jews could be trusted to be absolutely loyal to the emperor. With tremendous rapidity they joined the Catholic Church in thousands, and tried in every possible way to make themselves into good Viennese. Consequently the Germans of the empire, who thought themselves able to do every task better than the Jews, had to compete with them for jobs high and low. Therefore, in Austria, anti-Semitism was against all who by blood were Jew. In this judgment, conversion to Christianity did not make them less Jew.

My hostess said that her father and grandfather and their friends discussed various theories as to what should be done about the German position in the empire and in the wider world. Their circle had been liberal, broad-minded, easygoing. They had not stirred themselves to do more than talk. The Hapsburg Empire had its defects, yet it had been able to hitch along for seven hundred years, and the

German position in it was strong, probably predominant. In addition to nationalism there were other things of importance to occupy the minds of thinkers.

In Austria there was much pondering about the real meaning of life. Books were written on this, and they had to be read and considered. There were art, music, and seasons of Vienna Society. Also the fortunate had wakened to a sense of responsibility toward the less fortunate, and attention was given to charities and social reforms. There was plenty to do.

My hostess thought that, of all the political views she had heard discussed in her youth, those of only one man had direct bearing on the Austrian present. This man was Georg Ritter von Schönerer. He had not seemed of any particular importance while he lived, although he had made a great deal of noise. When he died, some years after the Great War was lost, few had taken notice of his passing.

Now he was important because of an Austrian who perhaps had never met him. My friend had noticed that in *Mein Kampf* Adolf Hitler mentions von Schönerer. All that she knew of the Führer of the Dritte Reich made her feel that he puts into practice the theories von Schönerer advocated.

Von Schönerer's father was one of the men who brought the steam railway to the Hapsburg Empire. In the national uprisings of 1848 he organized the transport of troops by train, in the efficient Prussian manner, and was of aid to his emperor by getting soldiers quickly to the places of trouble. The royal arms were drawn against Hungarian, Italian, and other insurgents within a few hours of the time the news of rebellion reached Vienna. Railway Director Herr Schönerer was rewarded with a knighthood.

He was a man who did not approve of the way youth in Austria was being brought up; there was too much uncertainty and aimlessness. He admired the self-confident optimism found in Prussia. He decided that the best schools in the world were there, and, being a wealthy man, sent his son Georg to Prussia for both high school and university.

These were years when Prussia was making rapid strides forward in things military, political, and economic. Young Georg returned home in the seventies to suffer for the remainder of his life because his native Austria was not like Prussia. Austrians found him vain, opinionated, hard to live with. His father had acquired a large estate on the Danube. Georg had this and was rich besides. The time was that of parliamentary democracy. He chose to combine a career of country squire with that of politics, and entered Parliament elected by his home constituency. Later he lost this constituency, and then he secured one in Bohemia. He represented Egerland year after year in the Austrian Parliament.

He started in as a democrat agitating for universal suffrage, spoke fiery words in every debate on railway problems, was anti-Semitic with the downrightness of a *Junker*, and took an active part in movements against the Hapsburg aristocracy, the church, and the non-German nationalities of the empire. He secured some following among university students, and became for a while the leader of an alliance of nationalists and social reformers. He was one of the chief promoters of the Programme of Linz, a

complicated document coupling demands for universal suffrage with a plan which would give the Germans a majority
in the Austrian Parliament every time, and ending with an
extensive programme for social legislation. Georg Ritter
von Schönerer never became the actual political leader of
German nationalism. He had magnetism and could attract,
but those who were attracted soon dropped away, put off by
his intolerance and his conviction that he knew the right
in everything.

Did the Crown defend the claims of non-German
nationalities? Down with the Hapsburgs! He spoke of
William I of Prussia as "our holy Emperor" and tried to
start a cult of the Hohenzollerns, linking this campaign up
with the most violent anti-Semitism. He lost friends.
Even the most ardent nationalists in Austria felt that everything hateful was embodied in what the Hohenzollerns
had made of Prussia.

He uncovered serious corruption in the building and
management of some railroads in which most of the
capitalists were Jews, and started a violent campaign that
brought him into conflict with the Liberal Party and
Jewish-owned newspapers. From then on he never ceased
to flay the press and pursue a relentless anti-Semitism. Because some Jews were wicked he would put away all who
had Jewish blood. No fate could be too cruel for them.
When a universal suffrage admitted Jews to Parliament he
turned against parliamentary democracy.

In the nineties he launched a vigorous campaign with
the slogan "*Los von Rom*" (Away from Rome). The
Catholic Church protected Jews, even baptized them as
Christians. It smiled on non-Germans everywhere. It

was the church of the hated Hapsburgs. Break from this strangle hold! He offered to join the Protestant Church when one hundred thousand Austrians had gone over to Protestantism. He roused no Reformation.

Finally, cold-shouldered out of Vienna, he retired to his country estate. Hearing that he was not well, the father of my hostess had once gone to see him, and found a lonely man, bitter in condemnation of the present as immoral and decadent, vindictive against parliamentary democracies, busy with musings about the ancient Germanic religion.

"Georg Ritter von Schönerer could collect no following in Austria. Adolf Hitler, an Austrian boy, went to Germany and found soil there for this seed. He will soon be lord of life and death in Austria. Thus do ideas, good and evil, live longer than men."

Like his wife, our host always referred to the *Anschluss* with the Dritte Reich as inevitable. These are among the thoughts he voiced: "We are not a large or rich land, and shall be of no economic advantage to the Nazis. We are not Nordic. This is the crossroads of the Teuton, the Slav, the Magyar, and the Latin. Despite our German nationalism, we Austrians have never been interested in inbreeding. We have married where our hearts led us. Far more than in Germany have we wed with the Jew. For my part, I think that union of Jew and German produces a fine combination of intelligence and feeling. I do not find the Teuton so perfect that he should be kept pure Teuton. He is improved by a dash of the Orient, and something of Latin, Slav, and Magyar.

"I am not taken in by this propaganda that the leaders of the Dritte Reich look on us as brothers. They look down on us as hybrids, and will treat us as inferiors as soon as they have won possession of this land. Their Führer is Austrian-born. I have seen him several times in Munich. I listen to him on the radio every time he broadcasts, and I have read his book most carefully. I think he is more Slav than Teuton. In *Mein Kampf* I can find nothing but contempt for Austria. There is no hate so bitter as that against one's own relatives. I do not think we shall fare well in his hands. We are wanted in the Dritte Reich for no other reason than that he who stands master of these crossroads is a stage forward on the way to mastery of Europe.

"Austria will be a Nazi military outpost, and Vienna will become a commercial city, her extraordinary possibilities as mistress of the Danube fully developed. In Bavaria I heard that they have a plan ready drawn up to connect the Danube with the Rhine, and make our Nibelung stream a trade way to the wealth of the Balkans."

Before the Nazis came to power in Germany our host had been a German nationalist all his life. He had gone over into Bavaria to stay with relatives, that he might spend three months in the Dritte Reich. He had come home ready to work either for an independent Austria with a constitution protecting the democracy it established or for a union with the Republic of Czechoslovakia. When I expressed astonishment at the latter idea, he assured me that he was not the only Austrian thinking that way. He had followed his three months' visit to Bavaria by three months in Prague, and had returned from there an ardent admirer of the way the Czechs had made a success of democracy, at which Germans had failed.

"In Austria we have tried out a number of ways politically and economically during the last eighteen years. There is now no escaping union with the Dritte Reich. But it is a pity, since union with a German democracy proved impossible to achieve because of the behavior of France and the support that nation had from Italy and England, that we cannot try out something with Czechoslovakia. Germans, Italians, and French in another part of the Alps have achieved a republic in which they are contented Swiss."

"*Vati!*" exclaimed his Nazi boy and girl. Two others of his five children sided with him. The anti-Nazis of the family made the Nazis a wager that by 1940 they would agree with their father's opinion.

"Long before 1940 both independent Austria and the Republic of Czechoslovakia will have bent the knee to the Dritte Reich," declared their uncle.

"That is an absurd idea," said the youngest son, talking to me alone later. I thought so too, then.

When we left Salzburg we took with us a neighbor who wanted to go to Vienna. We did not go by the new and more direct road. We went to Linz and followed the swift-flowing Danube through Pöchlarn, Melk, Dürnstein, where Richard the Lion-Hearted was held prisoner long years, by Krems and Tulln. Then we left the river to see Klosterneuburg. Finally we looked on Vienna from the last spur of the Alps, a cliff called Leopoldsberg.

Our Austrian guest proved himself very German in his willingness to inform.

Austria is about the size of Scotland. It is highland, with a narrow share of the fertile plain which lies at the foot of the Alps. Lordship of the land is divided between nobles, the Catholic Church, and peasants. Some families have a lion's share in title to more than one castle and the surrounding acres. The monasteries of Melk, Admont, and Zettl rank among the largest landowners. Between the great estates are the many small holdings.

The country is rich in water power, beautiful scenery, and fine forests. There is some iron ore, lead, copper, magnesite, graphite, occasional deposits of gold, and lignite, but hardly any coal. More than two million of the population work at agriculture, either tilling their own soil or as laborers on estates. In the Austrian share of the fertile plain, sugar beets are grown. In the sheltered valley of the Danube, fruit thrives. In the Alps the farmers keep cattle, and manage to get bread for themselves, and winter fodder for their cows, from steep and stony soil.

"The agriculturist is probably better off here on the whole than any other group. Our League of Nations loan was largely used to reorganize farming. Herr Dollfuss came from Alpine peasant stock, and before he was Chancellor he served ably in an attempt to make it possible for farmers to live and to produce food for others of our starving population. The breaking up of the old empire set national barriers across many peasant customs, including that of fattening Alpine cattle on the Hungarian plain below, and the habit of bringing from Yugoslavia new stock for breeding.   Despite the fact that they are better off than our industrial group and the people of Vienna, who administered the old empire, many of our farmers are so poor that salt is a luxury on their tables."

Textile, paper, leather goods, and confectionery factories; mines and steel mills, power plants and electrical appliance manufactories; sugar making, and a thriving business in winter sports, are the industries.   To one traveling in Austria the factories are not very noticeable.   The mountains are sprinkled with inns, and many a man finds it possible to earn more from teaching foreigners to ski during a few weeks in winter than from his labor at other things during the remainder of the year.

This is a lovely landscape, dotted with picturesque towns and villages, cream-washed churches, painted houses with wide eaves, occasional factories, castles, and great monasteries.   The people passed were mostly dark-eyed and not very fair in complexion, and, while some were tall, the average was short.   They resembled Bavarians more than other Germans.   Their clothes, no matter how poor and shabby, had a chic style.   All walked with an air.

The material standard of living appeared decidedly below that of the Third Reich.   I asked about wages.   What laborers got in Germany for hard toil had appeared to me microscopic.   When I heard what they got here, and what it would buy, the wages men had over there seemed large in comparison.

"Toil is not well enough repaid there either," said my instructor.   "The great point of advantage is that our Hitler has been able to get a workable economic plan started in Germany.   It is a plan in which the employer has no opportunity for great profit-taking. Wages will steadily improve there as markets are achieved and production increased. And it is far better to have won by honest toil a rough shelter and a slice of black bread without butter than to have no chance to work, as is the case with thousands here."

He longed for the day when Herr Hitler would come home to Austria. He had no faith in any plan by which Austria could stand alone, nor any confidence in the good will of the democratic powers. On his fingers, date by date, he checked off incidents of their conduct to Austria since the defeat, "all done in the name of loving friendship," and asked me if, hearing this, I could fail to understand the fanaticism of Adolf Hitler and those who follow him. These dates and incidents were so many, and given so rapidly, that I found it impossible to recall them for record in my diary. I had but a confused memory of an impassioned outburst.

"We Austrians may not look it, but we are a passionate people. There will be blood and thunder here when we join the Third Reich: massacre of the Jews; serious rising against the Catholic Church, which is hated by many peasants and others — and not without cause; and old grudges against the Hapsburg aristocracy will be paid. We will need the German army to save us from ourselves."

I was astonished at his vehemence. He assured me that he knew his homeland, and then abruptly turned the conversation to history. The Germans have called the land we know as Austria by two names. First, *Ostmark*, or East March; then *Österreich*, or Eastern Realm. Near the close of the eighth century, Charlemagne battered down

the Avars, who lay athwart the middle Danube, in a series
of campaigns which caused them to vanish from the earth
forever, and took into his own treasury the wealth they had
sacked from Balkan cities. He created *Ostmark* as a
military frontier for the protection of Bavaria.

When Charlemagne's life was over, the Magyars came up
from the Hungarian plain and drove the Germans out of
Ostmark. Magyar and Slav occupied this Alpine district
until the tenth century. Then that same Saxon Otto who
went to Rome for the crown that made him Holy Roman
Emperor set resolutely to the task of regaining what was
counted historically German land. In fierce battles he
drove the Magyars back. His successors, Otto the Second
and Henry the Third, continued this task, pushing the in-
truders through the wild mountain forests.

As the territory was reconquered it was given into the
keeping of nobles, bishops, and abbots, who were pledged
to defend it. The landlords brought in serfs, mostly Bavarians. Fields were cleared, seed planted, cattle pastured,
churches, monasteries, castles, and villages built.

But the proud spirit of the Magyars did not break.
Again and again they stubbornly counter-attacked. The
peace of German settlers was menaced, and civilization
could not advance. Then in the eleventh century, when
German authority had reached a halt at Pöchlarn, on the
Danube, the management of *Ostmark* was given to Leopold
of Babenberg. Generation by generation, with relentless
vigor, the Babenberg Margraves forced the foe down the
river and held what they had conquered. They had their
castle at Pöchlarn, at Melk, then at Tulln. Finally they
stood in command of the last spur of the Alps and over-

looked the Hungarian plain. Christening the cliff Leopoldsberg, they built a mighty stronghold.

The rear guard of nobles, abbots, and serfs had advanced closely behind the conquerors. Sword and plough and prayer book had made this a German land. All the way back to Bavaria it was German. Thus was Charlemagne's *Ostmark* reëstablished.

Eight hundred feet below the Leopoldsberg the Danube, hurrying to the far-off Black Sea with water from the Alpine snows, swings round the mountain spur at a sharp angle, and the tiny river Wien, running out to join it, completes there a triangular cove. In this strategic place, walled on the north and west by steep wooded hills, bounded on the south by the Wien, and protected from the east by marshes and the mighty Danube, Celts had a settlement nineteen centuries ago which they called Vindomina.

The Romans drove the Celts away, to establish a military camp known as Vindobona. Vindobona grew to be a municipium, and was queen of a line of fortified Roman posts connecting the Danube with the Rhine. Marcus Aurelius died there in 180 A.D.

Time flowed on as steadily as the river. The Romans passed. The Avars had possession. Charlemagne came; then the Magyars. Finally the Babenbergs chose this site, guarded by the Leopoldsberg, as their permanent capital. Drawing revenues from a domain that extended to include Styria and Carniola and reached to the shores of the Adriatic, they began the building of the beautiful city we know as Vienna, and the Germans as Wien.

Frederick Barbarossa, when Holy Roman Emperor,

raised *Ostmark* to the dignity of a duchy. He bestowed upon the duke privileges almost equal to the rights of an independent German prince. Then was the name changed to *Österreich*, or Eastern Realm. The capital of this outpost of German civilization soon had a reputation as a place of pleasant living. The poetry of chivalry developed here earlier than in other German provinces. Walther von der Vogelweide was its shining star. Here the *Nibelungenlied* took its final form. The culture in the little walled city of Wien gave satisfaction to Germans far beyond the borders of the duchy.

The Babenberg line became extinct. The keeping of their domain passed to Ottocar, King of Bohemia, a wealthy, vigorous Czech of the Přemyslide dynasty. Our informant said that he did not think history exactly clear on how this happened, but one account is that spokesmen for the duchy asked the King of Bohemia for protection when left without a ruler. Ottocar built in Vienna a cathedral to Saint Stephen.

The duchy was under Ottocar's protection for twenty-six years. The office of Holy Roman Emperor was not hereditary, and it had come to be a position to which eligible princes were elected by vote of a college of seven electors, three of whom were ecclesiastics and four laymen. There was much jealousy about the appointment. No strong prince wanted a strong rival to get the Holy Roman Crown. So it happened that it was given to Rudolf of Hapsburg, a minor nobleman from the Swiss Aargau. Those who elected him did not judge him ambitious. But when elected he immediately coveted strategic Vienna for his capital, and wanted the former Babenberg lands to make up for the fact that he had practically no land of his own. He found opportunity to cause a war against Ottocar, who, as the rich and mighty King of Bohemia, had many enemies. In the encounter on the Marchfeld before the city of Vienna, Rudolf killed Ottocar.

Dante in his *Divina Commedia* writes of these two as seen in the Valley of Kings in Purgatory: "He who sits in a higher place and looks as if he had left undone what he should have done, and who moves not his lips to the others' song, was Rudolf the Emperor who could have healed the wounds that are the death to Italy. . . . The other, who seems to be consoling him, ruled over the land where the waters rise which the Moldau carries to the Elbe, and the Elbe to the sea. He bore the name of Ottocar."

From history it would seem that Rudolf of Hapsburg, when he had power as Holy Roman Emperor, was too busy establishing his own family to give attention to the needs of Italy. The other German princes permitted him to have the Babenberg properties, but forbade his taking possession of the Kingdom of Bohemia. Bohemia belonged to Ottocar's son. The sixty-year-old Rudolf moved his family to Vienna. Before he died he had contrived that every secular electoral German prince, and the son of Ottocar, whom he had slain, were his sons-in-law.

"He must have had a lot of daughters!" I exclaimed.

"He did. All the Hapsburgs were prolific."

Rudolf laid the foundation of Hapsburg greatness. He started on their long career that famous family whose policy was consistently that of preference for acquirement of land by marriage rather than by battle; who demanded of their subjects revenues, adherence to the Catholic faith, and loyalty to themselves; who left their peoples free to follow their native customs, and stood for centuries as a bulwark against the advance of Magyar, Slav, and Turk into western Europe. From 1278 to 1918, Vienna was their capital.

While the men talked about the Hapsburgs, my fancy took flight to the towers and roofs on the cove below the Leopoldsberg. Long ago my imagination had made this the loveliest city in the world. It was the only city in Europe that I had ever desired to visit. Out of tales told me when I was very young I had built my Vienna. On a November afternoon I stood at the door to the city of my dreams.

XII

VIENNESE INTERLUDE

We lived in Vienna from November 1936 until June 1937. Shortly after our arrival we went to call on Madame S., who had been a star at the opera when Gustav Mahler was Director, and she asked if we had found a place in which to live. I had been looking, but I had not yet been offered one with a good music room.

There were several people in her studio. When we had answered as to what we planned to pay, they all discussed the possibilities. A young musician went to the telephone. He returned to say that he had made an appointment for me to look at an apartment on the Jacquingasse next morning at ten o'clock.

When I saw the apartment I knew at once that we should be well situated if we had it. It belonged to an attractive woman who had lived here seventeen years. Loving hands had made a home of these rooms. They held happiness as well as good furniture. She had come in as a bride. Her son and daughter had been born here. She told me that her family had long been Catholic, but because they had Jewish blood they would be destroyed if the Nazis came.

Her father-in-law had concluded that the Dritte Reich would acquire Austria. He had spoken, and his kin were obedient. They loved Vienna. They were Catholic. Yet they were leaving. Arrangements for their exodus had been made. What could not be taken away with them was to be quietly sacrificed. Her husband was already in Bucharest; she must follow him. She was sending the fair daughter, who sat beside her, to England for a little while. The boy had already been settled in a boarding school. She could not bear to break up their home. "We are Viennese, and Vienna is the only place in the world to the Viennese."

It was not right that we should have this woman's home. Circumstances which should not occur in a civilized society forced her to beg me to take it. She wanted to leave it just as it was, so that they could all come home when the scare was over. We took over her lease and her cook. She left her wedding silver and other treasures of sentiment, which I did not like to use, packed away in a room we did not need.

She thought the moving a folly, for she was certain that the Great Powers would not surrender Austria to the Dritte Reich. She believed that the democracies treasure civilization. The world now knew how barbarism held all Germany in thrall. If the Nazis got Austria, it would be but a step to control of Czechoslovakia. Then the whole of Central Europe would be within their easy grasp. That would give them dominance over Europe. The leadership of England and France would be in eclipse. A dark age for European civilization would have begun.

But it could not happen. England and France had clever statesmen. They would not let it happen. Italy would continue to aid in preventing this. Italy had acted promptly when the Nazis murdered Chancellor Dollfuss on July 25, 1934. Italy's dictator was not barbaric. He could be trusted. Thus she spoke her thought.

I had lived too long in China to have the faith she had in the Great Powers. But in Germany I had for the first time come in contact with the Catholic Church. I had been charmed by the beauty of the church services. I was puzzled as to why Catholics did not make a sanctuary within their church for their members whom the Nazis persecuted. Now I had met a Catholic who came of Jewish people, and she seemingly did not expect protection from her church.

I asked her if the Catholic Church in Austria permitted the destruction of its members who had Jewish blood. She said that the Pope was against the Nazis. He recognized them as anti-Christ despite their profession of support from God. But she had no hope of shelter from her church, if there was need for shelter. "The Nazis might destroy the church if we were hidden away inside," she said simply, and added, "None of us would want to cause the church to be destroyed."

On December 8, when we had lived in her apartment just a month, I happened to see an article in a newspaper stating that Monsignor Waitz, Prince-Bishop of Salzburg, had issued a declaration that nothing had changed since three years ago when the Austrian Bishops denounced National Socialism; and that Monsignor Gföllner, Bishop of Linz, had ordered all priests in his diocese to read a declaration from their pulpits repudiating the idea that any change had come in the attitude of the Church toward National Socialism.

The account emphasized the fact that the episcopal manifesto of December 1933 was still the opinion of the Church. It reminded readers that the manifesto strongly condemned the methods which National Socialism was then using to obtain control of Austria, with particular reference to political murder, and uncompromisingly rejected National Socialism, especially condemning four of its main characteristics — racial hatred, anti-Semitism, aggressive nationalism, and tendencies toward the establishment of a religion based on nationalism.

I cut this out and sent it to Bucharest. I thought it might give the refugee a reasonable hope of an early return to Vienna.

At Vienna we found a vast company of German men and women who had fled from other German lands. They had come from Munich, from Dresden, from Düsseldorf, from Hamburg, from Berlin. There was not a state of the old German Confederation which did not have its representative in Wien, the German city on the Danube.

German Jew and German "Aryan" had brought their talents here. Toscanini, that brilliant advocate of humanity in the arts and in living, was here, as were a galaxy of lesser men and women from all over the world. They were an unpremeditated company celebrating a festival of German music to which no invitations had been sent.

Until the deluge swept them away, tossing more than one into a Nazi concentration camp, they maintained in a German land the *Freiheit* tradition in German music. Vienna was their capital, Salzburg their summering place.

The musicians whom I met at Vienna believed that if

civilization is to live, the arts must be free and creation must be encouraged. They listened eagerly to new compositions, or new interpretations of the classics. The *Komistenbund* arranged chamber concerts at which the young had an opportunity to perform before an audience. Oswald Kabasta, first conductor of the Vienna Broadcasting Company, was tireless in his efforts to further musical talent. Although appearing two and three nights a week at the director's desk at the Opera, Bruno Walter had leisure to rehearse at the piano with singers, and was ever on the search for fresh voices.

The Opera was the centre of musical interest — one might say the centre of Vienna life. Night after night the great building at the end of the Kärntnerstrasse was crowded from the stalls to the highest gallery. The state supported the Opera. Tickets were cheap enough for all but the poorest, and even they could get gift seats. I shall never forget a hungry man to whom I had given food in our kitchen. I asked him if he would have another cup of coffee. He answered, "No, thank you very much, but I should like a *Säulenplatz* to hear Knappertsbusch conduct *Elektra*." In Vienna a *Säulenplatz*, a place behind a pillar from which one could hear but not see, was half price.

A host of performances that lifted opera to the mountain peaks crowd my memory. *Fidelio, Don Carlos, Die Meistersinger von Nürnberg, Margarethe*, and *Der Rosenkavalier* are among them. Knappertsbusch, formerly of the Munich Opera, and Bruno Walter, were the regular conductors; but they gave place at the director's desk to others of the galaxy of star musicians gathered at Vienna. Wilhelm Kienzl's eightieth birthday was celebrated by the

Schubert belonged to the Friends of Music, and gave his only public concert in their hall. After his death it was a fellow member, Joseph Herbeck, who discovered the "Unfinished Symphony." The original manuscript of this work, and six other Schubert symphonies, were preserved in the society's library. In 1838, when Robert Schumann came to Vienna, he so greatly admired the manuscripts and publications collected by the Friends of Music that he wrote the librarian a letter urgently asking permission to revisit this wonderful collection.

Mendelssohn was to have given a gala performance of his *Elijah* in the society's hall on November 14, 1847, but was prevented by death. Johannes Brahms was conductor of the society for many years, and bequeathed to them his entire collection of music. His example was followed by his friend Johann Strauss. When we were in Vienna, the librarian of the Friends of Music treasured manuscripts and relics of almost all the great German composers from the baroque period up to our own time. They had a library of about 12,000 books on the history of music, and a collection of about a million pieces of published music. This music not only was used for the society's own concerts, but was also lent to other societies and individuals.

The Friends of Music had their own *Singverein*, an amateur choir of high artistic standard which was started in 1858; also a music school of which Hugo Wolf, Gustav Mahler, Joseph Joachim, Hans Richter, and Arthur Nikisch were pupils. Anton Bruckner was one of the teachers. The aim of the *Gesellschaft der Musikfreunde* from the day of its foundation was to make music on a grand scale. The friends of music, gathered in Vienna from every German land, made every concert while we were there an event. The Philharmonic Orchestra gave us beautiful music. The "Musica Viva" and "Ravag" are not forgotten. There was so much that is memorable that twenty volumes would be needed to tell about it adequately. The concerts that return most often to my mind are the following: "Missa Solennis," conducted by Toscanini; a performance of a symphonic poem, "Penthesilea," written by Hugo Wolf when he was twenty-three, given by the *Gesellschaft der Musikfreunde* under the baton of Kabasta; the Philharmonic, led by Klemperer, first violinist Herr Rosé playing Bruckner's Fifth Symphony; and that triumph of Walter and orchestra with Gustav Mahler's magnificent composition beginning with a funeral march and ending with a joyous rondo.

In Vienna I heard such music as I had never heard before, and can never hope to hear again. This was the music at the German sunset of that day of European civilization which was called at its dawn "the Renaissance"; was known at its high noon as "the age of reason"; and moved to its twilight through "the liberal experiment." Night had fallen on Germany when we arrived there. We reached Austria while the sun was yet coloring the clouds with brilliant light.

In music, in architecture, and in the spirit of the people living there, Vienna fulfilled my dreams.

Turning into a narrow way in the hope that this was a short cut on a housekeeping errand, I read *Himmelpfort-gasse*, "Gate of Heaven," on the street sign, and saw amid squalid tenements a most lovely palace. On asking, I learned that it had been built more than two hundred years ago for Prince Eugene of Savoy, distinguished for assistance given to Vienna against the Turk, and that it now housed the Ministry of Finance. I had a thrill of pleasure in this. It seemed right for a little state bravely struggling with economics to have placed its Ministry of Finance at the Gate of Heaven.

When my domestic affairs were running smoothly, and I had leisure, the first building I sought out was the cathedral that Ottocar the Czech raised at Vienna to Saint Stephen and the glory of God. Built without concern for superficial appearance, the *Stefansdom* is the church of the people of Vienna. It stands at ease in the very centre of the city, in no way withdrawn from the life of the streets, friendly, humane, cheerfully unpretentious.

Kings were crowned at the *Augustinerkirche*, and were usually buried in the *Kapuzinerkirche;* but there were few who between their crowning and their dying ignored Saint Stephen's. Many gave the cathedral rich gifts. Weddings and christenings, aristocratic and proletarian, were held here; festivals were colorfully celebrated, and here people gathered in times of sore distress.

The cathedral has a grand west front, with a magnificent Giant Door and two nice round Heathen Towers; a nave lifted heavenward on soaring arches, and a south tower reaching to the sky with a tall and slender spire; a stubby north tower held down to this good earth by crowning with a substantial cupola; a steeply sloping roof surfaced with bright tiles, highly glazed, laid in a clear herringbone pattern varied over the choir by the emblem of the double-headed eagle; and many smaller pieces in between these outstanding gifts to God. There is no unity of design.

In Mongolia, prayer mounds are built by each passer-by's putting on a stone as his thanksgiving for safety thus far along the road. The *Stefansdom* has been raised in the same way. It is a heap of gifts to God. Each generation has made its offering in the fashion of the time — Romanesque, Gothic, baroque, and nineteenth century. Each piece is beautiful.

A piercing east wind was blowing in on Vienna when I first visited the *Stefansdom*. In the lee of the south and west walls, cabmen dozed, each man's horse carefully wrapped in his driver's only blanket; and peddlers had a corner where they sold children's toys. As I pushed open the Giant Door a glorious organ pealed out its message in the music of Schubert.

Eighteen huge stone pillars held up the vaulted ceiling, baroque chapels gleamed on either side, and far up the dark avenue a candled altar glowed. When the music was over I walked about with a friendly woman who had stood beside me. Of the cathedral's many treasures she showed me those she liked best — the "Servants' Madonna," a lovely figure; a sandstone pulpit carved by Anton Pilgram of Brunn; and the pulpit from which, in 1451, Saint John of Capistrano preached a warning against the barbarism of the Turk.

On the Jacquingasse we were conveniently situated for the enjoyment of Vienna's architecture. Our front windows looked to the charming villa which the city gave to Richard Strauss some years ago in gratitude for his talent. We could pass the *Karlskirche* every time we went to the

Palast where our friend Madame S. lived. Twenty minutes' walking took us to the Ring.

We had but to go up our short street, turn right on to the Gürtel by the handsome residence and well-kept garden of a Polish nobleman, past the modest building where Dr. Kurt von Schuschnigg, Chancellor of Austria, lived and worked, and a little way on we stood before the lacy iron gates of the Belvedere. The Belvedere is the loveliest palace that I have ever seen in any land. It is a real palace, not a fortressed castle or an inflated mansion. From dawn until dark the gates are ajar. Anyone who wishes may go in.

Through these gates one enters a small, self-contained world of fantasy. Imposing yet unpompous, the palace is mirrored in a shallow circular lake, its fairy lightness enhanced by the sheen of the water. Seen from every angle, the Belvedere has a dreamlike quality, as if its three central blocks, each with a different roof height, flanked by wings and then by pavilions, had been dusted with alchemy. Yet so perfectly are fantasy and practicality combined that it is apparent at a glance that this would be a comfortable place in which to live. The façade away from the entrance is perhaps the finer side. From here the walled garden slopes to the Rennweg in gentle terraces ornamented with marble steps, baroque statuary, lawns, shrubs, and fountains.

Gray curtains were kept drawn at the windows. The Belvedere was uninhabited except by wild ducks who lived on the lake, rearing there in spring a charming brood. Lucas von Hildebrandt created the palace and designed its garden for Prince Eugene, who had his winter palace at the

"Gate of Heaven." At his death it was bought by the Hapsburgs. The last of them to live here was Archduke Franz Ferdinand, whose assassination at Sarajevo started the war of 1914.

The Belvedere has its own secret world. From this exquisite place the shining hills seem so close that one could almost reach out and touch them. Yet they are beyond the cross of gold on the *Karlskirche*, the Gothic spire of Saint Stephen's, and the roofs of Vienna half hidden in the treetops. From the uppermost terrace one can glimpse on the left the park and palace of the Schwarzenbergs, and on the right the lovely Salesian Nunnery. Finished in 1720, the Belvedere is part of the joyousness which spread over Vienna when, after standing for nearly two centuries as a bulwark against the Turk, the city was relieved by the impassioned assistance of Sobieski, King of Poland, aided by brilliant leaders from Germany and Savoy.

In Vienna, for the first time in my life, it was things built by human hands that gave me steadiness. Always before, when harassed, I had clung to nature. Perhaps it was because there is such satisfaction with life on earth expressed in Vienna's buildings. Also, it is impossible to be in this place and miss realization of how much that is lovely has been put up in thanksgiving for survival through eras of terrible suffering.

Like others here, I was bound to Germany by close ties. We felt impelled to listen to the radio. And the Nazis in power over there issued a continuous spate of decrees, putting out one by one the few remaining candles of freedom.

One edict declared the Hitler Youth, formerly a Nazi

Party organization, to be henceforth a state institution.   No boy in Germany, or in any of the lands over which the Dritte Reich might extend, would be able any longer to escape.   No parent could protect a child.   All would be ruthlessly drilled on the Nazi Primer.

Austrians reminded me, in case the fact had escaped my notice in reading European history, that the Spahis and the Janissaries of the Turks were Christian children taken as tribute.   Through long years the Turks demanded, and by menace secured, tribute of children from Christian lands. Trained in a passionate loyalty to the Turk, reënforced by a blind and fanatical adherence to Islam, they were the most formidable force the Turk possessed.   After passing through their Turkish education, these sons of Christians remembered nothing but what they had been taught in the Turkish drill.   Spahis and Janissaries retaken by their own parents had no will but the fanatical desire to return to their Turkish masters.

Another Nazi edict proclaimed as German law during this winter was the following: "A German citizen who, knowingly or unscrupulously from motives of gross self-interest or other motives, removes or leaves property abroad, thereby causing gross injury to the German economic system, will be punished by death.   His property will be confiscated.   The criminal is also punishable if the crime is perpetrated abroad.   The competent Court for the offense will be the People's Court.   The law hereby promulgated comes into force immediately."

A friend was listening at the radio beside me and exclaimed, "By such measures do the Nazis acquire control of more and yet more money with which to substantiate their power! When all property is brought home and registered they can seize it at their leisure. The People's Court is a Nazi creation which has no connection with the people except for use to punish them."

On such days it gave me comfort to walk by the *Karlskirche*. The serene green dome, the twin belfry towers, and the strong Trojan pillars spoke to me reassuringly out of time. Built as a votive offering for Vienna's survival through the Black Plague, this church was designed by Fischer von Erlach and is a triumph of mind over matter. To pass when troubled was to hear a chorus of angel voices sing a glorious hymn: "Have faith. Have faith whatever befall. It is but a plague. It will pass. It is but a plague."

In Vienna many voices spoke from the past. What was now the *Hohe Markt*, or High Market, was once the Roman Prætorium. Saint Peter's, standing splendidly in a little *Platz* off the Graben, although brilliantly dressed in baroque with an oval-shaped dome, was there in plainer garb long ago. The sturdy, sombre, ugly, yet strangely lovable *Minoritenkirche* reminded me each time I happened by that Viennese are not so foolish or so gay as the casual observer might suppose, and made me feel that Austria has in her stout heart strength to endure, even through a Nazi conquest.

The poor here lived in squalor more picturesque than sanitary. Their homes were crowded round every available courtyard, filled alleys and lanes, and pressed in tightly between beautiful churches and tall palaces. They had no air in their low-ceilinged rooms. They lived in a fusty smell of *Gulasch* and stale smoke, slept in a feather bed covered by a thick feather quilt if possible, and kept their windows sealed up from October until May.

Yet, despite the miserable housing of her populace, Vienna was saved from the areas of utter misery found in some cities by a habit observed throughout her history. The rich and the poor lived side by side; and the city had innumerable green squares, tree-laned avenues, and wooded parks used by everyone. The Wienerwald was kept a place of groves, orchards, and vineyards close enough to Vienna for excursions there on Sundays and feast days; and where the plain stretched away to the east, on the other side of the city, there was the Prater, a preserve of many acres with the Danube flowing by.

Since the war, the Social Democrats of Vienna had shown other Viennese what could be done about squalor. Two blocks of workingmen's flats in which families lived cleanly stood as models, even though riddled by bullets in an hour of civic strife, which I heard regretted on every side.

Light and airy schoolrooms, and fine swimming baths for the general public's use, were proof that the Austrians did not need to be taught twentieth-century building by their German cousins.

In the nineteenth century the Viennese made the Ringstrasse in one great gesture of creation. It is a triple line of roadways laned by wide-branched lindens, forming a horseshoe arc from the Danube Canal to the Danube Canal. The Ring occupies the place where the city's last wall stood. "The need for encircling walls is now over and we can live!" So it proclaims. Along the two sides of this triumphal way are buildings in Grecian, Renaissance, and Gothic styles adapted to nineteenth-century use; fine hotels; coffeehouses with upholstered seats from which the occupants can look out through the plate-glass windows; some residences; and a general air of spaciousness given by frequent parks and gardens with trees, lilacs, roses, flower-beds, statuary, and fountains.

The Opera House, in French-Renaissance style; the Burg theatre, a place where one could hear the purest High German in Europe used in the acting of great dramas; the white marble Parliament; the University; the enormous Town Hall, set well back in its own park; a church with spires of fretwork stone erected by Kaiser Franz Josef in gratitude for escape from assassination; the twin museums of art and history, facing each other across a stretch of lawn where Maria Theresa, a great queen hugely commemorated in stone, sits surrounded by small images of her admirals and generals; and a wing of the Hofburg, Imperial Castle of the Hapsburgs — all these are on the Ring.

The Hofburg was the winter and summer residence of the Hapsburgs until they built the Schönbrunn in a great park far out of town. It is a rambling building, enlarged again and again through seven hundred years. The nineteenth-century wing, an extension to reach the Ring, is surrounded by a *Heldenplatz*, or Heroes' Place, where a colorful ceremony of changing the guard was held each morning. Bronze eagles with spread pinions are outlined against the sky from every cornice. Its many parts include a lovely library and a Spanish Riding School. The riding school is a baroque hall where specially bred caprioling horses of purest white, with small heads, arched necks, nimble feet, and flowing tails, performed daily feats of infinite daintiness and grace.

Scattered throughout Vienna are the palaces of arch-dukes and princes, for whom artists built homes of beauty in eras of peace; and at every turn an arresting arch, a sculptured door, or yet another beautiful church — perhaps such a one as the *Michaelerkirche*, with its charming eighteenth-century front, or *Maria am Gestade*, holding up a lantern of great loveliness.

In Vienna, stern German feeling seemed everywhere softened by southern influences, and enriched by the warmth of the Slav. The sky was ever near. From nearly every street one got glimpses of the friendly hills. The city has a few Gothic spires, but not many. There is sublime beauty in the Gothic aspiration to reach heaven, but those who crane upward too ardently are prone to crush flowers beneath their heedless feet. A place with too many Gothic spires and Gothic people can be bigoted, inhumane, hysterical. I found the Viennese and other Austrians tolerant and liberal in architecture and in daily living.

Those who lived here had their dire problems. Vienna was the abandoned capital of a broken empire, the home of more than two million people suddenly cut off from former revenues, and not yet adjusted economically to the circumstance of the present. None denied that too frequently, since 1918, native strength had been wasted in foolish civic strife.

From November until spring I saw a cruel wind drive in from the east, and poverty stalk these beautiful streets. Beggars held out beseeching hands as in the streets of Peking. One could not walk twenty yards along the

Ringstrasse without being stopped and asked for alms. "The beggars are a Guild. Don't give to them. They really are quite well off," some people said, but I had to give to all lest I miss one in need. I can't bear to be fed when another is hungry. I noticed that the Viennese who had money gave and gave.

Beggars rang our house doorbell. Shaky, white-faced old men, humpbacked children, desperate women, stood there. "Don't give so steadily. They make a track to your door," I was advised. But I had to give food, clothing, and once a warmer blanket for a woman to wrap her baby in. We had to keep quarts of milk, and a pot of coffee ready on the stove, for those who were too starved to begin with solid food. Others gave in the same way.

One who had cautioned me against giving too much came one day to say: "I'm sorry I told you not to give so much. Last night I said no to a woman. This morning we found her dead of cold and starvation on our door-step."

The Catholic church across the street from us, just above Richard Strauss's house, gave charity every morning. It was impossible not to see the long, tragic queue that stood there waiting. On the way to town, down the Jacquin-gasse, at the last street before the Rennweg, there was a house at which the poor were given soup at noon. They brought their own basins, usually old cocoa tins, and when they had been served they sat on the curb, or on the steps of neighboring houses, to eat. They warmed their hands round the tins that held their steaming food.

Just off the Gürtel, behind the South Station, there was a place called *Obdachlosenasyl,* where four thousand men and women were given shelter every night. Those who stayed there had tickets. They had to undergo a medical examination once a week to guard against infecting the place with anything contagious, or spreading lice. I heard that there were several of these places in Vienna. They gave supper and breakfast. The sleepers had to leave at seven o'clock. During the day they sat on city benches, or got shelter where they could.

There were many places that gave free hot dinners at midday. The best were those of the *Elizabethtisch*. These were given by society women in memory of the Empress Elizabeth, who had in the nineteenth century tried to get help given to the poor. The cooking here was excellent. And there was the *Joseftisch*, a society not so wealthy, which also gave hot dinners in various parts of the city. The English and American Quakers gave relief from a bureau that has been helping ever since the defeat.

Thrust down into the fraternity of distress were many of the old aristocracy, and thousands of intellectual pro-letarians — people with faces wrinkled before their time, knees slightly bent, thin hands that trembled.

Long ago a wise woman in Philadelphia pointed out to me that the number of women soliciting for a livelihood is a barometer, not of a city's morals, but of its economic situation. On the Kärntnerstrasse one could count more in half an hour than I have ever seen in any other city in a like time. They were nearly all young. They had made themselves as lovely as they could.

Vienna had an excellent system of social services, but the city's means were not equal to the need. Before the Great War a good start had been made to help the aged, the sick, and the unemployed. Since the war, the Social Democrats of the city had made intelligent progress toward a solution of poverty; but unfortunately much that they had started had been ruined in a stupid political quarrel. Chancellor Dollfuss, unwisely listening to the advice of Mussolini, on whom he depended for support of an independent Austria, had let the Social Democrats be destroyed; and their work on economic problems, well begun, had been left unfinished.

Numerous private charities supplemented the state services. I did not meet a single Viennese who was calloused to poverty. It was the habit of those who were not well off themselves to share what they had with the poorer.

It was surprising how many charities were run by Jewish women, frequently entirely on their own money. I know three who gave every cent they had to small institutions, and toiled there from morning until night, often doing the most menial tasks after their charges were put to sleep. Orphanages especially belonged to them; one could get a needy child in without any question as to its blood. Neither the Jews nor the Gentiles I encountered in Vienna favored their own. It seemed to me that people there were neither Jew nor Gentile. They were Viennese.

Only occasionally did snowfall soften the bitterness of the winter. But these were not a whining poor. It seemed that nothing but the hand of death could extinguish their hope and cheer. Hunger did not silence their quick-witted humor, nor did the lack of a coat end their appreciation of the ridiculous.

Vienna had many political visitors. Among those who came were Count Ciano of Italy, several representatives from Herr Hitler, and Admiral Horthy of Hungary. Light-heartedly, with gay remarks, the poor who could arrange a decent appearance deserted their bread lines to work for the state whenever cheerers were needed to give each visitor a good welcome. For this service they got five shillings a day.

Since knowing these people, Mozart, always my favorite composer, speaks to me as never before. New vistas of understanding were opened for me; things that formerly escaped me in his music I now hear. Poverty has haunted Vienna through the centuries. Mozart lived here when this city was the capital of the greatest empire in Europe. He was recognized as of sufficient importance for the Court to take notice of him. He lived in dire material distress.

Kapellmeister of the *Stefansdom*, he ate the bitter bread of poverty. He died in December weather, and was buried in a pauper's grave, his coffin lost among the coffins of the poor. Yet he could enrich the world as few men have done.

Because I met the gallant poor of Vienna I can almost hear Mozart say, "Things have got nearly beyond bearing. I'll now retire into my own soul for a while and make some nice music for a comfort." He could put off the call of death until he had penciled the last note of a glorious Requiem, and, that done, take a gentle leave of life.

We lived under a dictatorship. They did not use the handsome Parliament on the Ring, a building in Greek style put up in the nineteenth century when parliamentary government was in fashion. This was explained in the following way.

"We have had to abandon parliamentary government because, instead of trying to make it work, we stupidly used every democratic device to sabotage it. It proved too high an intellectual concept for us, as it did for the Germans. We have fallen back to the most primitive form of government. That is government by mandate. We have loaded all our responsibilities on to the shoulders of one man. We call him Dictator. It would be more accurate to call him Burden-Bearer. We ought to be ashamed of ourselves. Many of us are. Given time, I think we shall get parliamentary government reëstablished. But just at present, with Naziism in Austria supported by the might of the Dritte Reich, it seems a good thing to have Parliament closed. A democracy is the form of government most open to seizure by those who have no use for liberty except as a license."

On February 14 the Chancellor, Herr von Schuschnigg, speaking at a meeting of officials of the Patriotic Front, expressed a firm and confident intention to continue the policy of Austrian independence, with a gradual trend towards a monarchist restoration.

After describing the slow but steady progress in Austria's economic and financial position, the Chancellor turned to foreign affairs. He did not stress the Berlin-Rome Axis, which loomed so large in those days in the words of Italian and German statesmen, but put great emphasis on Italian friendship for Austria and on the unconditional support which Austria, as the standard bearer of an ancient German civilization, could confidently expect from Italy. He declared that no Communist danger existed in Austria, showing thereby that he did not intend to join the anti-Bolshevik Front.

The Rome Protocol, and the Italo-Austro-Hungarian collaboration founded on it, the Chancellor indicated, remained the essential basis of the Austrians' foreign policy. While laying all possible emphasis on the unrestricted sovereignty of their state, he added, they felt themselves the most genuine kind of Germans, and the agreement of July 1936 with Germany thus filled them with satisfaction. Austrians had no differences with Czechoslovakia or Yugoslavia. They attached special importance to the cultivation of friendly relations with the Western Powers, England and France. The growing appreciation of, and interest for, Austrian problems which showed itself in England gave them especial pleasure.

On February 22 Baron von Neurath, the German Foreign Minister, arrived in Vienna. He was met at the station by Herr von Schuschnigg and Dr. Guido Schmidt, the Austrian Assistant Foreign Minister. Dr. Schmidt entertained him at lunch at the Grand Hotel, and that evening the Chancellor gave a banquet for him at the Belvedere Palace, which was opened, and decorated with palms and flowers for the occasion. Members of the present government, and several hundred of the old nobility, were asked to attend, and did.

Baron von Neurath was the first German Foreign Minister to visit Austria since the Nazis came into power. It was felt by many people we knew that Herr von Schuschnigg's recent speech had set a polite but firm limit to whatever Baron von Neurath wished to achieve here politically. They thought that the visit might be limited to cultural collaboration between the two German states.

I found von Schuschnigg's régime extremely tolerant in

contrast with what I had experienced with dictatorship in Germany. The Austrian Nazis turned out in force to welcome Baron von Neurath, cheering him jubilantly. The police, in deference to the day's distinguished visitor, had strict orders to bear with all their activity. The Nazis marched round the town with chorus cries of "Heil Hitler," and "One nation, one Reich." They sang *Deutschland über alles*, and the Nazi Storm Troopers' song. They were mostly young men and girls. Other young men and girls collected and marched through the streets shouting "Heil Schuschnigg" and singing Austrian national songs. The efficient Viennese police kept the two groups apart.

The Fatherland Front was the only political party officially recognized in Austria, but at no time did I encounter, or even hear of, any drastic efforts taken by von Schuschnigg's government to crush Nazis, Socialists, Communists, or anyone so long as he or she did no serious harm to another. I expressed surprise at this. A friend answered me that there was nothing strange in such tolerance, as the Fatherland Front should eventually spread out its wings to include all Austrians. It meant loyalty to Austria. Under loyalty to Austria there should be room for healthy diversity of political opinion. She assured me that, although a member of the government at the time the Social Democrats were slaughtered, von Schuschnigg had been appalled by this happening. She said he was intelligent, and every intelligent Austrian knew this act had a serious effect on Austrian morale, aside from the pity of it. Managing to have it happen was the shrewdest thing that could have been done by Austria's enemies. She despised Mussolini.

People in Vienna talked openly on every subject under the sun. Before I reached Germany, Nazi decrees for "the protection of state and people" had started the custom of elaborate preparation before discussion of anything political. In Vienna I never saw plasticine put in a key-hole, or a telephone detached. Servants came and went, and voices were not lowered against their hearing. No one ever rose when the last course had been served to put sofa pillows along the crack of a door. I never heard a warning whispered behind a hand, "Careful! Speak through a flower."

A German who was on home leave from China came to visit us at Vienna. In a restaurant the first time someone started commenting on the government, criticizing Chancellor von Schuschnigg for trying to negotiate with the Nazis, he sat there shaking like a leaf.

His explanation was, "My cousin has gone to a concentration camp for less than that."

Our Viennese friends quickly assured him that there was no need for apprehension here. They said, "We have a concentration camp, although we are ashamed to have it. It is a disgrace to have gone back on the old established system of arrest and trial. But as a temporary measure this seems necessary. Still, it isn't a measure taken to paralyze conversation. Nobody is put in except a person who throws bombs, sets fires, or behaves in some danger-ously unsocial way in the furtherance of some political philosophy."

They further explained that there were no floggings. No sadisms were practised. It was merely detention in a place safely separated from the rest of society. The detained was not worked as a government slave. He or she could have books to read and paper to write on. There was nothing to hinder the concentration camp inmate from producing another *Pilgrim's Progress*, or following the example of William Penn in composing *Some Fruits of Solitude* while in prison.

Hermann was beaming on them before they had done. "That is the sort of concentration camp Austrians would have." Then he sobered. "My cousin made his unwise remark in London and was reported from there."

"You are safe in Vienna," they told him. "We retain our freedom here. We criticize our government and the Dritte Reich whenever we feel like it."

He did not think this a safe policy. They retorted that safety is not a thing of first importance. I asked him how Germans were in China.

"Cautious. Mighty cautious," he answered.

He explained that Naziism was rampant among the Germans out there. A man couldn't hold a job if he wasn't a Nazi. His wife had to be Nazi. The children had to be Nazi. "You know how it is in small communities. Out East now, every time a person yawns some busybody reports it to Berlin, and it goes on the Gestapo docket." He thought that the reporters got something for their zeal, or perhaps had their reward in feeling patriotic. He told us that Herr A. had lost his job. *Ja*, they dismissed him from the school. The little ones must not be taught by a pacifist.

"I got a warning about three months ago for going to R.'s. I went there to play my violin as I always have. *Gott im Himmel*, where are we being led? Because I'm by chance born an 'Aryan,' and his grandmother was a Jewess, I'm not to go there any more. I'm not to play Beethoven with him. If I don't heed this warning, a better German than I am is to get my job." In the sentimental German way he was nearly in tears. "R. and I went out to China the first time on the same steamer. We were on home leave when the war started. We fought for the Fatherland in the same battalion. We survived. We went East again. We suffered that awful time when men who had been our friends would not shake a German hand. Germans could not ride or play tennis at the clubs with other nationals. R. and I had our music. We could play Beethoven together then. Now I must give up my friend or I lose my job."

"Will you give up your friend?"

"I can't live if I lose my job."

The faces of our Viennese friends registered scorn. Beneath their gayety is a hard core. Hermann went on speaking, expressing his amazement that there was any place in the world where Germans still dared to speak their minds on politics.

"We are Austrians here," Fritz reminded him.

"You are Austrian, but you are also German. You ought to be watching your tongues . . ."

One by one they drifted off. They did not go rudely or abruptly. Each had an excuse. Each said farewell. But soon there were no Viennese at the table. We were left alone with our German.

The economic situation pressed on my thought. An Austrian banker whom we came to know well felt that, while union with a large tariff-free area was sadly needed, any material gain that might be achieved by *Anschluss* with the Third Reich would be bought at too high a spiritual price. "Man does not live by bread alone," was his firm opinion.

He showed me with graphs and tables just what Austria was doing for herself economically. His drawings displayed a diminishing line of poverty, and the plans for the future sounded promising. They included a steady stimulation of the tourist trade, furtherance abroad of Austrian styles in dress, the promotion of arts-and-crafts goods for foreign sale, and innumerable things detailed through a sheaf of pages. Naziism he defined as emotionalized materialism, and hoped Austria would be spared Nazi conquest.

He said that the Nazi leaders of Germany had advised Austria to man and arm four corps. Germany, possessed of plenty of guns, but short in meat and butter, would provide the necessary aircraft and artillery in return for livestock and dairy products. Von Schuschnigg had refused to accept this offer with the answer that a peacetime army of that many men would mean an expenditure beyond the state's resources.

"Germany does not pay for things with money. Giving her our meat and butter in exchange for guns would not help our economic situation; but since then Germany has offered to allow German tourists to come here again; to pay film dues, patent fees, and authors' royalties long overdue; and to give us coal, coke, and other things we need in exchange for what they want. So a trade agreement which should be advantageous to both sides has been signed. Broad hints from German quarters of political conditions accompanied the opening of negotiations, but our Austrian officials have conducted the business on a strictly business basis."

During this year the German press and radio made much of the fact that Austria was a German state, close kin to the states of the Reich. Dr. Guido Schmidt, Austrian Assistant Foreign Minister, flew back and forth to Germany. He attended conferences at Berlin, and was invited to Berchtesgaden. He was lent General Göring's private aeroplane. After one of Dr. Schmidt's trips abroad it was broadcast that these meetings were "leading the entire German nation to new heights." Another time there was a report that the leaders of the Dritte Reich "found much still to be done in the psychological and moral sphere of our friendship." We were told that one of the reasons for this remark was that Herr von Schuschnigg absolutely refused to commit Austria to any anti-Semitic plan.

"The Nazis say that anti-Semitism is historic among Germans. So is walking on all fours," I was told.

Many people I met distrusted Dr. Schmidt, and censured the Chancellor for having him in his government. Many more were suspicious of the hospitable German Ambassador, Herr von Papen, who gave such nice musical parties.

By April it was known that since Baron von Neurath came to Vienna and found that all remonstrances fell on stony ground, pressure was being used in Rome to prompt Italian admonition. Soon the customary reaffirmation of Italy's vital interest in Austria's independence was absent from the Duce's official communiqué. Very soon Italy joined the Nazi campaign against Czechoslovakia, and, further, Austria was strongly advised to stand politically aloof from the "Versailles state." The Austrian Chancellor would not join this campaign. Instead he began, mildly, to cultivate Austrian relations with Prague.

Apprehensive Viennese continuously talked things over. Many said that they really had no cause for complaint. Nazi bomb throwing had stopped since von Schuschnigg came to office. Evidently he had the secret of arranging civic peace.

The people of Vienna spoke a language German yet not German. Viennese is German with the stiff endings broken off, the verbs put in where they fall easiest, harsh sounds softened, and the whole seasoned with a generous sprinkling of Romance words and phrases. It is used by everyone who belongs to Vienna, from dustman to archduke. All have melodious voices, and give expression a lilt and a swing, a drag and a drawl. Quick-witted, melancholy, gay, suddenly droll, the speech of the Viennese is a *lingua franca* as delicious as their coffee.

They talked of the possibilities of a Hapsburg return, and many longed for the color and ceremony this would bring. But Naziism was the subject most often on their tongues. Thought of it continuously bothered those I knew.

It was round a table in a park, when the lilacs were in bloom. Mina had said, "If we must go down under an inrush of the Northern hordes I for one will always be glad that we had as our last Chancellor a man of honor and principle. I am glad von Schuschnigg does not barter away our civilization piecemeal. Gentlemen are out of mode in world politics, but I am glad we have a gentleman as Chancellor; and it seems fitting that he should have musical talent and education far beyond those of the usual amateur."

Stephanie did not think it right to be lazing in a pleasant sunset. She felt that a determined crusade should be organized against Naziism. "It is a disease of the mind, a plague that will spread over Europe unless stopped," she said.

"Our Chancellor has inherited no easy job. He is doing better than any one of us might do in his place," Mina insisted.

"Bravely said," declared Fritz. "Our own wounds have to be healed before we can cure the world of Naziism. His mild policy is the medicine we need."

Then gradually, as happened with nearly every discussion to which I listened at Vienna, talk veered round to that ever-current question, "What is life? Why scourges, plagues, recurrent dark ages? And what makes mankind survive every peril, and rise after every fall to reach again for the splendor of the stars?"

Each time the Viennese answer was, "*Man weiss nicht* — no one knows."

One could overhear this pondering as to why men are on earth in the bread-line queues, in the cafés, during intervals at the opera, in one's own pantry, and in the salons of friends. Always there was the same conclusion: "*Man weiss nicht.*"

XIII

THE CZECHOSLOVAKIA OF MASARYK

WHILE we lived at Vienna, a mutual friend who had been in China took us to spend the Christmas holidays with people whose home is a castle on the river Morava. We left Vienna at three o'clock on the day before Christmas Eve. When we crossed the frontier into Czechoslovakia we came into the part called Moravia, a place of gentle hills, a storybook land of castles and villages, thriving towns and busy factories. The trees were frosted. There was skating on the ponds.

We passed happy-looking townspeople, and gayly costumed countryfolk. We were curious about the Czechs. We studied those we saw. We were satisfied by their appearance. It suited a people who could endure though crushed to the ground by might, take strength from the good earth in life as peasants, hide and cherish their books and their culture; and who, when fate freed them of their oppressors, would choose to establish a democracy in the ancient kingdom of their forefathers.

We went by well-tended fields, sleek horses, fat cows, and innumerable flocks of white geese who pleased me by snapping their yellow bills haughtily at motorcars that dared honk them a message to hurry off the road. At dusk we reached Hodonín, the birthplace of Masaryk.

It was dark when we came to the castle gates. We waited for clanking locks to be undone. We drove into a great courtyard. The wall that had opened was shut behind us. The castle enclosed us, a tower rising from each of its four corners.

We were shown to rooms where wood fires roared in tiled ovens. We got warm and changed. Just as I was about to pull a bell to ask where we should find our hostess, she arrived to greet us. She took us to a high room filled to the ceiling with books. There we met her husband and children, and relatives from Austria, Hungary, and Poland gathered for Christmas under this hospitable roof.

Early on the morning of Christmas Eve we went to a Catholic Mass. This was a day of prayer and fasting. Festivities began when the first star shone in the evening sky. The great salon had been closed. Now it was opened. We went in to find it illuminated by a candled tree that soared to the ceiling, and a crystal chandelier more beautiful than the celebrated chandelier at Schönbrunn.

This was a feudal Christmas. Castle and estate people joined in its celebration, as has always been the custom here. They were all Czech. They came to the tree gorgeously dressed in silk and satin of lovely colors, finely embroidered. The men and boys were as handsomely garbed as the girls and women. There was no servility in these people. I liked their quiet self-assurance.

The celebrations were opened by the children's going up to their parents and thanking them for love and care since last Christmas. The eldest, a son of fifteen, spoke first. He was followed by his brother and sister. This is an annual custom, but this Christmas the children added a surprise. They spoke their gratitude in German verse that they had composed. Then we had the presents.

Christmas Day was the day of a big dinner at noon, with visiting children and children of the family dining, in their best clothes, at table with adults. Festivities went on until the New Year had been welcomed. We had dancing in the evening, music, bridge, and visits to people in neighboring castles.

When wild lilies of the valley were in bloom across their estate, Count and Countess Y. asked us out again, and we had a lovely week of spring with them. By summer we were made to feel of the family. Our daughter came over from Pennsylvania, and we were with them from early June until late in September, our visit broken by two trips to Hamburg, and a week at Salzburg. The same relatives we had met at Christmas were there.

It was a time to remember all one's life — the lovely park with the Morava flowing through it, gayly garbed peasants singing as they made the hay, orchards heavy with apricots, an abundance of peaches and melons, roses, and every flower one could want, boating and swimming, long walks, conversation, music, picnics in forests where deer grazed in herds of hundreds spread out across glades as far as one could see, ghost stories told of castles we visited, and all round us peace and happiness.

We met people of the Hapsburg aristocracy who had taken oaths never to coöperate with the Czechoslovak state. We met others who had taken oaths to destroy it. The majority seemed content enough with their government, but gave no encouragement. Only occasionally did we encounter those who praised the republic and gave full coöperation. Yet none of these people welcomed the idea of union with Germany. Those who did not coöperate with the Czechoslovak state dreamed of a dynastic return, with the capital again at Vienna. They lived in a world that was gone.

In the summer of 1937 we went north the three times I have mentioned. We had introductions to castled people in Bohemia, Slovakia, and to a family in southern Silesia. So we came to know many non-Czech citizens of the state. In addition we had Czech contacts both because of my husband's interest in music and because of my China book, which had done well in its Czechish edition.

This democracy, formed of a union of the Crownlands of Bohemia with Slovakia and Ruthenia, was five hundred and eighty-four miles long, one hundred and seventy-four miles across at its widest place, and thirty at its narrowest. It was traversed by many roads, some of them macadamized highways built since the establishment of the republic, others dirt byways. All were kept in good condition. We found motoring comfortable right up to the boundaries of neighboring states.

Everywhere we went we chose a different road each way so as to get a comprehensive view of the country. We crossed and recrossed Moravia, southern Silesia, and Bohemia. We lost our hearts to Slovak folk music, and attended every possible festival. Ruthenia, called by the Germans "the Carpathian Ukraine," although south of Slovakia, was not far off. People we knew had the habit of shooting in the Carpathians from a hunting lodge they owned in Ruthenia.

The winter of 1937–1938 my husband studied music in

Dresden, about twenty-five miles from what was then the Bohemian border of Czechoslovakia. We took a furnished house where we frequently entertained friends from the republic, and from which we often went into Bohemia, sometimes only for lunch. We came to know well the part called now the Sudeten. We had three visits in Prague. Before we left middle Europe we felt that for foreigners we were fairly well acquainted with the Czechoslovak state.

In Ruthenia lived a people who had been poor and illiterate through centuries of Hungarian rule. From among them some had gone to the United States of America and enjoyed democratic government. They longed to give freedom to their people at home. When victory in the Great War fell to the Western democracies, the Ruthenes in America stirred their countrymen to break the fetters that held them to Hungary and form an independent state.

This they did. They claimed as their own a narrow strip of wild mountain, and plain enough for road and railway. It lay between Hungary and Poland, and reached down to touch Rumania — one of the Allied victors. Then, feeling unsafe alone, the Ruthenes asked to join the greater republic of Czechs and Slovaks. The Slovaks had also belonged to Hungary, and sponsored the Ruthenes as their little brothers.

Czechoslovakia had treated Ruthenia well. Little Ruthenia was too poor to build herself roads, hospitals, and schools. She was given them in abundance. Health services were opened. To relieve the Ruthenes of their pre-war dependence on moneylenders who filched from them with high interest, the parent democracy promoted coöperative societies at interest rates of 3 and 4 per cent per annum. All the land, apart from some state parks, was given to peasants. Schools in their own language were given to all who lived in Ruthenia. Their number was 459 Ruthenian, 110 Magyar, 61 German, 4 Rumanian, 4 Jewish, and one Gypsy. A well-patronized Teachers' Institute was founded at Užhorod. Under Czech and Slovak guidance the Ruthenes were being prepared for autonomy in their own state, and the performance of duties in the national Parliament.

The lovable Slovaks, less advanced intellectually than the Czechs, were coming on rapidly in republican learning. The Hungarians had denied them schools because they gave education sparingly to their subject races. Now they had enough schools for every child to attend, and schools for adults.

The heroes of the Czechs are scholars, not generals, and they aimed to produce students rather than soldiers. Learning was cramped by no narrow boundaries. They had freedom now for their children to study in Czechish; and while the language of the state was Czech all citizens had the opportunity to preserve their own language.

The Republic of Czechoslovakia was established in country that had been feudal right up to the end of the war. Nearly all the land was held by nobles, many of whom had thousands and thousands of acres worked by people called free who were actually very little freer than serfs. An uncomfortable part of the establishment of the democracy was a redistribution of land. Castled people were not entirely stripped, but they had to give up a percentage

to peasant ownership. In some instances this made bitter
feeling. In others, nobles felt that they did hold more
than was right, and gave up what they must without fric-
tion.

Czechs filled most of the government offices. This was
because there were not proportionately enough others who
could, and would. A growing literacy among Ruthenes
and Slovaks was helping to remedy this. The German
citizens of the state, and all the aristocracy, were literate
and able, but care had to be taken against the danger of
taking into civilian and military services those with intent
to wreck democracy as soon as possible. The state salaries
were very small, and the national budget thrifty.

The greatest thorn in the state was Egerland. In the
days when Georg von Schönerer represented Egerland in
the Parliament at Vienna, anti-Semitism and anti-Slavism
had been rampant there. Hotels had a sign "Czechs, Jews,
and dogs not admitted." Priests had been harassed and
beaten in the "Away from Rome" campaign. Egerland
was anti-democratic from the birth of the state, but would
not secede from Bohemia unless the Sudeten mountain
districts went to Germany with them. When I asked if it
would not have been better to have had the boundaries of
the state narrower, I was told by a German Social Democrat that the smaller and weaker the state the sooner it
would have been battered down. Leaving the Sudeten out
of the Republic of Czechoslovakia would have meant giving away the natural frontier of the Bohemian Crownlands. Then the democracy would have been open to
German military invasion from the outset.

So the beautiful town of Eger, with a virgin or saint at

every corner, was a sore trial to Czechoslovakia. Yet the
Egerland was treated with that trust and liberty which
must be given to all the parts of a republican democracy.

The Czechs did not struggle with contentious elements.
Tidy, thrifty, hard-working, and virtuous, the Czechs did
the work of supporting their democracy. In their leisure
they read. They have a passion for intellectual development. The number of books they published was amazing.
The bookshops offered and sold vast numbers of serious
books. They were a keen public for foreign books as
well as books from their own writers. The Czech range
in reading was wide, but predominantly realistic in the way
that the French are realistic. Although they must be ever
on guard to protect democracy, still they made of democracy a reality.

Conservatives and socialists formed a workable government coalition continuously, and even parties with theories
quite contrary to the tenets of republicanism were allowed
deputies in Parliament. Speech and the press were free.
The contents of *Die Zeit*, a paper published in Egerland,
were such that one could scarcely believe that even a
democracy would allow such statements. The passion for
democracy among them had a fervor akin to that of the
founders of the United States.

As we went in and out of Saxony and Bohemia, crossing
the frontier at various places, we saw evidence of military
activity on both sides. The Nazi arrangements were
concealed as much as possible, and if mentioned were
strenuously denied to consist of anything more than necessary new barracks, frontier improvements, and seasonable

manœuvres. Across the heights of the ancient Kingdom of Bohemia, the Republic of Czechoslovakia was laying a line of defense for democracy such as no other country has ever surpassed. Their preparations were open to discussion, and never denied.

The Nazi press and radio bombarded Czechoslovakia with relentless vigor, and no concern for truth.

"Lies and hate, murder and rape, attended the birth of the Czechoslovak state, and have never left it during its short life," so I read in the *Völkischer Beobachter*, doyen of Nazi newspapers, in October 1937. "The internal terror has driven tens of thousands of human beings into an early death, destroyed hundreds of thousands of existences, and condemned millions to hunger. . . . Prague had better learn that the days of German weakness are past."

They spread tales of Czechoslovakia as party to Soviet Russian military plans for a Genghis Khan assault on Germany and all Europe. They said that vast numbers of Bolsheviks were coming in. They made persistent allegations about Soviet aerodromes set up in Czechoslovakia. They reported civic unrest which did not exist, gave highly colored accounts of things that never occurred, and interspersed this disgusting campaign with broadcasts of the most beautiful Bohemian, Czechish, and Slovakian music. They poured money into the Sudeten, as into Austria; and called on Bohemian Germans with a subtle call of race.

The courage, dignity, and restraint of the people of Masaryk's republic in this time were such as to be worthy of the admiration of all civilized men. They were going through a period of economic distress, with a large body of unemployed, and the neighboring Reich was doing everything possible to excite unrest. I made a tour of work conditions in the Sudeten and in Saxony. There was dire distress in both places; but conditions were worse in the Saxon valleys.

Dr. Krofta, the Foreign Minister, reviewing the international situation at a meeting of the Committee for Foreign Affairs in the House of Parliament, said that in regard to Czechoslovakia's relations with Germany, recent negotiations on railway matters in the frontier districts, and a trade agreement which included the regulation of German tourist traffic in the Bohemian health resorts, had been concluded.

He reported that negotiations on both sides had proceeded in an amiable spirit, and that if it were not for the violent anti-Czech propaganda of the German press and wireless, relations would be still better. He had faith in Herr Hitler's repeated assurances that Germany wished to live in peace with her neighbors, and he hoped that the cessation of the anti-Czech campaign would lead to really friendly relations between the two countries.

We were with Germans in Saxony on Christmas Eve, 1937, when President Beneš broadcast: "Czechoslovakia is a democracy which has the mission to keep the flag of peace, freedom, and toleration flying in Europe."

He spoke in Czech. A German who had learned Czech for the single purpose of listening in on Czech broadcasts interpreted for the rest of us. There was not a dry eye in the room. Czechoslovakia gave citizenship to our greatest writer of the age, Herr Thomas Mann, when the Nazis rejected him — so these Germans who were our hosts were careful to explain to us. They looked on Czechoslovakia as a great state, and would rather have had Saxony added to Czechoslovakia than continue in the Third Reich.

Among Czechs with whom we talked there were people who were pacifist in the way that Quakers are pacifist. That is a pacifism which does not sit with idle hands, but is ardently active in making use of spirit against material might. This is akin to the thought of Mencius, who lived in what is called the "Era of Contending States" in Chinese history. He reached the conclusion that those who achieve a military victory have not really conquered. The opposition is merely resting because their strength has given out. None are conquered but those whose hearts have been won. Therefore it is quite futile to arm. Better, according to Mencius, let the conquerors come, and reserve one's own powers for use in civilizing them.

But the Czechs had been some centuries under the conqueror. It was only twenty years since the Allied victory had liberated them to form a state in middle Europe. Many thought that they should resist another conquest with armed might, and believed that France and England would assist them to preserve an area of democracy in middle Europe. They looked upon themselves as the keystone of the belief that men are individuals, with rights to liberty of conscience and freedom of action. They saw it as their duty to preserve democracy not only for themselves, but because, they reasoned, "if we fail, then the whole cause for which the Western democracies fought the Great War is lost. Democracy in Europe will be in twilight. We have to serve more than ourselves."

Among the people living on both sides of the boundary

whom I questioned, there was no will to war. Those whose homes were here were anxious about bombardments, and many prayed for a miracle to keep the nation from fighting.

It was a Hungarian noblewoman who told me the following things.

She is married to a man whose castle stands on the tableland where Moravia rises to meet Bohemia — not far from a place where Czechs kept their books during the centuries when it was forbidden to possess them. They had all sorts of hiding places, as the Chinese did in the eras when the books of Confucius, Mencius, Mo Ti, and others, were burned. In Czechoslovakia they put theirs in the hollowed legs of four-poster beds, in the walls, in the double linings of cupboards, and in well niches. Just here on this tableland they kept them behind rocks in a stony place in the forest. Generation after generation of Czechs gathered here in secret meeting to read and study.

My friend had the utmost admiration for the democracy of Czechoslovakia. "Czechoslovakia is a remarkable venture," she said. "Cool heads and brave hearts have dared establish in middle Europe liberties such as the people of France, England, America, and other Western democracies have long enjoyed. Against great odds a system of freedom for all has been maintained here for nearly twenty years. I doubt if any outsider can realize what a wonderful thing that is, or how marvelous it is that when they got liberty they did not crush those of the race that had oppressed them."

About fifteen million people resided within the boundaries of the republic. All had citizenship. Power rested in the people. Voting was obligatory. The ballot was secret, and each citizen was absolutely free to vote as he or she chose. The suffrage was truly universal, with no discrimination against any group. It was the duty of persons over twenty-one years of age to elect a Chamber of Deputies; and the task of all over twenty-six to elect a Senate. The Chamber of Deputies had three hundred members; the Senate one hundred and fifty. The two houses of Parliament meeting in joint session selected the President. His term of office was seven years. Assisted by a cabinet of ministers responsible to Parliament, the President governed the country.

Following this system, the state had enjoyed stability in the very centre of storm-tossed Europe. It was one of the few states to have been entirely free of Communist uprising and labor strikes. Handicapped at the start by a large body of citizens eager for democratic rights, who had never had the privilege of learning to read and write, and by many members who took full advantage of the benefits of their position yet gave no assistance to the establishment of the state, a republic had been achieved in which there were civic liberty, equal rights, and honorable justice.

My friend felt that the republic stood in a very dangerous position now that the Nazis, heirs to the pre-war Pan-Germans, were in power in Germany. She said that there were many Germans who had never conceded that the Great War had been lost. In proof of this she read to me from *Der Wahre Staat*, a book published at Jena shortly after peace had been declared, written by Professor Oth-

mar Spann, a social economist then at the University of
Vienna: —

I foresee a revival of the period of the mediæval German
emperors. Germany has come out of the World War the
largest and ablest of the continental powers, for the future of
France is merely that of another Spain. Europe has been
Balkanized right up through Prague and Warsaw. No one
but Germany can, in the long run, bring order out of this
chaos and quell the disturbances of the small nations of Eastern
Europe.

England is certain to support Germany in this work, for so
long as Germany is busy on the continent she will not aim at
sea power or oversea possessions. Indeed, it is only in eastern
Europe that Germany can find her true destiny. To-day
we understand clearly why Poland, Bohemia, Hungary, the
southern Slavs, and even Greece, were at one time German
fiefs. That is how it must be again.

Among Germans everywhere the teachings of Dr. Spann
and others like him found a following. They kept alive
the old Pan-German ideas. In the democracies of Germany, Austria, and Czechoslovakia their disciples went
busily about working against liberalism, pacifism, humanitarianism, "Americanism," Bolshevism, democracy, the falling birth rate, and the development of individual person-
alities. They wanted disciplined masses pledged to execution of the Pan-German dream.

In August 1920 several of these young men met in a
Pan-German conference at Salzburg. Herren Hitler and
Drexler were the Reich representatives. Herr Hitler went
away to get the aid of German industrialists and the coöperation of what was left of the German army.

In Bohemia young men dreamed enthusiastically of the

German mission. They believed that on Germans rested a duty to save the world. Their thought split into many ideologies. Among them were two named Rutha and Heinrich, pledged to the practical execution of Dr. Spann's ideas. Rutha realized that political power in Bohemia could be best achieved through the *Turnvereine*, or gymnastic associations, and he chose Konrad Henlein, then employed as a bank clerk in Reichenberg, to work through them. From then on Herr Henlein gave his full time to the job, which included trips to England to tell of wrongs the Germans suffered within Czechoslovakia. Herr Henlein did not apply for the government permit to take money out of Czechoslovakia for expenses for these trips. Yet he traveled first class, dressed well, and could entertain in London. In Czechoslovakia one heard it presumed that his expenses were paid by the Third Reich. But right up to the end Herr Henlein proclaimed loyalty to Czechoslovakia and that his mission was merely to get rights within the state for Germans who had been denied them. He wanted these "rights" for a party opposed to humanitarianism, liberalism, democracy, "Americanism," within a democratic state.

Until the spring and fall of 1938, a liberal dictatorship and a republican democracy, both unwilling to accept and practise the theories of Naziism, lay athwart the Pan-German path in middle Europe. The Nazis believe that they are a *Herrenvolk*, born to rule and guide others. Their rule and guidance now extend over all that wide and lovely part of the earth that we have called Austria and Czechoslovakia.

At the close of my Czechoslovakian experience, it was

my opinion that this part of *Mitteleuropa* was fortunate in its government. That is still my opinion. This republic was founded by civilized men who believed in the principles on which good democracies are founded. They lit a candle for civilization. Evil winds have blown it out. It was a true flame to the last flicker of its burning. In Austria people were vague. They theorized on life. They summed up thought in "No one knows" why things happen. But here people did know. Many Germans, loyal to democracy, were supporting it. It was a moderate government, and humanitarian. Certainly it was a "disciplined" democracy in that moderate precaution was exercised to guard against its possible destruction from within. Aside from its Czech significance it was a stronghold of German freedom, and furthermore the keystone of all European democracy.

In Sweden, France, England, and every part of Europe the twilight presses closely now. Yet I sincerely believe that men will rise, from somewhere on this earth, who have the strength to light such a flame of freedom as will dispel this night. Perhaps a remembered spark from the Masaryk candle will help get that flame alight.

The writing of this book and assuring the accuracy of the scenes have been as much the work of others as of myself. This chapter was sent to Czechoslovakia for criticism and correction. Read by one of my favorite friends, it has also been read by her son of seventeen, and he has had word sent me that it is not good enough to be called "The Czechoslovakia of Masaryk." Born to a castle and a title in the land which became a republic after the Great

War, he has sent from that castle statements I should have put in. These have been telegraphed to me in England, with no counting of expense, because he was anxious lest my book go to press without them. I have hastily sent them on to my publisher without trying to incorporate them in my own text, as he suggested: —

In the book of things Masaryk said to Karel Čapek you can read, "What we did not like to have done unto us we shall not do unto others," and they did not. After their defeat at White Mountain they were deprived of the right to be nobles in their own land and their property forfeit to the victors. Castles, office, privileges, and everything were taken from them and they earned their bread as peasants until after the French Revolution, when ideas came to Europe which made it necessary for a state that wanted to be called civilized to let them begin to come up a little. When the victory of democracy gave them freedom and power in 1918 they only took enough land from others to give peasants small farms and took no castles except for government offices. While Beneš was president his brother continued to farm with his own hands. Yet this land was originally theirs and they had lived in subjection three hundred years. What they did was to establish the thing for which their forefathers had fought and been defeated, that is, the right for every man to have spiritual and intellectual liberty, civic equality.

Czechs are not primitive people. They had a literary language at the end of the thirteenth century. King George of Podebrad, a Czech, in case the Nazis may have claimed him, too, when they were being so historical as to forget that Berlin was once the not-counted-much-use property of the Kings of Bohemia, had thought up the League of Nations and had it established in the fifteenth century, and the reason it did not work was the same reason as caused this last one's fall. The Christian rulers in the alliance were only named Christian. Long before it was customary for people to travel much Czechs went to learn at Strassburg, Basle, Geneva, Netherlands, and England until Charles Fourth founded Prague University, the oldest university in central Europe and not founded by Germans. They just left in a body when studying there they learned that they could not have more voice than all the others put together. Some Germans have admired the Czechs as I do and they include Goethe, Leibnitz, and Herder. About their culture, the Pope of the Reformation time was surprised to find that these lay folk could read and quote the Bible better than most priests, and that women and men could both do it. Defeated at White Mountain they conversed with their conquerors in French. The weakness of the Czechs is that they never learn that other people who are supposedly Christian are not Christian. When Christianity came to them from France, Germany, Italy, they supposed it was to be lived and that is what they have done. If you want to know what Masaryk and Beneš were you must imagine a living of Christianity. There is an ancient Czech warning addressed to the west of Europe which did no more good then than recently; it is, that we are your wall against the pagan nations, and if we succumb and our house be shattered then you will face a danger; but none cared any more than to-day. As long ago as the fifteenth century Czechs were considering if a Christian can use the fist, and Chelcický renounced force, even if used to do evil that good may come, and chose pacifism. Masaryk resorted to force to establish a democracy. We had democracy started here. Democracy is not ruling but a laboring to create a good life for all. Let alone we would have protected it; given fifty years we would have had a Garden of Eden in central Europe and those who have not seen central Europe may not realize what an accomplishment that would have been. This was not just a Czech republic; it was a republic of various people ready to sacrifice their property, comfort, and life for Masaryk's ideals and Herder's dream to fill the earth in one small place with true Christian love and keep before us the definition of a nobleman: which is, that a man is noble who lives nobly; he may be found in cottage or castle; there was no difference in nobility between the Czech Thomas of Stitný in his castle of the Middle Ages and Thomas Masaryk of Hodonín in his father's cottage.   From your loving

JOHANN

XIV

IN A BLOSSOMTIME

DURING our winter in Dresden, we had a comfortable house with plenty of room and the skiing was good on the Saxon hills, so I asked Otto and Rüdiger to come for a visit.

They arrived equipped to ski. As I have said, we were but twenty-five miles from what was then the Bohemian border of Czechoslovakia, and their desire was to combine sport with seeing as much as possible of conditions in the Sudeten. I asked if they had visas for Czechoslovakia.

"The visa is not the difficulty," explained Rüdiger. "It is money. As you know, one can take only ten marks out of the country. We have been trying to go over there for a long time. We have been refused *Devisen*. But if we are careful we can perhaps manage three days."

"We have brought chocolate and biscuits from home to help out with the food, and if you will fill our thermos bottles . . ." began Otto.

"That part is all right," I interrupted him. "I have American dollars which I am glad for you to have, but the skiing is just as good, if not better, on this side. Why do you want to go into the Sudeten?"

"Our purpose is not altruistic," confessed Rüdiger. "We're not going because we feel particularly sorry for

Germans there, and would carry them comforting assurance that they will soon be gathered into the Dritte Reich. Our desire is purely selfish."

"By a sagacious and persistent use of propaganda heaven itself can be presented to a people as hell, and, inversely, the most wretched existence as paradise," came from young Otto. "I am quoting from Adolf Hitler in *Mein Kampf*."

"What has that got to do with it?"

"Everything. Absolutely everything, and you ought to know why it has. One of your own Presidents gave the answer, *Tante Hühnchen*."

Since we gave these boys a lift on the road from Remagen to Bonn, I have become as fond of them as if they were my own nephews, and I think that they are fond of me. They had been ardent in efforts for my education, but their nickname for me is *Tante Hühnchen*, or "Aunt Chickabiddy" — scarcely respectful. They take delight in answering me in confusing ways.

"You shan't go," I threatened, "unless you are clear as to why."

"All right! I'll now quote Herr Abraham Lincoln" — Otto was enjoying himself. "You can fool all the people some of the time. You can fool some of the people all the time. But you cannot fool all the people all the time."

"I am sure you haven't got it quite accurate."

"It will serve," put in Rüdiger. "The point is that we have heard so much about the hellishness of democracy that we have to visit where it is. We do not want to do our investigating in a place like England or America — even if you decided to give us the trip. We want to talk to Germans who have experienced life in a democracy —

we want to speak about it in our own language — we want to observe how they live under it. We have read a book written by this chap Beneš — archscoundrel of our age, a villain outranking Anthony Eden in wickedness. And we have read more than one book by the evil genius who taught him, the terrible Masaryk."

"We know full well, *Hühnchen*, that in such reading we do a great wrong." Otto likes to talk. "If caught with any such book, or discovered harboring ideas such as they contain, we shall be immediately arrested and taken to a concentration camp for reëducation. And if we do not learn there we shall be put to death. But some of us in Germany to-day are becoming more cunning than foxes. Brought up as we are, — preached at constantly that we must be ready at a moment's notice to give our lives at a Führer's command, — well, some of us are acquiring a different attitude toward death than our parents have. Death is not to be feared, so we are repeatedly told."

"Our parents were born in *einer Blumenzeit*. They are babes-in-the-wood even now. We were born in a burned-over field, and are educated by tigers."

They would have talked all the morning if encouraged. I had housekeeping to do. I told them I would take them into Czechoslovakia by motorcar after lunch, and leave them with money enough to stay there two weeks, paying the people who put them up a proper amount. I would not countenance giving poor people who sheltered them as little as possible; and I expected them to eat properly, too, and not return to me half starved.

They had German money, and went to do some shopping. I thought they were right in wanting wind jackets, and Rüdiger's gloves were too thin. They were late to lunch. When they did come, Otto's sleeve was torn, and the knuckles of his right hand were bloody.

I have often wondered about walking on air. Otto was doing it. His hair stood up, electrified. His face — no words of mine can describe it. Sixteen years of age — a clumsy, overgrown, flapping-eared lad, he tiptoed on air.

Rüdiger was nineteen. His face was grave — ashen. His is a more sober nature — to my delight he has chosen forestry as his career.

"You had better tell me about it."

They told. Busy about their own affairs, they had come on Jew-baiting. Dresden is the Saxons' town, and they are Hamburgers, but the victim being tormented was a woman — an old woman. A German-Jewish woman with some spirit. Her back was against a wall and she was answering. She was not defending herself — in no uncertain words she was defending the honor of a Germany some people think dead.

A crowd had gathered. Taller than Saxons, the boys could see over the crowd. The baiting was being done by a boy in the Hitler Youth uniform. Otto pushed in, and told him to stop. He did not, so Otto warned him; and when he continued Otto knocked the boy down. A man then came at Otto.

"He had fine teeth. They are now in his stomach," Otto informed me.

Rüdiger silenced him, and continued the narration. A policeman had taken charge of Otto. They had walked a long way. They had presumed it led to jail. But in a quiet street the policeman had suddenly released Otto.

He had shaken Otto's bloody hand and said: "Congratulations. I envy you youth and courage. Now be off — quickly."

After lunch I took them into Czechoslovakia. They had their fortnight of skiing, came back to me, and I waved them off to Hamburg — relieved to see them go, that I must confess. They seemed too much, just then, for my pacifism.

The longer I stayed among the Germans, the more necessary I found it to look into their past if I was to understand their present. They have many libraries, picture galleries, and museums in which rich harvest from the past is stored. Their learned men and women are tireless in assisting a stranger to education. As I looked at pictures, read books, heard music, and went to plays, I came to feel that from the middle of the eighteenth century until the Great War people lived very pleasantly here.

In the realm of mind and spirit, Germany was a garden of the earth. For a hundred and fifty years the stars sang to these people. Armed strife, famine, and pestilence followed in the wake of their Reformation; but when dogmatic rigidity gave way to the practice of Christian love, Johann Sebastian Bach was born to them, gifted with pietic genius to distill from their pain lessons in tolerance and compassion. Beethoven composed eternal symphonies while Napoleon conquered and lost in the material world. When Disraeli was busy adding "Empress of India" to the Queen of England's titles, Liszt was arranging a choir score for Herder's "Prometheus." And through one of their number, a German-Jew, they were given *Das Lied von der Erde* — the saddest, most beautiful music with which heaven has ever blessed mankind.

Madame de Staël had the good fortune to visit the Germans in their *Blütezeit*, or blossomtime. She arrived in an epoch which had opened with the first three cantos of Klopstock's *Messias*, and was finding its noblest expression as Goethe's *Faust* took form. Entertained first at Weimar, she was hospitably received among the Germans everywhere. Although few foreigners in the world at that time could speak German, she found that many of the cultured among the Germans knew French. In 1813 she published her observations in a book entitled *De l'Allemagne*, which was at once translated into English for London publication, and was reprinted in New York the following year.

She told of a new idealism, spiritual and intellectual, lived by a community of cultured people of all classes and creeds — a society which placed its faith in the power of education to elevate man, and had chosen naturalness and good sense as guiding stars. She eulogized philosophers, poets, and musicians. She devoted a chapter to German universities, the most learned in the world; and gave an account of elementary schools — where attendance was compulsory — which provided all the people, rich and poor, with intellectual and moral training.

She heralded a German Empire far greater than that of the Middle Ages, an empire of the spirit so wide that everyone of good will throughout the world possessed the right to citizenship. Her book had an influence on Western civilization both vast and beneficial.

Madame de Staël inspired foreigners to learn German

that they might read at first hand the works of the poets and philosophers of whom she wrote. In America, years later, Margaret Fuller taught herself sufficient command of the language to read Goethe and Schiller. Following the way pointed by Goethe, she published *Woman in the Nineteenth Century*, a book which has been a power in bringing about the American woman's status in present-day life.

Emerson, Edward Everett, George Bancroft, and many other Americans read *De l'Allemagne*. It affected New England transcendentalism and the Concord School of Philosophy. It led to the translation of De Wette's *Introduction to the Old Testament*, and the works of a host of other German theologians whose views — varying from extreme radicalism to strict orthodoxy — profoundly stirred the minds of American Christians.

George Ticknor, Spanish scholar at Harvard, tells in his journal that the reading of *De l'Allemagne* first gave him the desire to study at a German university. He was not alone in this. Within a few years of the time Madame de Staël's book was out, Frenchmen, Englishmen, and Americans were knocking at the door of German learning. Of the many who studied there during the nineteenth century, it is amazing what a large proportion returned home to live lives of distinction.

Idealism and individualism were features of German thought. Their universities had developed an *akademische Freiheit* which did not exist elsewhere. This academic freedom applied to professors and students alike. Students chose their own studies, and were masters of their own lives. Professors were secure in their positions, and free to teach what they believed to be truth.

Catholic and Protestant kings, still conceded divine right, ruled in the states of the German federation. A tradition had developed among them by which academic freedom was the palladium of the universities. Neither church nor state interfered with studies and investigations. Germany had what was as yet lacking in other lands — freedom of thought, and unselfish devotion to science and learning. The seminar method had been developed — a training ground for original scholarship, where professors and advanced scholars met to discuss problems and find a solution.

The French government sent Victor Cousin to study the school system that Madame de Staël praised so highly. His report proved another sensation, and led to the adoption of the German system of education, with some modifications, in France. Sarah Austin translated parts of it into English, and pressed for general education.

Calvin E. Stowe, Horace Mann, Henry Barnard, Miss Elizabeth Palmer Peabody, Mrs. Carl Schurz, Daniel Coit Gilman, and a host of ardent men and women transplanted to America the ideas that nineteenth-century Germans had created for raising the moral and intellectual level of civilization. Our kindergartens, elementary schools, high schools, normal schools, and universities are in part modeled on their pattern. In their homeland these ideals to-day lie prostrate under the fist of Naziism. From the Germans we received a great gift, and for them and all mankind we hold a noble tradition in trust.

Henry Philip Tappan, first president of the University of Michigan, writing in 1851 of the German system of education, says: "We cannot well be extravagant in its praise. Thorough in all its parts, consistent with itself, and vigorously sustained, it furnishes every department of life with educated men, and keeps up at the universities themselves, in every branch of knowledge, a supply of erudite and elegant scholars and authors, for the benefit and glory of the country, and the good of mankind."

Miss Catherine Maria Sedgwick, who traveled in Germany in 1840, wrote in *Letters from Abroad to Kindred at Home:* "It is impossible to witness the system of general instruction in Germany without asking if the rulers are not making an experiment dangerous to the maintenance of absolutism." She observed intelligently. A revolution occurred in 1848, but it appears to have been half-hearted.

People do not revolt seriously against absolutism unless they are pressed too hardly by it. Life can be very comfortable under an absolute ruler who is a good father to his subjects — dangerously so, because the subject does not develop a sense of civic responsibility. All goes well until the good king is succeeded by another. Then, if the subject finds himself in peril, he is bewildered about how to act.

In France, England, and America democracies were established by men who won their rights hardly, and held them with stout will. In Germany, men who fought for civic liberties were put down like unruly children, and accepted their reprimand docilely.

Searching in German libraries, one finds absolutism was

comfortable in the era of German enlightenment. People lived under a liege lord — a king, a prince, or a duke — to whom they owed devotion and fealty, but it was his Christian duty to rule with benevolence and wisdom, exerting himself for their benefit. *Der Goldene Spiegel*, written by Wieland, is outspoken on the duties of princes. He is ably supported in his statements by other authors. All kings and *Fürsten* were Christians — Catholic or Protestant. Germany was a Christian land — there is no doubt of that.

Liberty of conscience was allowed, and among intellectuals there were agnostics, radicals, and pagans. But such departure from Christianity was merely intellectual. The absolute ruler and all his subjects habitually practised the Christian virtues in their daily living. Compassion and practical kindness were the custom of the day, so widely accepted that its rightness was never questioned.

No slums were allowed to fester. There was concern about humanitarianism in prisons. Social services protected the old, the sick, and the orphan. Both man and beast had legal rights to humane protection. Jews were put on a legal equality with other citizens, and amply repaid the state by devotion to culture and science, and the state's material advancement.

The ruler was born to serve his people; one who failed to do so would have been scorned by the other dukes and princes of the federation of the German states. Liege lords were expected to provide theatres, operas, libraries, and schools. Prussia, an "enlightened and energetic despotism" according to Professor Stowe, husband of the author of *Uncle Tom's Cabin*, did "more for the education of the whole people than has ever been done by any other government on earth." In Schaumburg-Lippe the ruling prince always paid the imperial taxes out of his own pocket, because he was privately rich.

It was an age when suffrage and parliaments were fashionable. Karl August of Weimar gave his subjects a constitution, and other rulers followed his example — civic liberalism was a gift from the king.

But the ambition of Freiherr vom Stein "to bind everyone to the state by conviction, sympathy, and coöperation" was not achieved; and in vain did Herr von Schoen give warning, "If we do not use the time we have, and avail ourselves of the good that is in it and help it to develop, then time will bring its own punishment."

Rulers sometimes took away what other rulers had given, as when the newly enthroned King of Hannover suspended his predecessor's constitution in 1837. Then the famous Seven of Göttingen, including the brothers Grimm, shook the dust of the state from their feet. There were many political differences in this era of individualism. But clash of opinion did not lead to brutality. There is scarcely a writer or musician who did not spend some of his time in exile from his native place. Exile was no such serious thing as it is to-day. Private property was never forfeit to the state. Man could take his money and his goods along, and men of talent, even if penniless, were always welcome in a neighboring state.

The absolute state encouraged trade and commerce, bringing a modest comfort into every house. People worked hard, but considered it essential to reserve a part of their time for intellectual pursuits. Intellectual curiosity was lively and universal, as nobleman, farmer, and stonemason all received an education. From among the families of merchants and craftsmen sprang sons of genius who were welcomed at the courts. Faith in human progress acquired an almost religious character.

The kings and *Fürsten* competed in fostering genius. Each strove to make his court a Parnassus known for the men of talent it sheltered. Munich, Dresden, Hannover, Weimar, Kassel, Berlin, Mecklenburg-Schwerin, and all the others had their fame. The ducal house of Meiningen supported a company of players renowned throughout the German lands. Coburg, too small to attract genius, collected rare prints.

The old popular folk songs, fairy tales, and sagas were revived. The brightly lighted Christmas tree became a custom in German homes. Poetry was the only rival to music. Composers and authors were constantly giving to the world new operas, plays, songs, and short stories. Philosophy vied with science for attention. Schlegel finished the translation of Shakespeare's complete works. Wagner set the *Nibelungenlied* to music.

Kant stirred other thinkers by his efforts to overcome the antagonism between inclination and duty. Hegel and Marx spun their political theories. It was a time of individualism. Men of *Sturm und Drang* abandoned themselves to their feelings; men of restraint practised self-control. Pseudo science grew up side by side with sound research. There was preoccupation with "attempts to raise self to the greatest height of human nobility," but life was not wholly serious. There seems to have been plenty of fun — *Knittelverse*, birthday celebrations, heart-shaped valentines, picnics, and fiction with tender, happy endings. There were whipped cream, butter, and white bread for everyone.

As time advanced, every young man was conscripted for a year of military service. But gentlemen did not have to live in the barracks; they took rooms in the nearest town. Bismarck engineered three short, victorious wars for causes on which few citizens appear to have felt serious concern. He made the King of Prussia Emperor of Germany, with a nominal sway over the liege lords of the federated states. And then there was a new Kaiser who wore glittering uniforms.

Life continued to be pleasant. Perhaps people never do assume the burden of civic responsibility so long as they can comfortably avoid it. It may be that only when intellectual life is in danger of extinction do the intelligent arouse themselves to the task of self-government. Up to the Great War absolutism in government, combined with the greatest intellectual and spiritual freedom, was the peculiar characteristic of German life.

After the war, when their liege lords were gone, the German people were children suddenly flung from strict parental care, uneducated for the task that confronted them.

When I arrived in Germany government was absolute, but whether or not intellect and spirit were to be fettered had not been definitely settled. In the press one could watch the progress of argument on this matter. I was interested in it as a general subject, and also as it related to special men.

I meant to hear Professor Karl Barth lecture, but before

I could do so he had gone. This newspaper item explains his departure: —

Professor Karl Barth of Bonn, who was suspended in November, has now been dismissed by the disciplinary court at Cologne, to whom the matter was taken. The Court decided that Professor Barth should be granted relief to the amount of half the normal retired pay for a year. Dr. Barth, aside from his request for change in oath to suit his conscience, was charged with observations hostile to the state a year ago, and failure to give the Hitler salute in his lecture rooms after having been ordered to do so last autumn. Dr. Barth's reply was that as a professor of theology he could not do so because it would be tantamount to the recognition of a "totalitarian" state in theological classes. He has enjoyed unforeseen support among his students, 300 of whom issued a statement at the time of his suspension refusing to recognize a change in professorship.

Dr. Wilhelm Furtwängler's decision of whether to stay or go also concerned me, aside from the ethics of the matter. His way of conducting an orchestra as if he were playing an organ, phrasing with passion and restraint, speaking intimately through the language of the composer, has an emotional beauty which seems to me fundamentally German, and we were here for German music.

His contest over the freedom of music is illustrative of what happened to other forms of art.

On November 25, 1934, in the *Deutsche Allgemeine Zeitung*, Dr. Furtwängler published a spirited defense of Paul Hindemith, the composer. He declared himself concerned not only to defend Hindemith, but to bring up the whole question of interference with artistic life by political zealots. The theme of the article was "What shall we come to if political denunciation is to be turned against art without check?"

On December 4 I saw in *The Times:* —

Herr Furtwängler has resigned the vice presidency of the Reich Chamber of Music, the leadership of the Berlin Philharmonic Orchestra, and the chief directorship of the State Opera. Dr. Goebbels has accepted his resignation of the first two posts, General Göring of the third. Early in the National Socialist régime, he addressed a letter to Dr. Goebbels expressing the opinion that in music there should be no distinction except that of a good or a bad artist. Men of ability like Reinhardt, Klemperer, and Walter, must continue to have a voice as artists. Dr. Goebbels expressed his different opinion, and the matter dropped.

In the past eighteen months the majority of Jewish artists have been eliminated; and Herr Furtwängler, despite his known opinions, has been made much of by the National Socialists as an example of Aryan genius. The issue is over the work of Hindemith, which may not be used in Germany because "for years before the National Socialist seizure of power he had adopted a deliberately un-German attitude, which makes his collaboration intolerable in the National Socialist work of reconstruction." Herr Furtwängler's resignation leaves a Jew, Herr Leo Blech, whose original appointment was made by the Kaiser, the best-known conductor now remaining at the State Opera.

Herr Blech remained there, under General Göring's protection, until he reached the age of retirement.

In the *Völkischer Beobachter*, on December 6, Herr Alfred Rosenberg, designated "Special Supervisor of Intellectual Training and Head of the National Socialist

Culture Committee," wrote of the resignation of Herr
Furtwängler, stating that his unforgivable offense was to
conduct the first performance of Herr Hindemith's new
work, *Mathis the Painter*, and then, when this caused a
violent conflict, to publish a spirited defense of Herr
Hindemith as an artist.

When a talented musician like Hindemith, after German
beginnings, lives and works and feels himself at home in Jewish
company; when he associates almost entirely with Jews; when
he lends himself, in accordance with the spirit of the Republic,
to the worst kind of tawdry imitation of German music, then
that is his own affair. But it gives others the right to show him
and his circle that a revolution has now removed the entire
human, artistic, and political associations of Herr Hindemith.
It is deeply regrettable that so great an artist as Herr Furtwängler should have interfered in this dispute. But as he persisted in his nineteenth-century ideas, and evidently had no
further sympathy with the great national struggle of our age,
he must take the consequences.

On January first it was announced that Herr Furtwängler
had not gone abroad as rumored, since it had been pointed
out to him that to do so thus soon after his resignation might
be harmful to German prestige.

Then an order was printed in the professional journals.
It forbade German artists of all kinds, and German lecturers,
to accept engagements abroad without the express authoriza-
tion of the president of their own subchamber of music,
painting, sculpture, speech, or literature. "To disobey
means ineligibility to work again in Germany. This is to
ensure that only persons who will leave behind them a really
deep impression of German intellectual activities go abroad.

Such men as Dr. Furtwängler, if they do not wish to become exiles, are affected. He has canceled concerts in Vienna and London."

Some months later Dr. Furtwängler accepted the government offer to return to conducting. Herr Erich Kleiber, his associate at the State Opera House, conducted for the last time, handed in his resignation, and left the country immediately. Despite ardent appeals, he refused to return. Next, Professor Knappertsbusch, who had a life contract as musical director of the Bavarian Opera House, was criticized for "nebulous views" and turned his back on National Socialism.

And so it went on in all the arts, the government always winning, until the Propaganda Minister announced at a "festal sitting" of the Nazi Chamber of Culture that he had issued instructions forbidding from that day criticism of art, literature, music, and drama. The command against critical expression extends to remarks about stage, cinema, and concert performances. The government decides what is good and what is bad; the people's part is to be grateful for what they are given.

Art is not neglected, or even treated as a side issue, in the Dritte Reich. Art from the German past has not been repudiated. It has merely been "cleaned up" — the Jewish contribution given back to the Jews, and liberal, pacifist, and other "decadent" tendencies removed for "the benefit of the people." Aryan creation is energetically encouraged and supported. The state provides generous prizes, and promotes cultural groups. Genius is not readily producible, as we all know. So far in mankind's experience it has, according to my researches, never yet been possible to force or anticipate it, or even breed it from known variables. But this is a *neue Zeit* — a new time.

Dispute as to whether or not propaganda is an art has been settled. Propaganda is art, and presides over all other art; it ranks a Reich minister, — similar to a cabinet minister in a democracy, only of course far stronger, — and the Senate of Culture is one of the departments in his organization.

The *Führerprinzip* among Germans stands on three legs — the Propaganda Bureau, the Gestapo,[1] and the Army. When I was endeavoring to find the good in Naziism, I did not shirk looking at all three of them as intelligently as I could. I collected an enormous amount of data, so much that it is difficult to select from it.

Of the Propaganda Bureau, I have only space to tell that it is housed in a great white building in Berlin, and is equipped with more than one can imagine. It has a fine collection of books on psychology, shelves for every foreign book published about Naziism, and files for newspaper and magazine clippings from foreign lands. The staff are mostly young, and appear healthy and as if they enjoyed life. Under threat of death should they make a mistake, they seem to obey implicitly. When anything of unusual importance occurs, it is the duty of the Propaganda Minister to meet with those of them who are news writers and tell them exactly how the news is to be handled. They have, therefore, no excuse for endangering either themselves or the internal tranquillity of Germany. This mother-bureau has a little daughter at Stuttgart busy trying to bring all

[1] *Geheime Staatspolizei* — secret police.

people of German blood now living abroad into the fold of Naziism.

The young man who assisted in my education in Nazi propaganda told me that "the propaganda is thoughtfully arranged. It neglects nothing — not even the songs on the lips of the people. It is not destructive, but definitely constructive."

Everything is subject to the pressure of propaganda: painting, music, literature, sculpture, architecture — even God. All are in the process of Teutonization.

Count Gobineau's book on the inequalities of human races, esteemed by Wagner, and *Foundations of the Nineteenth Century* by Houston Stewart Chamberlain, who married Wagner's daughter, are used as aids in this tremendous task.

"We are working for generations to come and we take into account the needs of the future," the Führer has said. "The art of the new Reich shall be given a character which generations to come will see at once has sprung from this epoch."

His own book tops the best-seller list, climbing now toward its fifth million. Edition follows edition, each new edition generously expanded. "All 'Aryan' Germans are given a copy on graduating from school, and every 'Aryan' bride gets one with her marriage certificate," my instructor assured me.

I had noticed that for some weeks the newspaper my husband always takes — *The Times* of London — had had columns of letters debating as to whether *Mein Kampf* has any importance now, as it was written some years ago. The able Propaganda Minister misses nothing. He an-

swered it firmly with a statement radioed to the world:
"We go forward with the book in one hand and the sword
in the other."

And to safeguard everyone from misunderstanding as to
what art is, the Führer's definition has been published. He
has made it quite clear. "Whether it is a matter of architecture or of music, of sculpture or of painting, one fundamental principle must never be lost sight of: every true
art must give its products the stamp of beauty, for the ideal
for all of us must lie in the cultivation of the healthy. Only
the healthy is right and natural; and so everything right
and natural is beautiful. It is our task to find the will to
true beauty, and not let ourselves be led astray by the
chatter, half silly, half impudent, of decadent literati who
try to decry as trash the natural and so the beautiful, and to
put forward the unhealthy and unsound as interesting,
remarkable, and therefore worthy of consideration."

The newspaper which I had bought clearly stated that
the rumors people were spreading about the concentration
of German troops on the Austrian border were without
foundation. Anyone who believed in this report believed
in a mirage.

"There," I said to the news vendor. "See what a liar
you are — self-committed. Yesterday you wasted my time
telling me about this mobilization, and to-day you sell me
a paper telling me that what you said is untrue."

He winked at me. Another customer was approaching.
I waited while he sold wares to several people, taking my
revenge by reading one of his magazines with no intention
of buying it. Finally, we were alone.

"How long have you been in this country?" were his first words.

"Nearly four years — off and on."

"And you have not yet learned to read the newspapers. Somewhere I got the idea that Americans are quick — it must be a mistake. Let a Saxon give you a lesson. You are not cheated when you buy my newspapers. These are the papers of a new time. You read the news, and then you enjoy the mental exercise of taking each item and transposing it. What is printed is the opposite of what should be there, but there is enough truth mixed in it to confuse and give zest to the solution of the puzzle."

When I wrote to Germans in other parts that I had to spend the winter in Dresden, I received considerable sympathy. There was not one who failed to tell me that the people of Saxony are *sehr komische Leute*. All mentioned *Blümchenkaffee* — the coffee of a people so stingy that one can see through the pale liquid the flowers in the bottom of their Dresden china cups. On the German comedy stage the *Sachse* occupies the same place that the Philadelphian does on the New York stage.

My self-pity soon wore off. I was at home here. And not since I left my friend the coppersmith on the Taku Road at Tientsin had I met anyone near to being his equal until I met this news vendor at Dresden.

"When you are in a serious mood," I asked him, "what is your opinion of present-day printing in Germany?"

"The words I customarily use about that could not be said to a lady, but I will mention that those who are proclaiming themselves leaders of a new culture are without culture. Therefore, they underrate the intelligence of their subjects."

"Now that is nonsense," I retorted. "The head of your Bureau of Propaganda and Enlightenment is a university man. I have heard him broadcast that he has had a classical education."

"A little learning is a dangerous thing," was the answer. "Have you ever seen him?"

"Yes — in a hotel. As I was paying our bill I happened to hear a page asking for Herr Doktor Goebbels's bill, as he wanted it taken upstairs. I felt acquainted with him as a radio voice, and was curious to see him. So I sat down in the lobby and waited."

"How did he look?"

"Well scrubbed, neatly dressed, pleased with the morning. There was a man with him, but merely there; your Propaganda Minister was the person present. Dr. Goebbels gave the lobby a swift glance as he stepped from the elevator — the glance of a man accustomed to looking before he leaps; then smiled cheerfully and shook hands with everyone — the elevator man, waiters who came in from the dining room, pages, hotel guests, desk clerks, and the doorkeeper. He said 'Thank you for everything' to all, and was gone, gliding away in a car which had been waiting at the door."

"Very interesting," commented my news vendor. "Dr. Goebbels is scheduled to speak here next week, and people won't take the tickets. It is going to lead to trouble. Last time we were insolent we were punished. The Senate of Culture issued an order that singers at the Dresden

Opera were not to sing at the *Hofkirche* any more because
it took time needed for their proper work. In Dresden
under the kings, it was always in the opera contract that
singers must sing in the church on Sunday. That continued up to January of this year. If we do not rally to this
meeting we shall probably be told that we cannot drink
from flowered cups. But we are *sehr komische Leute.*
People are not taking the tickets."

"Is Saxony likely to start a revolution?"

"I hardly think so. Haven't you heard that we were
slow starters in the Great War, and not very much use
when we got there? We are a plodding people, quiet
and industrious; we wouldn't like a revolution. Our last
king, when taunted, would not take part in one. When
approached by revolutionists, he merely said: 'Good-bye,
have a republic if you want a republic. I won't be responsible for bloodshed in the *Schloss Strasse.*' Sometime
later he was traveling from one place to another in Saxony
on a train, and at one station a lot of people had gathered
to cheer him. The conductor told him that they were
there. He went out to the platform, and all he did was to
look them over and say, 'You are a fine lot of republicans!'
and return to his carriage.

"Our kings were in business like the rest of us. His son
is in business — one of the best businessmen in Saxony. Our
kings were not dependent on monarchy for an occupation.
We had our democracy. Now we have our *Führerprinzip.*
The fact that we do not revolt against it does not signify that
we endorse it."

As I walked home I thought, "I shall never understand
the Germans," and something seen when we were traveling

in the Riesengebirge returned to memory. To the side of the road, a little way ahead, we noticed a patch of blue, and coming up discovered that it was lupines. They covered the space of a clearing right up to the edge of the wood — tall and in full bloom, as well grown as in a tended garden. In serried ranks, thousands of them stood holding up spikes of intense blue, of lighter blue with white-tipped petals, of bluish purple, of reddish purple, and of pure white. Their beauty, in this unexpected place, was such as makes the heart leap up when the eyes behold a wondrous sight.

Someone had placed a banner in their midst, a long white strip of cloth stretched taut between two posts that were neatly painted green and firmly planted in the earth. In broad black letters the white cloth bore the words, in German: "He who does not stand with the Führer is no longer German" — words seen in many places.

On this banner set amid the lupines another hand had written below the bold letters, in a delicate script, as with a fountain pen, also in German: *"Et tu, Brute."*

XV

DRAGONS' TEETH

The sentiment of a people is the most energetic element in national action. Even when material interests are the original exciting cause, it is the sentiment to which they give rise, the moral tone which emotion takes, that constitutes the greater force.

— ADMIRAL ALFRED T. MAHAN, U.S.N.

FROM the time of the proclamation of conscription, March 16, 1935, life in Germany was punctuated by events great and small which kept the thought of war recurrent. During the summer before the reoccupation of the Rhineland, men in neat uniforms who called themselves "the war protection service" came to give us instruction as to exactly what to do in case of falling bombs. They had sand, and such, which they wanted to put in our attic. I was at home alone; I explained to them that I do not take part in wars, and refused to have the stuff brought in. They listened to my speech and went away without dispute; but they came again when I was not at home and arranged the attic exactly as they had planned, giving the "household instructions" to our German maids.

That winter, which was our second in the Rhineland, our daughter went to school in Cologne, bicycling to and fro. She was often late for her lunch because of some "war protection" lesson. My diary holds several pages written in her hand about the different gases that might be used, how to protect oneself against them, and how to give first aid to the injured. She also put there a description of the "air-raid cellar" which all her class were taught to enter without panic, with instructions on how to conduct themselves when there. There is something very touching as well as terrible in the *Gemütlichkeit* of that cellar, with its place for a foreign girl, two small books for each child, — good books, — and packets of concentrated food to be rationed sparingly. My child has written in my diary: "It is really cosy. Our teacher will read aloud to us, and we will take turns in reading."

Friends of ours who were building an apartment house had in their plans arrangement for a laundry, in the basement, for each apartment; but they had to abandon this to make a bombproof and gasproof room large enough to hold all the persons that might be in the building when the sirens gave warning. They had also to furnish it and equip it with an "air-refreshing pump" (the pump alone cost about three hundred dollars). Others, who had inherited a large house and decided to convert it into four apartments, had also to provide such a cellar.

Before the sudden occupation of the Rhineland by the army there were Gestapo arrests, and this time I knew of one case where the secret police broke the house lock and were standing by the bed of their victim when they announced their presence. Gestapo arrests were made again before the march on Austria. And I was told that they recurred before the order for the conscription of labor to refortify the Western Front last summer, and before the march into Bohemia. Each time, key people who might lead rebellion were taken.

When the reoccupation of the Rhineland occurred, I was at Bremen. My sister, who lives at Shanghai, had been visiting me, and I had waved her off to China, sad to see her go and wishing I could go along. With German friends who had accompanied me to the boat, and were now taking me to my Cologne train, I was walking in the main street of Bremen when a loud-speaker announced that German soldiers were again in the Rhineland. There was plenty of time, and we stopped to listen to the dramatic broadcast of how the soldiers had got safely in under cover of the night, and how the happy people had welcomed them with flowers, cheers, and song.

On the train I shared a compartment with people who mistook me for English and began to thank me for the reoccupation. They were all certain that England had sanctioned this before it took place. They had no apprehension of war, being sure that England would restrain France. Cologne looked as usual when I arrived about eight in the evening. The next day as I went my round of household shopping, and to call on various people, I met intense apprehension. Some were prepared for bombs to drop at any minute. There was more interest in peace than delight over the reoccupation. I learned that the local *Gauleiter* had given a dinner for all the foreign consuls, and kept them entertained while the troops got themselves fairly well in. No one with whom I talked seemed to consider this so clever, but most told me of it. The length of the dinner and the after-dinner speeches was detailed as if the narrator had been present.

By the time we came to live in Dresden we were accustomed to preparations for possible war, and gave one of our most successful musical evenings on a *Verdunklungs-abend*. Silence was not compulsory; the only restriction was against showing any light. Bishop and Mrs. Perry, of Rhode Island, were our guests of honor at this party.

Strengthening the German army was not to us just the recruiting of so many men; it was conscription of Fritz and Hans, Otto and August, Friedbert and Lutz. If a person called was a "conscientious objector" it meant his arrest. The families of boys who had no religious objection did not talk of war; they avoided that subject, and spoke of the discipline and order soldiers are taught.

After they had gone into barracks we heard of double-decker beds, with eight men in some rooms and fewer in others. We learned that each man had his own cupboard, with a porcelain shelf on which to keep stores of food received from home. Letters read aloud explained that, besides morning coffee, they got a hot dinner at noon — usually very good — at the canteen, sometimes with cabbage and sausage, sometimes three eggs and spinach, always plenty of potatoes, and on Sunday often roast beef, carrots, and peas. Once a week they got a large loaf of *Kommissbrot* and butter, and this was eaten in their own room for other meals, with whatever they had from home added to it. They were not allowed to leave barracks except on Saturday and Sunday, and by permission on Wednesday. They could go to the canteen in the evenings, if they had time, and buy beer and play "skat." They received fifty pfennigs a day from the state, and they reminded their parents that this would not allow many drinks of beer. They had to do their own laundry, also to sew names in their garments — and if this was not well done underofficers pulled the work out as many as nine times; they had to press their uniforms and clean their boots, shave early, clean their nails, stand up to be inspected, and bear it if ordered to take off a boot and sock and display a foot so that the underofficer could see if it was clean. German boys are waited on at home, and mothers used to smile as they read such things and say, "The poor darling!"

As discussed, the army was a very domestic affair. Keen interest was taken at home in how the bed must be made to pass inspection, and just what clothes the state provided. There was a uniform for exercise, and a uniform for street wear, with white gloves, underwear, socks, boots, and nightshirts. We heard all the details of fights against these nightshirts waged by sons who preferred pyjamas, and of a boy put in the guardhouse for redressing in his home pyjamas after he had got into bed.

To begin with there were two salutes, one to the forehead after the manner of the *Reichswehr*, and the Hitler salute given with the right arm stretched out to the front. One boy complained of this, saying that it is the salute slaves had to give in ancient Rome. His father shook his head as the letter was read because he did not see any need to change the old customs of the army. When home on Sunday the embryo soldiers complained of endless lectures and lessons in National Socialism, and of continual grumbling, especially by farmers and workers.

"Grumbling would not have been permitted in my time," fathers would say, "and we had no hours to waste on lectures. We were up to learn to handle our guns."

"The peasants have been told so often that they are the earth's best that they grumble at the state in a way that could not be stopped except by putting them all in prison, and they know they cannot be spared from food growing. As for learning to handle our guns, we do that all right, and have plenty of drill, but we have the lectures piled on top." Discussions of then and now would go on for hours. Only in time of tension was there ever talk of war, and never to the boy. Fathers did not talk of the Front. Asked questions, they skirted away from the subject and would soon become silent, with a far-away, sad look in their eyes, often a bewildered look. Nobody ever mentioned conquest, not even the reconquest of former German lands, although the regaining of these lands was the principal propaganda subject.

Once we visited the family of an old *Reichswehr* officer, and he gave me an armful of copies of a paper his men had printed during the Great War. They were full of verses, pictures, brief stories. There was scarcely a mention of battle or military prowess, and no hatred of the foe; few referred to the horrors and calamities happening about them. They were marked by a terrible homesickness for the remembered homes, children, gardens, forests, and rivers they had gone forth to defend. They had no resemblance to the German war propaganda which, like that of the Allies, pictured the other side as horrible men. This poem by A. J. Hentze, who fell in 1917, is an example: —

> *Mein Dorf, ein Haus, ein Lindenbaum,*
> *Aus allen Gärten ein Blütenstrauss*
> *Steht Tag für Tag in meinem Traum:*
> *O, wär' daheim ich wieder!*
>
> *Ein Kinderlied, ein Mutterwort*
> *So weh mir im Gemüt erblüht.*
> *Wie weit, wie fern der Jugend Hort!*
> *O, wär' daheim ich wieder!*

Die Glocken schlag'n den Sonntag an:
Ich sehe ferne die Strassen ziehn
Dort hin, wo ich zu Hause bin!
O, wär' daheim ich wieder!

Und drückst du mir die Augen zu,
Gott, gib auf blutigem Feld allhier,
Gib, Vater du, mir Himmelsruh;
Dann bin daheim ich wieder!

(My village, a house, a lime tree,
From every garden a bunch of flowers,
Appear day by day in my dream.
Oh, if only I were home again!

A childish rhyme, a mother's word,
So sadly blossoms in my heart.
How far away are the days of youth!
Oh, if only I were home again!

The bells chime the Sunday in;
I see from afar the road winding
Thither to where I am at home.
Oh, if only I were home again!

And if thou close my eyes,
God, give me on this bloody field,
Give me, thou Father, heavenly peace;
Then I shall be at home again!)

I am sure it is not a windy boast when the Nazis proclaim that they have a peacetime army which is the most powerful striking force that any nation has ever possessed. When Germans undertake a thing they do it well.

Under a Führer who has absolute power, and is keen on arming, they have become the most thoroughly fortified and armed nation in all history. When we were first in Germany many around us spoke of the *Reichswehr* as the most conservative group in the land. Immediately on the death of Field Marshal von Hindenburg, the armed forces swore an oath of obedience to Adolf Hitler. This allayed the worry of many who had been anxious about Nazi deeds, as they interpreted this army action as foretelling the end of Nazi radicalism.

From then on, there were periods of gossip about what might be happening inside the *Reichswehr* — whispers that the generals were not in favor of things planned, and not always satisfied when these plans were accomplished without bloodshed. But the Führer progressed successfully to possession of absolute power until he could retire generals with thanks for services to Germany in the past, and have them accept a signed photograph of himself as a retirement gift.

The Führer's power is now said to be absolute. My travels were wider than those of many of our German friends, and were not bounded by any class or group limits. Many anxious about the possibility of war used to ask me, "Do you think the army would march at his command?" To them I always presented a copy of Joseph Conrad's *Lord Jim*, and recommended its reading.

Under Nazi direction the army has increased in size and strength very rapidly. It has a million men standing at arms, an ever-increasing number of trained reserves, and the entire resources of the Dritte Reich — including all food stuffs, and women and children — ticketed and docketed ready for war at a moment's notice if their Führer decides war is necessary.

The army is systematically conscripting all men of military age in accordance with the contention that Germany would have won the World War if the imperial authorities in pre-war years had made full use of Germany's man power. In addition to the conscripts who receive a full military training of at least two years, the annual classes which escaped conscription in the post-war years get a short military training of at least several weeks. The classes born in 1906–1907, who missed conscription, have been instructed to report to the authorities at the beginning of next year preparatory to receiving military training.

There were more boys born during the latter years of the Weimar Republic than during the war and the years immediately following. These are coming on toward military age; in each succeeding year that elapses there will be more to conscript from; and many state measures aim to encourage the increase of births.

Machines and soldiers, mostly technicians, have been detailed to Spain for testing out in actual warfare — "a better preparation than any sham manœuvres," I was told. It was also explained to me that one of the reasons for calling officers home from China, aside from the fact that the Dritte Reich had made an agreement with Japan, is that these men have had valuable experience and are needed at home. They, with those who had been in Russia before conscription was reëstablished in Germany, were spoken of as General von Seeckt's men.

All the forts that were destroyed have been rebuilt far better than before. Heligoland, the submarine base marveled at by engineers sent to destroy it, is much improved, and there are other bases. Nazis have told me that there is nothing in the Anglo-German Naval Treaty to disturb their ocean plans. The ratio is a ratio of tonnage, and while England builds large vessels, Germany concentrates on smaller ships — largely "undersea" craft of the destroyer category.

The Germans have finished the Wilhelm Canal, which makes it possible to shift their navy safely from the North Sea to the Baltic at desire, and will soon have the Black Sea and the Mediterranean linked up with their system of inland water traffic. They have a network of *Reichs-autobahnen*, and the railways are under government control. As for their bombing arm, Field Marshal Göring, its creator, has declared, "Germany's aviation industry is now organized in such a manner as to ensure German superiority in the air for the coming years. Whatever the aircraft production of other countries, Germany will increase her air force correspondingly."

Munition factories are tremendously expanded, and are working day and night, as are the navy yards. Miners work a fourteen-hour shift, or longer if there is a press. Not only are iron and steel made from ore such as was formerly used, but there are new processes for getting raw material out of what was once discarded as useless. Foreign exchange is devoted to the purchase of things needed for armed strength, and to the stirring up of German racial consciousness. At home, whipped cream, white bread, and personal liberty have been sacrificed. Butter rationing has been accepted. Steel railings from parks and private gardens have been used for war preparedness.

Broadcasting from all German stations, the Propaganda Minister has declared: "We live too fast in these stirring times. The years are filled with dramatic thrills, and as fast as one great event is over another follows it.

"Owing to this abruptness and speed we are often inclined to forget the difficulties involved. We take the success of the régime for granted. If, in the course of a year, we reap an unprecedented historical harvest, we suppose that it is only the result of luck, or of some sort of historical miracle.

"There is no doubt that luck is necessary to obtain historical success, and in its totality the work of the Führer must be regarded as a miracle. But miracles come not when one just waits for them, but when one works and fights for them. That is what happened here. The Führer did not wait. He collected the forces of the nation, organized, and boldly engaged on the big historical decision of the year. He succeeded."

The great mass of the people, he proclaimed, "possess a primitive, unspoilt capacity for believing that all is possible," and then remarked that "unfortunately, in certain circles, this faculty had been somewhat blunted, particularly among men of possessions and education, who trust more in the power of pure and cold understanding than in that of the glowing idealistic heart."

These intellectuals he characterized as knowing so much that they did not know what to do with their knowledge. "When the Nazi movement was fighting for power," he exclaimed, "they could not believe in its victory. And now, too, they cannot bring themselves to believe. They only recognize what is, but do not see what will be.

"Difficulties for them are not things to be overcome, but things to capitulate to. With such feeble-spirited elements one cannot make history, but happily, in all peoples, and particularly the German, there is only a very thin top layer of intellectuals and 'society.' They will never lead the nation.

"Formerly they encountered in our country willing and grateful disciples. To-day they can only fling a few cues to members of the intellectual bourgeoisie who live behind the times.

"The people do not want to hear of these intellectual grumblers. The people live under a nerve-racking tension, and they are happy about the great success the Führer has gained."

Field Marshal Göring has appealed to the German people to continue making sacrifices under the Four-Year Plan: "The year 1938 rises like an obelisk of granite above the centuries; like a tremendous oak tree it overshadows all events of German history.

"Nineteen thirty-nine too will be a year of hard labor. The third year of the Four-Year Plan demands the utilization of the entire strength of the people, because the strength of the nation always depends on the determination of the individual to work on and his willingness to make sacrifices. Every single individual is important — that is the watchword for 1939."

In the Dritte Reich, to harbor Bertrand Russell's book on roads to peace behind the clock may lead a shoemaker into prison. Arrested without warrant, and held without trial, he may pass into that Nazi darkness called a concentration camp, and may not be seen again by his kin. They may be allowed to send blankets, soap, home-cooked food. Receiving a message, "Be brave," they must forever question, "How came that slip of paper with his handwriting on it to be posted at Berlin?" — because no other word of him comes.

But it is permissible to have *Der Christliche Staatsmann*, by Wilhelm Stapel, which ends thus: "*Wenn nun der Germane, der nordische Mensch, seinen Fuss auf den letzten Streifen eroberten Landes gesetzt hat, so nimmt er die Krone der Welt und legt sie Gott zu Füssen, um sich von ihm damit kronen zu lassen.*" (And when the Germanic, the Nordic, man has set his foot upon the last strip of conquered land, he will take the crown of the world and lay it at God's feet, in order that he may be crowned by the Almighty.)

From reading this I turned to reading Ibsen. That is a natural turn. Radio and press repeatedly stressed the Nazis' feeling of the necessity to cleanse themselves, and all other Germans throughout the world, of every characteristic which is not Nordic. The National Socialist Students' Union has been entrusted with the task of cooperating with the Nordic Society in the promotion of Nordic ideals. The plays of Ibsen are in the repertoire of nearly every theatre.

And this is what I read from Ibsen, in words not quite so simple as those of Matthew: "If you won all, but lost yourself, then your whole gain was nothing but a wreath around a cloven brow."

"We have struck the word 'pacifist' from the German vocabulary" is a remark which I heard frequently from people of the Reich who felt that way. They were using something coined for them by Herr Franz von Papen, last German Minister to Austria. A peculiar thing was that I often heard, even from those who used these words, another statement: *"Ich habe alle Quäker in mein Herz geschlossen"* (I have locked all Quakers in my heart).

This greeted me in castle and cottage. It was said by ardent supporters of Naziism, as well as by German men and women, who whispered their pacifism; and by folk who went courageously forward as pacifist until arrested, and then continued pacifism in prison. In fact, I got the impression that pacifism might be out of the vocabulary, but that the Germans have not done with its practice yet.

Pacifism has been a German tenet for a long time. I have seen letters and journals which show that similar revelations on the ethics of living came to practical mystics in Germany simultaneously with their receipt by George Fox and others in England. These yellowed pages record a generous exchange in which the Quaker faith received tenets from German thought. William Penn had no difficulty in getting Germans to join in his "holy experiment" — the founding of Pennsylvania. In present-day Germany no one ever drew away from me because by the fortune of birth I belong to the Quakers. Quite the contrary happened. When Germans discovered that I am a Quaker they received me with a readiness to love me, and often treated me with a warmth far beyond my personal merit.

I do not think the Germans are a people of short memory. Whenever I was told by a stranger, "I have the Quakers locked in my heart," I always queried, "Why?" The answers, often from men in uniform, were all like this one: "When we were defeated and forsaken, the Quakers came to us. They fed starving children, but not only did they bring food, they brought us friendship. They were quick in love, they restored our faith in human goodness. They came as friends." I was humbled by this remembrance, ashamed where I had been impatient.

Narration of the reason for this twentieth-century Quaker action must begin with a "declaration from the harmless and innocent people of God called Quakers," presented to King Charles the Second of England on the twenty-first day of the eleventh month, 1660: —

We utterly deny all outward wars and strife, and fightings with outward weapons, for any end, or under any pretence whatsoever: this is our testimony to the whole world. And whereas it is objected: "But although you say that you cannot fight, yet if the Spirit move you, then you will change your principle and fight for the Kingdom of Christ," to this we answer: that the Spirit of Christ, by which we are guided, is not changeable, so as once to command us from a thing as evil, and again to move unto it: and we certainly know and testify to the world, that the spirit of Christ, which leads us in all truth, will never move us to fight and war against any man with outward weapons, neither for the kingdom of Christ nor for the kingdoms of the world.

This explanation must further include a minute of the Quaker Monthly Meeting of March 1760, which sets forth a testimony regarding victory: —

As we cannot join in shedding the blood of our fellow creatures, neither can we be one with them in rejoicing in the advantages obtained by such bloodshed; as we cannot fight with the fighters, neither can we triumph with the conquerors.

On my desk as I write lies a small book which I have made for my personal use. It contains a selection from the testimonies of Friends' minutes on war passed by groups in every country where they have dwelt. From 1660 to the present day not one minute deviates from that position. In the crisis of last autumn (1938) the Society of Friends in Great Britain held a meeting at its headquarters in London to consider the Peace Testimony of the society and its implications and interpretation to-day. The meeting was the largest in the history of the society in Great Britain. The final minute, which reaffirmed the Quaker Peace Testimony, stated: —

We have looked over the world and at home, and we have seen everywhere the denial of those standards of human relationships which Jesus Christ showed to us. Some evils stand out clearly, some we know that we are only just beginning to recognize. God has met us here, and in His presence we have reaffirmed the testimony of our society against all war for whatsoever purpose and have determined to make that testimony our own to-day.

Looking back across the centuries, I am thankful to the thousands individually unknown to history who have held true to that belief. Friends neither take part in wars nor celebrate the victories of armed might.

Guided by this spirit, Quakers of the Allied victor countries did not rejoice in a victory for which they had not fought, nor did they tarry for peace terms to be arranged. They hurried across the frontiers to their friends, the Germans, to give what aid they could, both spiritual and material, bringing sympathy and loving reassurance as well as food.

They stood staunchly by the Germans through the sad time that followed. During the occupation of the Ruhr in 1923, English Friends sent a special mission which by intervention with the French military authorities obtained certain privileges for the imprisoned German officials. The Centres in Paris and Germany, through coöperation, were able to alleviate in some measure the tension between the two countries. Exchange of visits was also arranged between Germany and France of people of influence in their respective countries. Friends took considerable interest in the movement in both countries for improving Franco-German relations through school textbooks, and German Friends translated from French into German *The Struggle for the History Book in the Schools of France.*

In the years 1925–1928 the Warsaw and Berlin Centres planned together a series of Polish-German Conferences held in Danzig, Warsaw, and Berlin. These resulted in the forming of Polish study groups among students in Berlin and Königsberg, and helped towards an unbiased understanding of such thorny problems as the Polish Corridor.

Through the medium of the Quaker Centres in Germany and other contacts, Friends were in a unique position to receive information on current tendencies in German thought and the economic situation of the country. As early as 1922 a statement was published on the "peril to all stabilized civilizations involved in the condition of Germany to-day." The increasing anxiety among members of the Germany Committee of the Friends' Service Coun-

cil in London led them to arrange for the publication in
1931 of a series of leaflets by well-known authorities on the
direct effects of reparations payments.

In 1933, through the intermediary of the Frankfurt Centre, a number of children of German unemployed were
entertained by French peasants in Alsace. That year also
marked the beginning of extensive work among German
refugees after the coming of the Nazi régime. Within the
Dritte Reich the Quakers have centres from which they
give help to those in trouble; and a "Rest Home" where
come many afflicted by the bitterness which so often ac-
companies great suffering when it is felt to be undeserved.

There again, as in the post-war era, something very beautiful has been shown in the German character. The
thanks of these people are not so much for the good food,
warmth, and freedom from financial cares, although these
are mentioned with gratitude, as for having their faith in
human goodness restored to them once more when it had
been lost.

Outside Germany, many people have asked me if there
are any German Quakers. Germany, the land that gave
Thomas à Kempis to the world, has its practical mystics
still, men and women who have seen a vision of the true
way of life, and want to be true to that vision, cost what
it may. Some of these people have their spiritual home
among Friends.

It may seem to people in other countries that it is impossible to be a true Friend in a totalitarian state. They
need to remember that this era in Germany is not the only
time and place where a minority holding deep convictions
on the way peace can be achieved have found themselves

in opposition to the established order. Followers of Confucius faced that peril in the reign of Ch'in Shih Huang-ti
— some were buried alive, others had "traitor" branded on
their brows and, chained together, were taken north to toil
at building the Great Wall of China. He who was born
at Bethlehem, and gave us the Sermon on the Mount, did
not have an easy time. Not so long ago men were burned
at the stake for what they believed. Later, George Fox
and other Quakers were in the English gaols in company
with men and women of other sects courageous in suffering
for their convictions. Neither side was kind to pacifists
during the war of 1914 to 1918.

The coming of the Nazi régime in Germany has meant
difficulties for Quakers, as individuals, and for other Christians. But in times of suffering the spiritual feeling of true
Christian groups rises. This is certainly true of the Germans. The sons of those Germans who preached against
the occupation of Belgium protest from their pulpits with
a courage that does not shame their fathers. Catholics,
ably encouraged by the Pope, are fearless in devotion to
Christ's teaching.

I have sat in Quaker Meetings in Germany in various
places. What we call a "living" silence was seldom absent. God seemed more present than in meetings where
life does not call for the bravery that it does here. The
German Quakers go forward led by the Spirit — a loving
fellowship strong in Inner Light, able to believe that virtue
lies in every heart, even the hearts of those who oppose
them.

I have been present when the door has opened and an
official stepped in. I have never seen a German Friends'

Meeting broken up. It has been my experience to have
the official bow his head through what remained of the
hour of quietness and inspired speech. In the time of per-
secution in England, meetings were ruthlessly disturbed
— Milton writes of dust thrown on the silent worshipers.
There are records of children who held meeting alone
because all the grown-ups were in gaol.

It is the Quaker belief that peoples can be a society of
friends living peacefully and profitably together in a frontierless and unfortified world. Those who are born to
an environment where great thoughts are a daily commonplace often are not impressed by them until experience
makes them real. As a child in the United States I had no
contact with forts or frontiers — even when we went to
Canada I did not notice any. The first sentence in this
paragraph was to me but a copybook task — something
written down by Grandfather which I must copy neatly
twelve times before I could go skating. That was when
I was what my niece Brenda calls "suffering an education."

While I lived in Germany, that copybook sentence became real to me and, although I saw in process the building up of the most powerful army the world has ever possessed, I did not get the impression that the Germans have
done with pacifism. Instead, there grew deep within me
a faith that Germans will be a powerful force in the making
of a frontierless and unfortified world.

Our guest had noticed that Christl, who had let him in, was an Austrian woman, and asked how she came to be with us in Dresden. I told how she has been with us, in about the same capacity as Bald-the-third, our old Chinese serving matron, ever since a winter day when she rang our doorbell in Vienna. She had gone along with us to Czechoslovakia, and was going to England. Then my husband, who dislikes domestic conversation, turned the subject to literature and music; and we expressed our admiration of the heights Germans have reached in things of the mind and the spirit.

We enjoyed our guest. After he had gone, I thought of how short human life is, how there are good and bad in all of us, and what the more energetic in each generation do to others. I considered Mr. Hitler. Memory of three incidents concerning him came back to me on the rays of the setting sun. Two had to do with wayside villages. One happened in East Prussia, where we all went to spend three weeks with the friend who was Marie's governess at Tientsin. The other occurred in the Rhineland.

The people of a hamlet had long disputed with the people of a neighboring *Dorf* beyond the hill regarding their respective rights in a wood. There seemed to be no end to this quarrel. Now that they had a Führer, the people of the hamlet decided to present their case directly to him. They drew up a list of their grievances. The schoolmaster wrote the petition on a scroll in fine script. It was rolled and tied with Nazi ribbon. The Führer was due to go through on his way to a great assembly.

The tallest man was chosen to wave the petition. Early in the forenoon of the day, the whole population dressed

in their Sunday clothes and lined up along their street.
It was considerably after country dinnertime when their
Führer whizzed by. He was in a powerful car. He left
ill feeling behind him. "Adolf Hitler was born to the
people, but he is a mighty man now. He does not see
folk like us — except when he wishes to use us."

Until evening they grumbled. Then, shortly after
Abendbrot, a young stranger arrived on a motorcycle.
Their Führer had seen the petition waved. He had some-
thing so important to do that he could not stop for it.
But he wanted it. He had sent this messenger to fetch it.
They gave it gladly.

In less than a fortnight they had their answer. The
disputing was to stop at once. It is forbidden for Germans to quarrel with each other. The man who brought
this reply was to hear both sides, and the people were to
abide by his decision. Enough German strength had been
wasted.

The investigator went about his task quietly. He wrote
his decision in two copies, and gave one to each set of
citizens. He did not set down any details, the interpretation of which could lead to further dissension. The sum
of his decision was that what the wood produced was to
be divided without selfishness. He held a joint meeting
which everyone from both villages must attend. He led
them in singing songs together. The people did as he
decreed. The quarrel, two decades old, was over.

The second incident is about people who wove a carpet
of flowers from their gardens. They placed this on the
road over which their Führer was to pass. Either word
of it reached him somehow or, as one old man in that

village is certain, he has very long sight. His car and those that escorted him halted. He got down. Wheels were not allowed to crush the blossoms.

The cars and the escort went around. The Führer walked through the village. He spoke gently to men, women, and children. He took the hands of two little ones who ran to him. Babies went into his strange arms fearlessly.

No one who saw this could correctly call it play-acting. He was moved by the gift of flowers put on his road. He was grateful for love. Goodness shone in his face.

When he had gone, they said: "He is our true German Führer. He would not let a flower, a bird, or a person be crushed if he knew it was to be done. He is enthroned in our hearts. Heaven sent him."

This village had been troubled. A few days previously a minor Nazi official had put up a sign: "Jews must go." The village had just one Jewish family, who had been there as long as anybody else. The head of the family is an old man, a shoemaker. His son married Anna, the postmistress, and they have a fair child named Hans. Although possessed of very slender means themselves, this family have been very charitable to others in times of distress. In the wartime, people who had no money had their shoes mended and never had to pay. Now, in the butter shortage, the old man and his wife were giving more than half their allowance to a neighbor who was sick. One of the fair babies whom their Führer had taken into his arms was little Hans. These village people accepted that as a sign. They took down the anti-Jewish poster.

The third incident was at a review of soldiers. Some

people gave a party in their offices, and we were among those invited. Food and wine were served inside, and from a large balcony, through glasses, we could plainly see the officials' platform as well as the marchers.

A company of aged veterans came along, one of them so feeble that I had just thought, "He ought not to be walking," when I saw his Führer take notice of him. Herr Hitler had him taken out of the line. A chair was placed for him on the platform. Aglow with pleasure, the old soldier enjoyed the remainder of the review from a seat beside his standing Leader.

My packing was as near finished as it could be until just before we started. I had idleness to spend. Enchanting April called me out of doors. Fed by freshets, the Elbe was running high. A white cargo boat went downstream at fine speed, brilliant laundry flapping on the line, and a little brown dog sitting at the prow like a sentinel.

I crossed over to the *Weisser Hirsch* side, intending to walk a way and then take a tram up to the *Kurpark;* but the newly grown grass was a lovely green on this bank of the river, and a group of pretty children played a spring-time *Ringelreihen.* Rosy-cheeked, they joined hands and circled. Confidence of life was in their every movement as they sang: "*Wir drehen uns, die Wange glüht und Freude füllt die Brust.*"

A well-dressed woman came on to the path. Her small, neatly shod feet paced back and forth restlessly. She stared at the river, and then, as if drawn by their happiness, she stared at the children. Her sensitive face was pale, her eyes bewildered. She began to pace again. Although a stranger, I had decided to go and ask her trouble when I felt someone looking at me.

Turning, I met the gaze of an elderly policeman. I had begun to wonder why he measured me when he strode off toward the pacing woman, who was now going upriver with her back to us. He caught up to her, and walked by her side to the second bridge and back. I could see that he was talking persuasively as they returned.

I sat down on the grass and opened my book. Soon I was interrupted. The policeman stood before me. He paid me the nicest compliment. He said, "You have a look one can trust," and asked if I would do a kindness. I replied that I would answer when I knew what he wanted.

He wanted this woman to go to a café he named, and stay there reading the papers all day until five o'clock. It was now about eleven in the morning. She must not go home to her own house until after five o'clock. Then she would find what she had lost; it would be in the upper right-hand drawer of the desk in her *Frauenzimmer.*

She must not be allowed to stay out of doors. He feared she might throw herself into the river. He needed to be quickly about what he had to do, and wanted me to escort her to the café and sit there with her until she was quieter. I said that the café idea seemed dreary. I would take her home with me for the day if she would come.

She burst into tears when I asked her, and sobbed, "You are both too good." Then she was concerned for me. "I must not get you into trouble — are you married to a German?" I told her an Englishman. That reassured her. The policeman called us a taxi. We took a ride over the *Weisser Hirsch* and back, because I thought that sight of the leafing trees would do her good. We had the top down, and the air brought color to her cheeks.

Some time ago the Nazi authorities had called in her German passport, and had not returned it. Then they had sent her a notice to be out of the country in a fortnight. She could not go without her passport. No other country would let her enter without it. When she asked for it they told her that they had never received it.

She acted as wisely as she could. She was a widow. She asked aid of her husband's brother. He plainly did not want to be mixed up with anyone who was in trouble with the government. She asked friends. They drew away as soon as they knew her plight. She appealed to every possible official, but to no avail. She was told that she lied if she said that the government had her passport. The very man to whom she had handed it accused her of either hiding or destroying it. They exchanged remarks in front of her about her being neurotic.

Her fortnight was up to-night. She did not know what they would do to her if she was here after the hour when she had been warned that she must be away; but she was sure that it would be better to be dead than found. Germany was her homeland. The homeland of her fathers. She did not think these Nazis, many of whom are not German born, had any right to dictate as to who shall live on this part of the earth. But they have seized power in the Fatherland. As a child she had played that same springtime *Ringelreihen* children were playing now by the Elbe, and had been as confident as they. She did not know why she was in trouble. No one would tell her.

She explained about the policeman. For years he had

been on the beat by her home. He was their "family policeman." Somehow he had heard this morning about her lost passport. When he did not find her at home, he looked for her by the river. He had promised to get the passport and put it in her desk. She did not believe that he could do it. Her faith in things was worn out.

I felt sure that he would do it if he said he would. My husband was away for the day. He was visiting some musical people a little way out in the country. I was to meet him at the opera and go to a supper afterwards. In the Dritte Reich one cannot telephone about anything private. I decided that it was no use bothering anyone else until the policeman had failed.

We had a quiet day. We played chess, and read aloud. At half past five her passport was where the policeman said it would be.

I helped her pack. She took a small trunk and two bags. She left a nicely furnished house. Both her father and her husband had willed her comfortable fortunes. She could take but ten marks out of the country with her. Still, she was glad to get away even if it proved that all else was forfeit to the Nazis. She gave me good clothes, warm bedding, all the extra cash she had, and a list of poor people she had been helping. Sometime after seven I saw her depart for Paris, where her sister lived.

I felt in a horrible trance as I dressed for the opera. I was so slow that I did not slip into the seat beside my husband until after the bell had rung for the last act. *Tosca* seemed less tragic than present-day life.

From Paris I got a telegram announcing her safe arrival.

On the morning we left, beautiful Dresden was daubed with the yellow paint of anti-Semitism, and hung with scarlet in commemoration of the Nazi Führer's birthday. We went to Kassel, stopping at Weimar for lunch. In obedience to a command broadcast from the Propaganda Bureau, every habitation displayed the banner of the hooked cross. If anxiety and sorrow dwelt anywhere on this lovely landscape, they hid themselves. Only joy and satisfaction were abroad.

We went by orderly fields, neatly painted houses, trim gardens, and well-kept forests. It was a gala day. People were marching, singing, and cheering. At Weimar we could not drive into the square by the Hotel Erbprinz because it was filled with men in black and brown Party uniforms, who had gathered for speeches and luncheon.

We were politely shown a place at the side of the Duke of Weimar's castle where we could park. We had come early because I wanted to put flowers on Goethe's and Schiller's desks. We went first to Goethe's house, intending only to go to the little room where he used to work. But as we were coming down the stairs a teacher with a class of schoolboys went into the museum, and I had curiosity as to how he taught them. When here with Marie I had wished for other aids than the collection of relics arranged in chronological order in the big hall. Following this teacher past Herr Hitler's statue, I found that he did not need aids. Out of a full mind he was re-creating for his pupils the Weimar of Goethe's time.

Using vivid words, he arranged a background: one Duke of Weimar, and then another; this duchess and her successor; individuals gathered round them; their furniture, their clothes; a few sentences of reminder concerning the stirring of minds through the Reformation and the hard times that followed. He had his boys' attention, and mine. He noticed that I listened. I explained my eavesdropping. With that friendliness which I have found everywhere a German characteristic, he welcomed me to his class. He said they were from Bayern, and were celebrating Herr Hitler's birthday by this trip.

This stiff-necked, spectacled, threadbare teacher warned his pupils that the time under study was an era when state control, particularly in Weimar, was lax. There was no Bureau of Propaganda and Enlightenment to guide Germans. Ideas of freedom and liberty for the individual were loose in the air.

There was no Führer, and even Goethe failed to devote his genius to the furtherance of national discipline and obedience. Goethe made a hero of Götz von Berlichingen, beleaguered in his tower, defending personal opinion against the forces of law and order which pressed hard upon him. Schiller declared that an artist could follow no voice but the promptings of his own inner self. The little teacher made live people of these Germans of the past. Herder, urging men to be "masters of their own fate," went through the Weimar streets, his "blue coattails flying in the wind."

The teacher's range was wide. He did not bother about any of the labeled relics of Goethe's life. He concentrated on other things. He touched on Novalis, who defined the best state as one where individual men were powerful, not weak. He mentioned Wilhelm von Humboldt, who demanded that the state should limit its sphere of action to the safeguarding of the citizen's life and property. He dwelt longest on Lessing, influenced by the philosopher Felix Mendelssohn. He said: "The author of *Minna von Barnhelm* discounted patriotism. When very ardent he called it unheroic. Anything other than appreciation of all humanity he considered a weakness, a sign that a man was a coward, afraid of men not exactly his own image."

"I'm not sure these ideas are not right," said one boy, the tallest and strongest. He was promptly scowled at. Squelched, he became sulky, while the teacher impressed on them all that, as good Hitler Youths, it was their duty to keep their oath and give instant and blind obedience to the Führer's every command. Then he announced that for ten minutes they could look at things by themselves. After that it would be time for lunch.

When I had thanked him I went to find my husband. He was waiting in the hotel, which was considerably torn up inside. It was being enlarged because more accommodation for Nazi officials was needed at Weimar. The former duchy, once famous for the musicians and writers entertained there, was becoming an important government centre. Soon Weimar would be almost surrounded by military aeroplane fields, and a concentration camp called *Buchenwalde* for "undesirable and antisocial elements" of the German population.

Feeling that the old Weimar was about gone, except in memory, I asked to see again the little suite of rooms which we had occupied when previously here. They were as yet unspoilt. These were the rooms that the Duke of Weimar provided for Hans Christian Andersen.

In the countryside beyond Weimar we saw new barracks,

and many aeroplanes. Thuringia, the green heart of Germany, is one of the earth's charming places; we lingered in forested hills as long as we could, then hastened to Kassel. After we had booked a room for the night we went to find a stranger, of whom we had been asked to bring news to England.

She and her family had been working late in their field, taking advantage of the fine evening, so our plan to arrive after their supper did not succeed. Sitting on the doorstep, a board on her knees, the mother was cutting slices of black bread and smoked sausage. To her children's delight she was giving the food into their hands and letting them eat it by the haystack, or wherever they chose.

Five children were at home, in ages from sixteen to four; a daughter was away learning to be a nurse, and a son studying for the ministry. Her husband, a pastor, was in a concentration camp. She was grateful for the invitation for some of her children to come to England, although she herself was certain that Germans ought to stay in their Fatherland. She would not send any outside, but if they wanted to go they could. No one wished to leave. The "cause" would be lost in Germany if those with eyes that saw the decline of morals, hearts that felt it, and tongues that dared to rebuke it, went into exile.

The mother and two older boys talked to my husband, while I went with the younger ones to see their cow and newborn calf, three baby pigs a neighboring farmer had given them, and the stone mill, very like home mills in China, on which they had ground rye. This *kleine Bauernhaus* had been willed to their mother by her aunt. Formerly they had only come here sometimes in summer.

But when their father was taken their mother had brought them here to make it their home.

"Father could come out at any time," said the six-year-old. "God gives him courage to stay in. We pray for it. He asked us to pray because it helps him to know that we are doing so."

"To come out he has to sign a promise to support everything the Nazis do. He has to take the oath of blind obedience to Adolf Hitler. Our father is a Christian. A Christian cannot approve or be quiet in the face of the things the Nazis do," explained the daughter of eleven.

"Christianity is a religion of love," offered the tiniest solemnly. "Love and sorrow for all whom the Nazis hurt; and love and sorrow for the Nazis, too."

After Kassel, we went to a family who gave us an evening of a string quartette, playing Mozart. In this house they were enthusiastic about the Third Reich, and keen on the things their Führer has done. They knew that there had been cruelty, but "revolution is never bloodless." They believed that Germany would soon be invincible, and that Herr Hitler really does speak for seventy-five million people, whose strength is at his command.

"If you think otherwise, you are misinformed," I was told.

They talked with satisfaction of the end of unemployment. When I asked what will happen eventually about the multitude now making munitions, they said that the time will never come when they need be turned off. There will always be a market for arms — wars are natural to man; and besides, the larger the Reich grows the more need there will be to defend frontiers and colonies from jealous nations.

In the Rhineland we said *auf Wiedersehen* to many we knew well. Above Aachen we halted before the same red and white barrier that had been opened to us nearly four years ago. "Heil Hitler!" said the official. "Heil Hitler!" we responded to his country's convention. My husband went into the wayside office. I waited.

The formalities for exit were soon completed. The way was clear to leave Germany. "*Auf Wiedersehen*" — "*Auf Wiedersehen*." Until we meet again. As we exchanged that parting with the man who let us out, we knew that often we should be homesick for this land and its people.

En route to Ostend there was time for a detour to take a present to our godson in Eupen-Malmédy. He had grown splendidly, and could greet and thank us in English. His grandfather hoped for some assurance from us that union with his Fatherland would come soon.

"The Saar and Austria have got home." He had pride in this. "Probably it will be the Sudeten next, and maybe the Tirol. Then Memel and Danzig and the Corridor. Our Führer seems to be swinging round that way. Our time will come — but it is long. It is long, and I grow old in waiting."

His daughter-in-law did not want Eupen-Malmédy to be taken into the Reich. Belgium is her country. She was five years old when the frontier was fixed at its present place. She has a married sister living on the other side.

"Bibsi is better off under good King Leopold," she said. "Our king is of German race. He is a Christian king. I do not want Bibsi to grow up where Christ is rejected."

"I know English, French, and German," suddenly boasted Bibsi. He won't be four until June. His English words are less than a dozen, his French is decidedly limited, and German is his daily speech, but he has joy in being trilingual. "I can salute 'Heil Hitler,' sing 'Bravo King George,' say 'O.K. Roosevelt,' and wave the flag for my king."

His mother flushed. "Do you think he is too forward? It is hard not to spoil when there is only one. Perhaps we encourage him too much?"

The white cliffs of Dover welcomed us to England. Bluebells were in flower when we arrived. Almost immediately I began to prepare this account of my experience among the Germans. A concern has been on me to do it. Its purpose is to help understanding between Germans and people who live outside the Dritte Reich. We who inhabit this earth must draw closer together in brotherly love than we have done. We must take more interest in each other. Selfishness, ignorance, and fear have brought us to the pass we are in.

We ought to have helped the Germans to a wiser constitution after the war. The Weimar Constitution is a beautiful thing — a code for angels. They needed a code for earthly use. We should have known that they had never learned to carry civic responsibility. In writing this book about present-day life among the Germans I have striven to give a clear, true, and balanced picture. I hope it will rouse wise men to help Germans to get back into the vanguard of civilized people where, by merit of their talents, they rightly belong. In my portrayal I have not used actual names, excepting those of state officials, and I have changed the location of incidents wherever I have thought it necessary. While I have been working at this, German history has moved on in a tragic course.

We now live by a wood into which our gate opens to a path that leads through the wood and fields to Jordans, the Friends' meetinghouse where William Penn used to wait for the voice of God. His grave is in the yard. I am not homesick here as on the continent, because I never feel far off from Pennsylvania. The people round me hold the same views, and order their lives in the same way, as those among whom I grew. It seems as if I had come home; and it is good to be among one's own in months such as these have been.

Since we have been here, more Germans than we expected have crossed our threshold — each one welcome. We have had exiles, people on holiday, and advocates of Naziism. I know myself fortunate to be mistress of a house in a liberal land where one can listen and talk on neutral ground.

From the many things which my guests have told me, it is my conclusion that through the time of mounting tension up to the destruction of the Czechoslovakia of Masaryk, and on to the end of the year, havoc which has deeply stirred the German people has been wrought in all the lands over which the banner of the hooked cross waves.

Not all people have been stirred. During my experience I have met a fairly large number of men and women who give to their Führer a blind allegiance from which critical judgment is entirely absent, no matter what happens. One of them visited us late this fall. He is a man of education, and successful in business. He told me that Adolf Hitler is an *Übermensch*, a god-man. He said that the Führer willed Mr. Chamberlain to go to Munich so that war might be avoided, and that eight days before he flew there Mr. Hitler became quite calm and waited for his arrival. The people I know who have maintained a steady assurance that the peace of Europe and the future of civilization can be trusted to one man have all been middle-aged. Among youth I have not known anyone whose confidence has been so steady.

The destruction of Czechoslovakia upset me very much. When Mr. Chamberlain set off by aeroplane for Munich I was thrilled. I thought that he knew a way in which to adjust things differently than was done. I do not blame him for what happened. If there was no choice except between this and war, then this was the better. But I felt things should never have reached this crisis.

In my disturbed mood I wrote letters to a number of people, including young men I knew in the German army. From one — after some time — I got a lengthy answer. He said that he and a good many other young men did not like being moved around as chessmen in a game. He imagined that youth who feel like that are to be found in other countries as well as in Germany, and that if he had any choice in the matter he would order a complete disarmament of the entire world, erase all the frontiers, and have everything run for everybody's benefit by a committee of unselfish men devoted to the welfare of humanity.

He had not enjoyed giving two years of life to the boredom of army training. This is part of his letter, in translation: —

I know that things in my country could be ordered better than they are. Many of us talk about that, but none whom I 'know has devised any workable plan by which a change could be made. We shrink from a revolution which would cause great destruction, and leave us probably no better off than we are at present, and perhaps worse. We rescued Austria last March. Our entrance met with no resistance from a population counted German, but whom we found different from ourselves. They welcomed our soldiers with cheers, but no joy. Soldiers were given a special allowance — extra pay — to spend in the land of the poverty-stricken Austrians, and thus create a feeling of coming prosperity. In the countryside we could pay for nothing. With a courtesy which was somehow embarrassing, people gave us the best they had and refused our money. We had heard that they were poor. So they were in a way, but they had things we had not seen for years — many of us felt like locusts as we passed over their land. After the conquest Austria was as poor in butter, milk, white flour, wool, and the pretty things in shops, as Germany.

We had to let Nazis do things no German should be allowed to do, and then, when it had run a little time, bring them to order. The purpose of this was to make it look as if there would have been civic chaos in Austria but for the German army. The Austrian face reflected scorn. They saw through the whole thing. In Vienna such deeds were done as civilized men have never done before. Ballots were marked "Yes" for the plebiscite, but we know that it was no more than the acceptance of the inevitable — we were the barbarian hordes.

That was spring. The cuckoo announced the coming of summer. Men were conscripted in Germany to fortify the Rhine. We had a warning of what it means to be governed by mandate — a notice that man, woman, and child can be taken

from anything he or she may personally want to do and be set
to work at anything the government plans. As for soldiers, they
were kept at manœuvres through long weeks — waiting. And
again marched to meet no resistance, taking over territory and
property, the theft of which made many feel anything but
happy. We have all been to school. We know the historic
boundary line of the Bohemian Crownlands. We know how
Germans happened to live in the Sudeten, and we've no illusions
about Nazi interest in poor people. We've observed the *Win-
terhilfe* several winters.

Few have any illusions about propaganda. Some of us have
skied over there, and have never seen any Czech atrocities.
This time a proportion of the rescued ran before us as fast as
they could go. Others welcomed us, expecting to receive all
that they had been promised.

German soldiers are not beasts, whatever you have imagined.
It was horrible to have to leave Jewish sick unattended by the
roadside in no man's lands, and be forbidden to allow cars to
pass to them with food.

It may be a thrilling thing to make a conquest by battle —
the soldier risking his life to gain territory can feel himself a
hero, but if we don't find a foe soon who will fight when he
is encountered our fine army is going to fall to pieces. [In
other mood my young friend does not think this — knowing
him as I do, I am certain of it.] We have the guns, and although we may grumble about the lack of butter, that is really
not an important thing. It is something quite inexplicable.

And among us many are asking each other, "What is up?
Are we being decoyed as Napoleon was into Russia? We have
got 10,000,000 people and their lands. There is no bulwark
between us and the Ukraine, or the Black Sea — but we are no
better off in Germany than we were last year. We are poorer
by far."

This is the way another man has been affected. He is middle-aged, a prosperous manufacturer. He has been a supporter of the Party, and when I first met him he was sure that this was the way for his country. He was anti-Semitic then, and told me that most Germans were. Recently he has changed. "I am cured of anti-Semitism because I see now where it leads. We've got to learn to get along with, and protect, our fellow men even though there are some different from ourselves to whom we are not attracted."

He told me that men who knew better were among those who obeyed when ordered out of their beds to set fire to Jewish synagogues. He explained that the reflex habit of obedience was too highly developed in Germans in a time when absolutism was not unsatisfactory. He was deeply troubled that men looked on without action, although with apprehension, at Hitler youth destroying property with government encouragement. "We Germans have been a thrifty and frugal people, and developed a sense of the care of property. Even in the time of the Bolshevik uprisings, in the era just after the war, it was not like this. Although Bolshevik in theory they remembered that they were German, and put papers on polished floors before they placed guns on them. That may seem queer to a foreigner, but there is a Germanness in it which I like. I am not the only one lost to the cause. Those fires did not please the German populace. The whole anti-Jewish show was a strategic mistake. Five years of intensive propaganda have failed to rouse the German people to a spontaneous pogrom. Our people are humanitarian. They were the

happiest when led by kings who saw to it that they practised the Christian virtues.

"This blunder has won us the condemnation of the civilized world, and rightly. It has lost to the government the
adherence of vast numbers of people without ability to
stand against it openly, yet certain that it is wrong. My
workmen were not pleased about it, and other men have
told me the same about theirs.

"The people are not ignorant of the fact that ever since
the Nazis came into office they have taken as forfeit the
money in the treasury of every club and organization,
large and small, which they have ordered to be closed.
They know of private fortunes — 'Aryan' fortunes — forfeit to the state, and the sudden disappearance of good people. And now they see Nazi confiscation of £80,000,000
from the Jews. To peasants and workers that sort of
thing is plain thievery."

Angela is eighteen. She came to me in England because there was something she wanted me to help her do.
Three and a half years ago, when she first wrote me, she
was a child — a child in Arcadia. Her hair, the color of
ripe wheat, was in a braid, and her blue eyes shone as we
sat by the Rhine and she told me of National Socialism.
She was a Hitler Maid. Her selfless heart, her talent for
influencing others, and all her strength were her Führer's
to use.

She now held a Nazi job, which she combined with an
unofficial mission. Accredited as a Nazi worker, she could
move about with a freedom she said she would not other-

wise have. Her unofficial mission was "listening to the voice of the people."

She dialed my radio, picking up a succession of German stations. I heard nothing unusual. Other nations, including my own United States, were being portrayed as dens of iniquity. England happened then to be occupying the centre of the stage. Identical statements, in three different voices, from three stations, followed one after the other, quoting an Arab paper on the wicked behavior of British troops in Palestine. It was but a repetition of the reports, from so-called eyewitnesses or obscure middle European newspapers, of atrocities formerly broadcast as committed by the Czechs on the Sudeten Germans. There was good music. She let me hear only a few bars from Chopin and Bach. There was a weather report, and an interesting talk on cookery had my attention when she dialed off.

She said: "You may think that our radio is the voice of our people, but it is not. The voice of Naziism is trumpeted, but the true voice of Germany is a murmur so low that only the patient and gentle can hear it. Many of us who were formerly deaf to all but the cause that had enthralled us are listening now to news that is never published. What we learn we are passing from one to another."

Earnestly she endeavored to give a report which I would credit. With my young German friends I have a reputation for skepticism. This is owing to the fact that when I was young my educators were Quakers who counseled against too hasty enthusiasms. She covered the map of her country from Königsberg to the Brenner, from the North Sea into the Sudeten. Compatriots had assisted in arming her. I was not asked to accept a general statement for any district until the conclusion had been buttressed with specific incidents, in which she gave the occupation and home background of the person whose "voice" she reported.

Her record was written in her memory. In Germany they wrote nothing down. They passed what they learned by word of mouth. If record was found in the Dritte Reich, at the frontier, or by a German spy in England, the carrier would have endangered the people reported. Also, the carrier's chance to work toward the reëstablishment of civilization in Germany would be over.

Discontent is widespread. The Nazis never have represented all the people, and now many who were won by misrepresentation, or were conquered by fear, are stirring. While broadcasting to the world that they speak for the whole people of Germany, the leaders have had to arrest an ever-increasing number, until a total they dare not publish has been taken into concentration camps. They have to silence opposition by beheading; there is an unknown number of martyrs — many seventeen to thirty years of age — whose lives have been taken. Their death fans the cause.

Neither propaganda nor violence is the power that it was. People are uncertain as to how to effect a change, but they want a change. Fundamentally, Germans are good. People are making cults of men who stand against Naziism. Pastors who refuse the oath, and condemn wickedness from their pulpits, have a greater following than those who do not — and when they are taken into concentration camp that following increases. They are called blessed when they stay in prison, refusing to retract what they have said.   Lay folk gather courage against fear by the pastors' setting this example.

In the Sudeten, people who welcomed the union with anticipation are already whispering how much better it was under Beneš.   In Austria, people who discounted Herr von Schuschnigg as a narrow, bigoted Catholic take courage from his courage.   Peasants who did not know the name of this minor Tirolean nobleman when he was Chancellor tell stories of him: how he threw his service cap into the open grave of the murdered Dollfuss, pledging his life "for Austria," and how he has kept that pledge.   He could have flown before the arrival of the Nazis, — a plane was ready and his friends urged him to go, — but he stayed to drink the cup of bitterness with Austria.   Taunted, reviled, tortured, he has shown men how to keep faith with their principles.   Even when the Nazi Führer came to try to make him leave, because his presence strengthens the courage of those who have surrendered but not submitted, he would not go.

People in Germany, in Austria, in Bohemia, watch with growing apprehension the exodus of neighbors ordered to leave the Reich.   Despite what the Propaganda Bureau may try to teach, Hans and Gretchen know whether or not their own neighbors, Jacob and Rebecca, have been folk whom it is good to live beside through thick and thin.   They do not have the civic courage to stand by a neighbor, but every time a good neighbor is taken the government loses prestige with those who are left.

What she wanted was for me to be less silent than I had been.   She asked me to condemn in no uncertain terms every breach of the humanities committed in Germany, and combine this with outspoken belief in the goodness of the German people. She wanted me to ask all my friends to do the same. She said that it would help.

"You do believe in us, don't you?" she pressed.

I assured her that I have faith in the goodness, the courage, and the endurance of the Germans. They are a people whose true nature is not to hate, but to love all their fellow men. When they had passed through the fires of the Reformation their hearts were neither stone nor ash. They were pure gold. With this treasure they founded a kingdom so strong that they could fearlessly welcome Jew and Gentile, pagan and agnostic, to full citizenship.

In ages past the Germans have reached so high in getting truth for mankind that they have touched the stars. They have brought down for us gifts beyond estimation. That contribution is not ended.

Often I have heard it said that Naziism will last a thousand years. I think that those who speak for it overestimate the time of its duration. The good in this movement will endure. All other elements the German people will discard. They are not an ignorant mass. They are an educated populace. Their future history will be different from that of a less cultured people on whom barbaric emotionalism is used.

It is well to reconsider their past. Before the close of the eighteenth century, the intellectuals among their forefathers had dreamed of a system of education that would raise the moral and intellectual level of the whole people. Rulers were won to the movement. By the opening of the nineteenth century all the German states, led by Prussia,

had established schools — and normal schools for the training of teachers — to give the people, rich and poor, opportunity for education. And in 1819 state laws made attendance compulsory. Present-day Germans bear the
mark of this attempt so clearly that I am convinced of its
success. It permeates every class.

Circumstance did not seriously press their fathers to
sue, and die if there be need, for civic rights. The fact that
the Germans have to-day no political liberty is not a true
sign that they are a people too backward to assume the
responsibilities of government.

In past times, those of their number who made efforts
to secure a hold on the steering wheel of state could gather
but a feeble following. Ruled as they were, there seemed
no necessity to demand ruthlessly more than was benignly
given. Civic responsibility is a heavy burden — few cared
to assume it. One has but to look into the histories of
other nations to learn that we are all akin in this reluctance.

I have talked with many educated in the time of *Freiheit*.
Few of them ever considered the possibility that freedom of
intellect might lead to what exists under Naziism. They
did not dream that such liberty could result in suppression,
by men of *Sturm und Drang*, of all voice but their own.
Politics were never even considered seriously by many of
these descendants of nineteenth-century Germans.

When the war was over they lost their kings and other
liege lords so rapidly that many with whom I have talked
do not know how it happened; they blame it on the victorious democracies, and tell me that they looked on their
own democracy merely as something forced on them by

military defeat. Not all, of course. There were loyal supporters of the Weimar Republic, but not enough. The others, harassed by the unruly, who interpreted civic liberty as civic license, were only too glad to hand the responsibility of government to any leader willing to assume it, protect them from all bother, and give back the happier past.

But, alas, that beautiful past has not been restored to them. Some Germans never hoped for it, and warned others, sacrificing their liberty and their lives in order to do so. Many are only now waking to realization of what has happened. Even when they saw evil done they held on to a comfortable hope that everything would come out all right in the end. Few are evil, but a great number close their eyes to what goes on, and continue to hope. An increasing number do not.

Naziism is a materialism. My estimation is that a very small proportion of the Germans are materialists. They are mostly people whose poetic comprehension is more developed than their common sense — but they are not materialists. On the radio and in the press there is great clamor about a German demand for the return of colonies, but in non-Nazi circles there is a stirring concern regarding foreign affairs which has nothing to do with colonies. "Colonies" is a subject less important, in many German minds, than a very real concern for civilization. The German people's reluctance to war is not wholly fright that *their* land may be bombed, but encompasses a concern that other countries may be bombed.

Just as Nazi anti-Semitic propaganda has failed to do more than make many stay quiet, and others take part under orders, so the vile propaganda against other nations has failed to make the people as a whole hate them. To my certain knowledge three nations and their nationals are popular in Germany to-day — England, America, and Sweden. I have not tested out the popularity of others, but I can state that there is many an admiring word said for Herr Beneš; and it is remembered that he is of the people who gave to Germany, in the seventeenth century, Johann Amos Comenius, "the father of German common school education," a Hapsburg exile.

Even when in another land those of us who have a wide German friendship are kept continuously close to the civic troubles of Germans. Our situation is similar to that of all our English friends who have connection with those who dwell in the Dritte Reich. We never know from which German the mail will bring an appeal, "Help me to get out," or, "Will you take my children?" When telephone or doorbell rings we do not know whose voice will say, "I have had to fly" — we are now beyond all possibility of surprise. German-Aryan, German-Jew, and German-Czech are among those who turn to us.

A government does not stand long, without drastic modification of its tenets, when this begins to happen. It is but a warning of the unrest rising in the land the exiles leave. I learned this wisdom from the Chinese political philosophers.

Of refugees I give one example. Recently arrived from Germany, he sat at my husband's piano, playing as if we were not there — playing German music, Czech music, Russian music — playing with a feeling divinely inspired

— a man bewildered, seeking guidance from other musicians.

In the *Who's Who* of German music, a long list of celebrated accomplishments are recorded below his name. He was composing in early youth, and his music has absorbed all his attention until now, when he is no longer young. He was born of Flemish blood, and is on the census as German because his "speech in daily use" was German — that was the way their census report was made up. In these last years he has had his home in Cologne — a home furnished with things of beauty. He often played in Brussels, and some friend thoughtfully saw to it that he had a Belgian passport. He seems never to have thought of himself as anything but a musician.

My husband knew him, and we were privileged to be invited to his private musicals. Anyone looking over fellow guests soon saw that if his host had ever heard of the "poisonousness" of Jews he had brushed that foolish noise impatiently away. In April, when we left Germany, his name was one acclaimed by those who have German voice to-day — and he, deep in a cycle of songs, gave politics no heed.

In June, although he is of pure Flemish inheritance and has a Belgian passport, he received a Nazi request to state his political position. On the form he wrote, "I am an artist." In November, about to start on a series of concerts in German cities, — all arrangements settled, — he received a notice that he could play no more in Germany, and had a warning that if not out of the country in twenty-four hours he would be put in a concentration camp. He got this message by telephone.

He consulted friends — "What is an artist to do?"

"Fly — fly — you have the fortune to be a Belgian — you have a Belgian passport — go to Amsterdam, go on to England — to America — fly while you can."

"But is it right to fly before injustice — should I not fight it — go into *Konzentrationslager* for the freedom of music, if necessary?"

"An artist's first duty is to enlighten pathways with his art. That you cannot do from a concentration camp. Go abroad — tour America — help us all — you have a Belgian pass — you can get out — go quickly while there is time."

His German friends — "Aryans" — persuaded him. Leaving everything, he set forth. Luckily, from his last trip abroad to play in Switzerland he had a statement that he had brought in, and had permission to take out, 430 francs. All his other money, excepting ten marks, must be left in Cologne — most of the money of to-day's exiles stays with the Nazis.

Before twenty-four hours were up he was in Amsterdam. From there he brought the report: "The Dutch are alarmed — they arm — they arm — to hold this storm at bay if they can. They see the gathering *Götterdämmerung*. I was preoccupied with my compositions. I did not wake. The burning of the Berlin *Reichstag* signaled the start of *Götterdämmerung*. We have had our second warning in the firing of the synagogues. Fire is its theme. One hundred and twenty-six beautiful synagogues, all the synagogues of the German-Jews, burst into flame in one instant — oil and then fire. It will be the Catholic Church next, — the beautiful churches, — then the homes of the people.

It is a crash more terrible than Wagner foretold. Yet he is right — his music is right for it."

And he continues: "You remember Frau L.?" We nod. "They have taken her fortune. First they took her car, the car she used to send for my use; then they took her property — she is allowed one hundred marks a week. Frau L. a Nazi pensioner because she is a German-Jew! That lovely park at her country place — I wrote some of my best music as her guest, and she has had to go to her daughter at X. They will make a household with what they are allowed. A twilight of the gods comes on us all, and yet you say I must learn English."

"No, not *learn* English, but use English. Perfect your English. Don't fall back into German continually. German is a tongue few understand here," we press on him, attempting to make clear to him the futility of trying to make himself understood in his native language.

He will come through his twilight. He has his art. God has gifted him. Art is enriched by suffering — he will now have more to give mankind than before.

I, too, can see that *Götterdämmerung*. Much in Germany has already gone, but brave men and women there hold up the edifice of civilization, and their support is an educated populace, a populace waking to realization of the danger.

I do not share the view of those who feel that if that crash occurred it would mean the end of civilization. Nor do I think that a general European war would end civilization. We should have to endure it, as my dear ones in China endure, and those who survived would carry on regardless of which side had the victory. But much of great beauty, which should be the property of our children, and our children's children, would be destroyed. I am thankful for what peace we have to-day.

It is Christmas Day as I write this page. Logs burn brightly on my fire. We have a tree, and there is a smell of candles and hemlock. The landscape beyond our windows is white, with the laurel hedge gleaming, green and glossy. There is snow for my first English Christmas. Holly grows here as tall as trees. In our thicket it was adorned with a glory of berries ready for hungry birds to feast on.

There are many robins. They come to the kitchen door for crumbs. The English robin is small, friendly, and red-breasted. These robins are a great comfort to me. They have the same effect on our German friends. They have power to blot out awareness, even remembrance, of human affairs. Whether or not next Christmas has as much peace as this one, or more, depends too much upon the strength of the faithful among the Germans.

They need the aid we can give them — our prayers, our friendship, and all the recognition and support that our statesmen can devise.

Auf Wiedersehen, and a good New Year.